Queer Velocities

RETHINKING THE EARLY MODERN

Series Editors
Marcus Keller
Ellen McClure
Feisal Mohamed

Queer Velocities

Time, Sex, and Biopower on the Early Modern Stage

Jennifer Eun-Jung Row

Northwestern University Press
Evanston, Illinois

Northwestern University Press
www.nupress.northwestern.edu

This book is freely available in an open access edition thanks to TOME (Toward an Open Monograph Ecosystem)—a collaboration of the Association of American Universities, the Association of University Presses, and the Association of Research Libraries—and the generous support of the University of Minnesota. Learn more at the TOME website, available at openmonographs.org.

Printed in the United States of America

10 9 8 7 6 5 4 3 2 1

Library of Congress Cataloging-in-Publication Data

Names: Row, Jennifer Eun-Jung, author.
Title: Queer velocities : time, sex, and biopower on the Early Modern stage / Jennifer Eun-Jung Row.
Other titles: Rethinking the Early Modern.
Description: Evanston, Illinois : Northwestern University Press, 2021. | Series: Rethinking the Early Modern | Includes bibliographical references and index. | Summary: "This book explores the sensations of haste and delay as represented in seventeenth-century French theater. Jennifer Eun-Jung Row proposes that these disruptive velocities--occasions when the tempos of desire subverted society's rhythms and norms—sparked new queer attachments and intimacies"—Provided by publisher.
Identifiers: LCCN 2021057758 | ISBN 9780810144705 (paperback) | ISBN 9780810144712 (cloth) | ISBN 9780810144729 (ebook)
Subjects: LCSH: French drama—17th century—History and criticism. | Theater—France—History—17th century. | Speed in literature. | Gender identity in literature.
Classification: LCC PQ528 .R69 2021 | DDC 842.409—dc23/eng/20211130
LC record available at https://lccn.loc.gov/2021057758

To my parents, who gave me every opportunity to learn and grow, to pursue my passions and my dreams. Thank you.

CONTENTS

ACKNOWLEDGMENTS

This book was written slowly and quickly. The hasty version—the dissertation, or the embryonic form of the book—was pounded out frenetically over one summer with a view of Ithaca's nature, punctuated by CSA deliveries of vegetables and twilight jogs. The slow version was steeped in conversation during two luxurious academic fellowships, writing "hunkers" in community, and shared exchanges with friends. This book was written in Ithaca, Madison, Atlanta, Cambridge, Paris, Rome, and Minneapolis, and I am grateful to all my friends and communities who sustained and housed me and supported this project along the way.

This book would not have come to fruition without the brilliant developmental editing by Marie McDonough, who has tended this manuscript with a judicious hand for pruning my fanciful theoretical spirals while fertilizing with such care the best, truest version of my ideas; thanks to Marie my own writerly voice has been able to bloom. Marie deserves the Pulitzer Prize of developmental editing, if such a thing ever existed.

My gratitude to the Institute for Advanced Study, at the University of Minnesota, especially to Jennifer Gunn and Susannah Smith, who provided me a community and a physical place to write. Thank you also to Susan Stanford Friedman and Ann Harris at the University of Wisconsin–Madison's Institute for Research in the Humanities, for fostering such a warm and vibrant community during my yearlong Solmsen Fellowship. I am also grateful to Brown University, Cornell University, New York University, the University of Chicago, the University of Wisconsin-Madison, and Wesleyan College, for the invited opportunity to share parts of this manuscript in progress.

Fragments of this manuscript first appeared in the journals *Exemplaria* (introduction) and *Le monde français du dix-huitième siècle* (conclusion), as well as the edited volume *Autour de l'extrême littéraire* (chapter 2); thank you to these venues for offering me a space to work through my initial ideas.

Thank you to Ellen McClure, as the Rethinking the Early Modern series editor and as a mentor, who believed in an early version of my manuscript and shepherded it along with grace, wisdom, and care. Claire

Goldstein and Hall Bjørnstad were my two anonymous readers of an article version of my introduction, which appeared in the journal *Exemplaria*. Their comments helped me crystallize certain concepts of velocity and I relied on their insightful and careful readers' reports to pull together my book's anchoring concepts. Lewis Seifert, one of the book's manuscript reviewers, has been an indispensable source of wisdom and clarity, and truly pushed this book to be the best version it could be. Thank you also to the anonymous second reviewer for their valuable feedback. Gianna Mosser also supported and believed in this project from the beginning. Thank you to the Northwestern University Press team, including Elissa Park, Trevor Perry, Maia Rigas, and Patrick Samuel.

I would never have found seventeenth-century French studies were it not for the mentorship and guidance of Julia Prest, who so generously welcomed me into her graduate seminar at Yale while I was still an undergraduate student; when I was intimidated by the prospect of writing a twenty-page paper in French, which I had never done before, Julia encouraged me by saying, "I think you'll find it liberating!" and I took the bait, relishing in the invitation to explore deeper, more complex ideas about sexuality in Racine. My introduction to queer theory and my dedication to the field was fueled by Jonathan D. Katz, who mentored me and virtually exploded my mind about what queer theory could do, the state of the field, and my place in the field of queer theory as a scholar. Seth Silberman highlighted new and exhilarating racial and political angles of queer theory to me as an undergraduate. I am grateful to Barry McCrea, who taught me how to close read and to unravel a text's formal and beautiful mysteries.

To the Essique family (Louisa, Raphaël, Alexandre, and in memory of dear Bernard) who took me in and became my French family. Thank you for all the warm meals spent together, our trips to dear Bénévent and Vendée, the sustaining bowls of vegetable soup, and the evenings spent listening to music.

To my doctoral advisors, Mitchell Greenberg and Timothy Murray at Cornell, who challenged me to sharpen my overly abstract thinking and to pin my unconventional theories to the text itself. Thank you for pushing me to use seventeenth-century French literature to impact queer theory, instead of merely being satisfied with queering French literature. To Jenny Mann, whose class on early modern English drama opened my eyes to a world of critical approaches to early modern literature I never knew existed, and for sparking my love of rhetoric's infinite possibilities. Thank you to Petrus Liu, for propelling my grasp of queer theory to new heights.

Thank you to Anne Emmanuelle Berger, whose feminist theory seminar at the Université de Paris–VIII was like a dream, a wonderful, sunny semester of reading Derrida in your living room and eating strawberries by the Canal Saint-Martin. Thank you for curating a real *salon* of feminist-queer international misfits and scholars. Ophélie Chavaroche, my "grad sister," the best of roommates, the most caring of friends, thank you for being there for me. You inspire me to love and to think about literature and feminism deeply, in new and enriched ways.

Thank you to Katie Kadue, who has been a caring and thoughtful interlocutor, a meticulous reader of my prose, and an incredible collaborator! I always feel refreshed after every conversation we have together. Joanne Brueton Wilberforce, I am grateful for all of our glasses of rosé and our rich, deep discussions about our writing. Mariam Wassif and Brant Torres helped me in the editing phase of this manuscript. Thank you for being the metaphorical spatulas to "unstick" me when I most needed it. You were there to energize me through late nights working and our conversations galvanized the most critical intellectual growth spurts I had in grad school. To Julia "Danger" Chang, Adeline Rother, Sarah Senk, and Xine Yao, thank you for being such amazing friends and wonderful guides and interlocutors through graduate school.

Katie Laporta, I would not have finished this manuscript were it not for your cheerleading, chapter swapping, Google sheets work tracking, and more. I am grateful to other members of the Society for Interdisciplinary Seventeenth-Century French Studies (SE17) who have been my best interlocutors along the way, including Hélène Bilis, Jean-Vincent Blanchard, Juliette Cherbuliez, Katherine Dauge-Roth, Katherine Ibbett, Larry Norman Anna Rosensweig, Lewis Seifert, Christophe Schuwey, Christopher Semk, Jennifer Tamas, Anne Theobald, Ashley Williard and Ellen Welch. To the members of our little "Cambridge Circle," Topher Davis, Julie Elsky, and Diana Garvin, thank you for so many months of swapping work and reading through so many chapters.

To Boston University's "GenSex" group, especially Cati Connell, Jennifer Knust, Erin Murphy, Anthony Petro, and Carrie Preston, thank you for supporting me and creating a wonderful, vibrant community to share work and ideas. A huge thank you to Keith Vincent, who was an unbelievable mentor, friend, and supporter during my first years at BU, and whose dedication and love of literature is refreshing and inspiring.

Thank you also to Andrés Fabián Henao Castro, my wonderful co-instructor of a fabulous queer theory class, from whom I learned so much, and Takeo Rivera and Kareem Khubchandani, who were both incredible co-conspirators and resources in performance studies, queer theory, and critical ethnic studies. Thank you to the "Sexual Poetics/ Sexual Politics" research group headed by Ramzi Fawaz and Damon Young: you offered so many wonderful "workshop" venues for my own work, but I learned infinitely more from reading your own rich and inspiring writing in progress. Thank you, Kadi Amin, Katherine Brewer Ball, Zakiyyah Iman Jackson, Uri McMillan, Amber Jamilla Musser, Shanté Paradigm Smalls, and Jordan Stein. To the "Premodern Temporalities" working group at the University of Minnesota Consortium for the Study of the Premodern World, thank you to Mary Franklin-Brown, JB Shank, and Amit Yahav, who read and helped me through so many early versions of my introduction. Thank you especially to Dan Brewer who gave me so much mentorship, support, and feedback on my writing, especially getting me across the finish line to article acceptance when I needed it most. I appreciate your help immensely.

Thank you to Vivian Choi, Susanna Ferlito, Margaret Hennefeld, Jason McGrath, Candace Moore, Sonali Pawha, Ila Nicole Sheren, Tracy Rutler, and Elizabeth Wijaya for doing "work hunkers" with me, brewing me cups of tea, and for listening to me think out loud through some of my most "sticky" places in the book. Danielle Haque, you were the best "boss/mom friend-nagger" propelling me along just when I needed it. Thank you especially to PhD students Chloe Mais Hagen and Ray Balstad, who helped me with formatting and other editorial assistance.

Amanda Pearson was a true friend and cheerleader, offering me support along every milestone and step along the way. Thank you also to Joanne Brueton, John Paredes, Matt Gabbard, Tejas Srinivas and Andy Popovici, for being such caring, kind, compassionate, and supportive friends while I was in "book jail," offering meals, theater breaks, moral support, and physical places to crash in many cities all over the world.

Lastly, and most importantly, thank you to Lorenzo Fabbri, who kept me watered and fed during late nights writing. You have been my "rock" and my anchor when I felt adrift, and you believed in me from the very start. Ti amo molto tanto. The most brilliant insights and philosophical gems of this book are thanks to you. Thank you to Emma Momo, ever joyful beam of sunshine who brightens our days.

Queer Velocities

Introduction

Queer Velocities

Sex and the Stage

It is 1637 in the theater space of the Hôtel de Bourgogne in Paris. The air is thick with the smoke from the burnt-down suet candles that are being refreshed during the entr'acte. Spectators and actors alike know the hour is late; some tell time by the distant clang of the Hôtel de Ville clock.[1] The audience chatter is hushed when act 4 of Isaac de Benserade's *Iphis et Iante* begins. All are eager to see what will become of this nervously excited couple's wedding night. Onstage, while the bride Iante waits impatiently in bed, Iphis wrings his hands, struggling to express something to his new bride. With the smitten rhetoric of a Petrarchan lover, Iphis draws attention to the excess of emotion that he cannot possibly put into words, pointing instead to his heart, his sighs, and his eyes. How very poignant, then, that such a conventional rhetorical plaint points repeatedly to a body that is not, in fact, conventional. Seventeenth-century French theatergoers familiar with Ovid's *Metamorphoses* could have easily guessed the secret that Iphis conceals: Iphis is biologically female. Because Iphis's father had vowed to kill any nonmale progeny, Iphis was subsequently raised by her mother under a male guise to save her life.

Iphis's wedding night delay might appear at first as a mere sticking point, or a hurdle to be surmounted. After years of gender passing, for Iphis the hymeneal night not only a moment marks of nuptial consummation but also of gender revelation and sexual transgression. Addressing an impatient Iante, Iphis sighs: "Hélas! Ne sauriez-vous lire dans ma pensée / L'étrange mouvement de ma flamme insensée?"[2] (Alas, do you not know how to read in my thoughts / the strange movement of my senseless desire?). Iphis's anxiety regarding her own readability is of course important on the diegetic level, since it contributes to the emotive charge of this fraught revelation. In Iphis's "do you not know how to read (me)?" one can also hear a larger anxiety regarding the legibility of gender and desire. For Iphis, who has long been in love with Iante, this hymneal night marks a potential shift in their romance; Iphis must simultaneously reveal her true gender and gauge whether Iante will still love her.

And yet, this play depicts something more than gender transgression. Significantly, Iphis *delays* the moment of revealing her body to Iante and of engaging in the long wished for act, as if the delay itself, the slowed tempo leading to the desired moment, will allow Iante to intuit the secret of Iphis's sex:

> L'hymen qui convertit le crime en innocence
> À mes jeunes désirs donne toute licence,
> J'aime et si je possède, en ce retardement
> Ne vous doutez-vous pas de mon secret tourment?[3]
>
> (This marriage that transforms crime to innocence
> Gives full rein to my youthful desires.
> I love, and even if you are mine, in this delay
> Do you not suspect my secret torment?)

Shifting the focus from Iphis's gender identity to the very strategies of delay, we can imagine that the *retardement* (delay) goes beyond the traditional diegetic use of delay to create suspense. On the one hand, Iphis hopes that her deviant speed will lend legibility to her sexual and gender position, employing retardement as an instrument of revelation, a means of flagging the "strange movement" of her affects. On the other hand, retardement—in its "thickening"—begins to take on an erotic, affective quality: for Iphis, the slowness accompanying the revelation of the truth of her body enables a momentary reprieve from the temporal norms to which she has so far subjected her body and her desires.[4] Iphis's doubly deviant body (first deviant to her family because female, then deviant to her wife because transgender) is under threat by normative power structures that dictate the acceptable terms of marriage and inheritance. Because of this scrutiny, a new form of time opens up for Iphis, one that increases her pleasure or at least pauses over the possibility of a world made otherwise. What would it mean for *time* to feel erotic—replete with possibilities of rejection, horror, transgression, delight, recognition, and more? How might we read the queerness of an eroticism generated from temporal sensation of fastness or slowness, even if the act itself may not be explicitly "sexual"? And how does seventeenth-century theater, with its peculiar conditions of representing the body and eroticism, allow the spectator to sense and to feel temporality differently?

Queer Velocities: Time, Sex and Biopower on the Early Modern Stage is about the feelings that tempos can create: the supplementary, wayward affects generated by sensations of rushing, haste, delay, and drag—or what I call "queer velocities." In the seventeenth century, new ways of feeling and knowing time, from advances in early modern chronometry to the strict regulation of temporal duration on stage, allowed for new kinds of aesthetic and affective sensations, wrought in and around time itself. From a contemporary standpoint, we might grasp the concept of supplementary emotions concomitant with tempos, such as the impatience (or deliciousness) afforded by delay or the joy (or anxiety) relayed by haste. I underscore how the early modern staging of different speeds and slownesses of lived experience yielded unexpected affective intensities and a messy, inchoate constellation of relation and feeling. In so doing, I hope to enrich the historical dimension of queer critique of temporal norms: that time has not always "felt" the same, nor has it organized lived experience in the same ways.[5]

In my deployment, velocity is crucial to understanding the intertwined sociosexual dynamics of the early modern world. Velocity has been treated, in the realm of physics, as a vector quantity, meaning that it is comprised of a magnitude (speed or slowness) and a direction. The notion of a direction, or orientation, here becomes essential for an analysis of norms and deviations. Major innovations were underfoot in the seventeenth century, including new theater regulations that limited the represented narrative to a twenty-four-hour period, as well as groundbreaking advancements in chronometry that allowed for portable and precise timepieces for the first time. These innovations and more offered a new sensation of temporality and new awareness of time's passing. Velocities, in my analysis, are *directed* and often normatively oriented toward futurity, progress, production, and reproduction. Thus, velocity's dual figuration (indicating both speed and direction) allows both the intensity of temporal rhythms and the directional quality of sexual "ends" to be signaled. A wayward directionality is made present through affects and intensities of feeling (e.g., Iphis's trepidation or her embodied joy) that stray from a more appropriate rhythm or telos.

Directionality, as Sara Ahmed has contended, is more than merely one's orientation in space. The notion of direction also conveys moral, social, and even sexual orders or organizing principles. She writes in

Queer Phenomenology that "the etymology of 'direct' relates to 'being straight' or getting 'straight to the point.' To go directly is to follow a line without a detour, without mediation. Within the concept of direction is a concept of 'straightness.' To follow a line might be a way of becoming straight, by not deviating at any point."[6] Ahmed thus envisions that directionality is performative: it invites, guides, and coerces the properly aligned behaviors that produce, as an effect, directionality's normalcy. For Ahmed, "the lines that direct us, as lines of thought as well as lines of motion . . . depend on the repetition of norms and conventions, of routes and paths taken, but they are also created as an effect of this repetition."[7] *Queer Velocities* builds on Ahmed's work to imagine what stepping outside the "straight line" of conventional behavior might look like and to remain attentive to the queerness of directional deviances.

This book makes a bid for paying attention to the "differential speeds marking our becoming with the other beings and things that make up our world," to build on the work of anthropologists Vincent Duclos, Tómas Sánchez-Criado, and Vinh-Kim Nguyen,[8] and thus seeks to shed light on different kinds of velocities that are not always oriented toward heteroreproductive or capitalist ends. Anthropology has been attuned to varied scales of time, both large and small, and scholars such as Cymene Howe have urged thinking in "chrono-mashups with divergent scales: geological time married with temporal immediacies, crises, and catastrophes."[9] These scholars highlight how anthropology's attention to "differential speeds" allows us another way of thinking *relation* and "becoming with other beings" through erotics, intimacy, and sexuality. My book strives to serve as a model for how this might look in the literary and cultural domain of the theater.

In the seventeenth century, on the threshold of the "modern," a whole host of institutions, from dance manuals to the postal service, began to configure and choreograph life. Within this whirlwind of sociotemporal choreography, notions of timeliness, temporality, punctuality, or delay were increasingly threaded through everyday actions, from letter writing to theatergoing. A general normalization was taking place. As Elizabeth Freeman asserts, time was binding "flesh into bodies, and bodies into the social,"[10] while also calibrating these embodied subjects to "proper" affects, ends, and intimacies. These temporally inflected affects and desires allow me to foreground a way of thinking about early modern sexuality that dims the focus on identitarian categories.

It is perhaps an understatement to mention that temporality was one of the most oft-debated topics in seventeenth-century theater. French neoclassical theater was invested in an imagined set of "rules" from antiquity, which yielded dynamic spheres of theater criticism, dramaturgy, and theories of spectatorship that were all hyperconscious of a somewhat artificial and arbitrary constraint: that the tragedy had to unfold within the temporal span of twenty-four hours. Pierre Corneille writes: "La règle de l'unité de jour a son fondement sur ce mot d'Aristote, *que la tragédie doit renfermer la durée de son action dans un tour de soleil, ou tâcher de ne le passer pas de beaucoup*" (The rule of the unity of time is founded on the word of Aristotle, *that the tragedy should restrict the duration of its action to one revolution of the sun, or take care not to exceed it by much*).[11] On a straightforward, ideological-cultural level, the theater did invoke and model life's proper tempos, according to the coalescing sociosexual norms of the period. But I also understand theater to be a site of ambivalent resistance: instead of being solely normative, theater was itself part of distributing a new kind of sensation—the sensation of "rates of motion" or an awareness of speed itself. Therefore, theater became imbricated in this biopolitical management of the time of life by mapping out new ontological possibilities of time itself: *what temporality could even be*. In the theater, within this particular "frame" of the twenty-four-hour window, the focus is heightened on the very speeds of living and desiring that—with strange haste or delay—unhinged the monolithic nature of a single tempo of productivity or reproductive futurity. In the plays that I analyze, desires fail to conform to temporal norms, eliciting rushing or slowness that jars against prescriptive rhythms or deviates from heteroreproductive ends.

My objective here, then, is threefold. First, I highlight how queer velocities (the sensation of slowness and fastness that directionally veers away from a normative telos) are part and parcel of the biopolitical management of time. Second, I insist that we must think of temporality as a historically specific and variable category: the *type* of temporality founded by new developments in the theater and the sciences created new onto-epistemologies of time in the early modern period and catalyzed unexpected affective and often queer intensities. And third, I enlarge our understanding of what "counts" as queerness in the early modern period, moving beyond an identity-driven approach to premodern sexualities to one that emphasizes "differential speeds" as varied, rich, and subtle ways of belonging and being with one another.

I therefore use "velocity" to highlight a relationship between speed and power. Instead of focusing on top-down control, I zoom in on what Michel Foucault called biopolitical "capillary" management, in which everyday bodies and social groups become imbricated in the proliferation and investment in correct, socially acceptable tempos. The scholarship of Gary Ferguson, Carla Freccero, and Todd Reeser on queer sexuality in the French Renaissance and Joan DeJean and Lewis Seifert on seventeenth-century French literature and culture, among others, has already destabilized long-held assumptions regarding gender and sexuality in sixteenth- and seventeenth-century Europe.[12] While appreciating these contributions for their capacity to highlight the historicity of obscenity, male-male sodomy, cross-dressing, same-sex friendship, or queer prolepses of the early modern past, I wish to depart from an identity-centered approach to the study of early modern sexuality. Moving from the molar realm of identities to the molecular space of desires, this book considers a range of affects that did not necessarily lead to the establishment of fixedly transgressive forms of subjectivity. Thus, instead of focusing on a range of minoritarian sexual identities, my study traces desires, however liminal or ephemeral, that fail to sediment in any coherent subject.

Rather than matching contemporary queer identities to premodern analogues, I explore the more fleeting spectrum of temporal intensities and strange affects. I constellate an assortment of feelings, relations, and positions that, according to José Esteban Muñoz, "function as queer evidence: an evidence that has been queered in relation to the laws of what counts of proof";[13] counterintuitively, I unearth this evidence in some of the most canonical neoclassical tragedies. This book ultimately traces the grappling with and reappropriations of temporality that gives rise to desires, attachments, and intimacies that complicate not only the norm and the margin but also the very idea of "sexual identity," by destabilizing the biopolitical and affective terrain on which something like an identity comes to be established.

To return to my opening example, we learn later in *Iphis et Iante* that Iante is not completely shocked by Iphis's bodily truth and even finds it "doux" (sweet).[14] Iphis's and Iante's love would not have seemed immediately scandalous to the seventeenth-century audience. This was in part, of course, due to the Ovidian classical source, but it also could be explained by the fact that same-sex sexuality and gender expression were only beginning to be sedimented into identity categories. The lines between obscenity and propriety were only in the initial stages of being traced out; it was common to question if same-sex female acts were corporeally possible.[15] This presumed "impossibility" also adds another layer to Iphis's plaint, "do you not know how to read (me)?"

This moment in flux is of interest. I take a cue from Foucault's *History of Sexuality* to emphasize that, before the concretization of homosexuality as an identity, sexual behaviors both transgressive and normative were met with a range of reactions, from indifference to new kinds of scrutiny, which reveal a rich and complicated terrain of sexual surveillance. Sexuality was ambiguously caught between flourishing and suppression. Official discourse and practice (e.g., religious sermons or obscenity laws) curtailed unconventional sexual behaviors; for example, Théophile de Viau, a known "sodomite," libertine, and licentious poet, was subject to the first obscenity trial in 1623 and was burned in effigy. Later in the century, Louis XIV's own brother, however, could still openly enjoy the company of his many *mignons* (or boy favorites). Overall, deviant sex and desires were somewhat socially denigrated, but not fully stigmatized.

Rather than speculating about the causal or differential relationship between sexualities of the past and sexualities today, I am much more interested in the incoherencies of sexuality as they are rooted in a historical *moment*. I look to the ways that seventeenth-century French theater ignited new abilities to experience affective stumbles, deviations, and lags as erotic intensification: what Peter Coviello terms "earliness." Although Coviello's analysis bears on the nineteenth-century American context, his deployment of "earliness" offers a rich methodological approach to consider "the experience of sexuality as something in the crosshairs of a number of forms of knowledge and regulation *but not yet wholly captivated or made coordinate by them*."[16] Iphis's plaint, "do you not know how to read," reminds us of her affects and desires that remain uncaptured or inchoate —the sentiments that had not yet coalesced under a legible sign. Her slowness allows us to be arrested in a space that is more nebulous than that afforded by the easy erotic assurances such as fixed gender identity or the constellation of sexed signifiers around "lesbian."

For example, in *Iphis et Iante*, following the wedding night, Iphis's mother Télétuze anxiously asks what happened. Iphis dreamily recounts:

> J'oubliais quelque temps que j'étais une fille,
> Je ne reçus jamais tant de contentements
> . . . .
> J'embrassais ce beau corps, dont la blancheur extrême
> M'excitait à lui faire une place en moi-même
> Je touchais, je baisais, j'avais le cœur content.[17]

(I forgot [for] some time that I was a girl
I have never received so much satisfaction
. . . .
I kissed this beautiful body, whose extreme paleness
Aroused me to make a place for it within myself
I touched, I kissed, my heart was content.)

By foregrounding touch, sensation, and bodies, Iphis forgets for "some time" but also forgets "time"—ignoring the overarching temporal weight of sexual norms: the time of being married or not married; the time before or after gender transformation. In Iphis's case, swerving away from temporal regulation opens an erotic intimacy that skirts the norms of gender identity. Nonconforming velocities in neoclassical drama trouble the increasingly normative temporality underfoot and generate surprising affects and erotics through the very feeling of time.

While the primary focus of this book is temporality and biopolitics in seventeenth-century France, I am aware that this presumes a certain type of hegemonic, white, European time and excludes a discussion of what Johannes Fabian would call the "denial of coevalness" about colonial temporality.[18] The "whiteness" that Iphis idealizes is not incidental and shows how temporal normativity becomes increasingly yoked to not only sexual-gender norms but also racial "norms." Other discussions of the time of empire assume a certain imbrication with time-work discipline and ideals of progress, undoubtedly a crucial component of the history of temporality, but one that risks taking the focus away from the "microdisciplinary" nature of affects, sensations, and temporal intensities.

Queer Velocity and the Ends of Time

Foucault suggests that toward the end of the seventeenth century, a new governance paradigm—biopower—emerged, as power shifted from an executive force that wielded its authority through execution or clemency, to one that managed bodies through a regulated flourishing or calculating diminishing of life's capacities.[19] Foucault traces modernity's cultivation of a whole host of biopolitical apparatuses that fostered such microdiscipline of life, from the codification of labor (artisanal training) to the monitoring of health and wellness. As Eric Santner has underscored, biopower did not neatly supersede early modern absolutism.[20] Biopower, in fact, names a kind of relationality forged between the state and the people, regardless of the juridical form that the state itself assumes. This relationality hinged on harnessing the sexuality and temporality of individuals, cultivating specific rhythms in the life of the body politic while also encouraging self-regulation of the body's cravings, labor, and needs. Instead of power exerting its force through dramatic top-down thunderclaps, it infiltrated and was disseminated through multiple pathways of calibrating life. Drawing on this biopolitical perspective, *Queer Velocities* enriches and troubles the monolithic narrative of spectacular implementation so often associated with absolutist power in the seventeenth century. One contribution this book makes is to foreground spectacle as part and parcel of the production of new forms of embodied subjectivity, of new modes of dwelling in space and in time. In this sense, the theater did not solely provide an ideological legitimation to absolutist power, nor did it primarily subject individuals to certain ideals of social relations and political processes.[21] Drama, in my analysis, thus emerges as a modeling device, a *dispositif* (apparatus)[22] that affects individual bodies and shapes the body politic.

And yet, as Foucault and cultural historians explored this paradigm shift of biopower, they overlooked one crucial aspect, a missing piece that *Queer Velocities* endeavors to reflect on: the *changing nature of time itself* in the seventeenth century. The increased, minute attention allowed by chronometry enabled an intensified attention in the domain of biopolitics, especially in the disciplining of the sexed body. Foucault's attention to time-work discipline in his analysis of the Gobelins tapestry school, for example, highlights the progressive, continual nature of training that breaks down the craft of weaving into minute, masterable gestures. This fractured and serial temporality served to "bend behavior towards a terminal state [making] possible a perpetual characterization of the individual either in relation to this term, in relation to other individuals, or in relation to a type of itinerary."[23] However, Foucault's analysis does not fully account for the ways that temporality itself was itself in flux in this period. Conversely, cultural historians' accounts that do trace this chronometric transition tend to describe a triumphant temporal implantation, a focus on innovative precision that glosses over the errant or surprising modes of feeling that this temporal shift also produced.

The special strangeness of such an unprecedented experience of temporality in the early modern period cannot be underestimated. A brief digression to examine existing accounts of clockmaking innovations is necessary to discuss the affective dimension of time management. After

Christian Huygens developed the pendulum clock in Paris in the late 1650s, the device brought to light a measurement of time that was "so small as to elude all notice only a few years before," and this temporal advancement of the "change in scale amounted virtually to a change in kind," according to Stuart Sherman.[24] Carlo Cipolla has graphed the "dramatic" and "exponential" growth in precision occasioned by this new technology—the margin of error in timekeeping shifted almost instantaneously from a *thousand* seconds to a mere *ten* seconds per day.[25] Major epistemic changes in the ways of perceiving and conceiving the universe were linked to these technological advancements. After the development of the balance spring, a mechanism introduced by Huygens or Robert Hooke (c. 1675),[26] the watch "revolutionized time-discipline" and brought timekeeping performance "very close to the standard we now employ in ordering life and work."[27] Thus bodies, bodies-in-motion, pleasure, and gesture, all could be newly measured and calibrated in time and space. Such chronometries, David Landes suggests, ushered in an era of state and personal regulation of time. The major cultural historians of horology and chronometry, the most prominent of whom include Landes, Gerhard Dorhn-van Rossum, and Carlo Cipolla, all offer detailed analyses of clockmaking innovations, guilds, timepieces and trade, or time and the organization of public life, but lack a closer attention to the sexual and affective dimension of temporal management.[28] This is one gap that *Queer Velocities* seeks to remedy. The regulation of time was inextricably linked to the regulation of desires, embodiments, affects—and therefore, the theater, as a site of this temporal implantation, with its emphasis on the unity of time, and debates over (temporal) propriety, was a major force in the cultivation of proper kinds of sexualities.

Timing technologies offered new apparatuses for disciplining the population, new epistemologies of calculation and measure, and new modes of considering eroticism and desire. Taken together, these innovations prompted a new regulation of temporality—indeed, a new mode of temporality itself becoming proper—in the late seventeenth century. Here, I extend Patricia Parker's work on the gendered and sexualized connotations of the "proper" in early modern English literature and culture in order to emphasize how the tripartite notions of property, propriety, and place *also* became crucially imbricated with temporality in the French seventeenth century.[29] Temporality was becoming personal property in the form of the watch, rendered newly precise by the appearance of the second hand and portably small, thanks to innovations in watchmaking technologies. Temporality also took on qualities of propriety in the regulated rhythms of courtly life, down to the quarter-hour management of Louis XIV's daily rites and rhythms and in the dramatization of proper rates of seduction and marriage on stage. Time's relation to the properness of place emerges from the notion that the state, from domestic life to state politics, relied on a standardized and precise temporality.[30] Roland Racevskis, to give one example, traces the importance of nation-wide temporal coordination for the invention and development of the French postal system.[31] Timepieces themselves were favored gifts to the imperial courts in Beijing, and French missionaries to Siam were often as trained in horology as they were in their religious faith or diplomatic skills.[32] And later, in the eighteenth century, England and France dangled hefty monetary prizes to accelerate the national "arms race" for precise clocks aboard ships; with seaworthy timepieces, seafarers could calculate precise longitude, thereby enabling imperial expansion. In all these senses of "proper" time, timekeeping technologies and new ideologies related to the state, intimacy, and communication became intermeshed in new and surprising ways.

One commonplace of seventeenth-century French studies highlights yet another aspect of temporal "properness," in terms of ideological dazzlement. The king's body can be thought of as a *roi-machine* (king-machine). Jean-Marie Apostolidès builds on Ernst Kantorowicz's theories of the king's two bodies to assert that Louis XIV, as the absolute Sun King, had to ceremonially sacrifice his body mortal to sublimate into a body politic, with divine right to rule: the coexistence of two bodies, mortal and politic, thus present a paradox for the living yet divine king.[33] Apostolidès suggests that one aspect of this transformation that takes place in seventeenth-century France is that the king takes on machine-like qualities

> This glorious body that functions like a clock brings to the court a ceremonial quality mechanized to the extreme in the court . . . Saint-Simon notes that "with a clock and an almanac, three hundred leagues from the court, one knew what the king was doing, at a given hour." The gesticulations of the king-machine corresponded to those of the courtesans who daily approached him in the hopes of a favor or a kindly glance.[34]

Thus, the clock is not only the metaphorical figure of the king but also the condition of possibility of such a king-machine. The very precision of a clock and of calculable daily rhythms produced an absolutist, quasi-divine body, whose rhythms and mechanized gestures gave a ceremonial effect and elicited the attention and desires of the nobles surrounding him.

This book detours from the straightforward association between clock timeliness and kingly power—beyond the equation between temporal regularity and political regulation[35]—to consider the ways that clocks inaugurated a new *kind* of biosocial temporality. I build on the work of Roland Racevskis, who argues that these "newly accurate timepieces" that ticked away the minutes and even seconds of quotidian rhythms actually permitted a special kind of privacy, a richly detailed interior life, ever new possibilities in "mapping the microitineraries of private experience."[36] This privacy cannot be underestimated. Cipolla notes that before the seventeenth century, towns benefited from one public clock that loudly (and rather inaccurately) clanged the hours away. These public clocks, a source of community pride, required a civically appointed governor who regulated and manually reset the clock to the correct time. In contrast, personal timepieces in the seventeenth century appeared to be *self-governing*, and the clock's self-automation similarly metaphorized and metonymized new possibilities of individual self-governance.

The increased, minute attention allowed by chronometry can be thought of as the individual-level operations, representative of a larger-scale intensified attention in the domain of biopolitics, especially in the disciplining of the sexed body. The significance is on the level of scale. Sex, for Foucault, served as a *dispositif* (apparatus) of dual management. On the disciplinary level of the body, sex was invested in the "harnessing, intensification, and distribution of forces, the adjustment and economy of energies," as well as being threaded through the "regulation of populations, through all the far-reaching effects of its activity."[37] All this yielded "infinitesimal surveillances, permanent controls, extremely meticulous orderings of space and time, to an entire micro-power concerned with the body."[38] Thus, to fold Foucault's assertion back to the early modern moment, as time became more precise, so too did the body's "meticulous orderings." Gone were the public clock and the clock's governor, and in their place emerged a new, proper and personal time. In this light, the body becomes both an effect of power and the contested site itself of control, in terms of its productivity and activity. We move here from the *roi-machine* as clock (whose bodily rhythms were deployed for dazzling ideological control) to the new timepieces as generating another kind of subjectivity and intensity, and therefore another type of embodiment, ripe to be seized by biopower.

As mentioned before, the "properness" of time was increasingly directed toward reproductive ends, appropriate objects of affection, or future progress. Elizabeth Freeman and Dana Luciano have suggested that the *chrono*biopolitical merges a biopolitical control of life practices and orientations with a particular attention to the temporal management of life. Such coordination, Freeman argues, "extends beyond individual anatomies to encompass the management of the temporality of entire populations . . . in a chronobiological society, the state and other institutions, including representational apparatuses, link properly temporalized bodies to narratives of movement and change."[39] Foucault underscores that his notion of biopower hinges on the organization and calibration of multiple forces—not just the imposition of force, but the attunement of intensities of life.[40] Given the increased importance of chronometric technologies to everyday life in the seventeenth century, it is easy to see how emergent temporalities could present a major contribution to this network of biopolitical force. This early modern moment offers a window into a chronobiopolitics coalescing.

This is not to make a case for straightforward techno-determinism, or to contend that technology was responsible for provoking a change in the sociosexual sphere. Instead, I want to highlight two interventions: when "temporality" is invoked by queer theory, it is often a modern sense of temporality rather than one that allows the richness and strangeness of the premodern confrontation with temporality to fully emerge. Second, and perhaps more radically, we can consider the theater in seventeenth-century France as constituting no less than a new onto-epistemology of temporality, specifically through the representation of velocities. By showing a range of speeds, a spectrum of "chrono-mashups" on stage, and by awakening the audience to the disruptive nature of haste or delay, the theater could present new ways of knowing, feeling, and sensing time. A range of time-inflected social, historical, and cultural developments were knotted together in the seventeenth century, from the invention of chronometric precision to much broader theater regulations, and this matrix yielded new possibilities for aberrant feelings or surprising erotics onstage.

Queer Temporality's Blind Spots

In the past two decades, queer theory has certainly considered the relationship between time and sexual normativity. *Queer Velocities* participates in this conversation by specifically highlighting speeds and tempos. A brief digression is necessary to examine the preexisting positions that queer theory has taken in relation to temporal norms. In 2004 Lee Edelman's polemic *No Future* argued for a stand against "reproductive futurity" and the "coercive belief in the paramount value of futurity"[41] as emblematized by the figure of the child that we are consistently enjoined to protect, to fight for, or to (pro)create.[42] Those who "opt out," or—worse—refuse to fight on behalf of the child are then blamed for the "fatal lure of sterile, narcissistic enjoyments understood as inherently destructive of meaning and therefore as responsible for the undoing of social organization, collective reality, and, inevitably, life itself."[43]

The mere lack of biological heteroreproduction would be a rather clumsy, obvious way to tie nonreproductive futurity to queer existence. Edelman, however, goes beyond the equivalence between childlessness and a politics that opposes this "coercive" futurity. He does so by drawing on psychoanalysis and the death drive, highlighting that for a person to cohere as a self, that person must foreclose a certain sense of negativity, perpetually racing toward an "eventual" realization of meaning that is impossible to obtain.[44] Therefore, instead of pushing toward unattainable ideals in a fruitless race, queerness amplifies a negativity that has long been associated with it, thereby hijacking the otherwise stigmatizing association between queerness and nonreproduction. Futurity only makes sense in relation to the social, and the social is constituted by *definitional conditions of possibility* that allow and disallow certain bodies, genders, and sexualities to cohere. In this manner, queerness must outright reject the future and the terms and conditions of social legibility, under which we are compelled to "fight for the child." For Edelman, "the death drive names what the queer, in the order of the social, is called forth to figure: the negativity opposed to every form of social viability."[45] This has been termed the "antisocial thesis" because it refuses the presumed good of the productive bonds and intimate ties that undergird and constitute the social.

In contrast to this antisocial negativity, José Esteban Muñoz powerfully invokes queerness's relationship to a futurity, or a not yet. The opening lines of *Cruising Utopia* stand as a rallying cry:

> Queerness is not yet here. Queerness is an ideality. Put another way, we are not yet queer. We may never touch queerness, but we can feel it as the warm illumination of a horizon imbued with potentiality. We have never been queer, yet queerness exists for

> us as an ideality that can be distilled from the past and used to imagine a future. The future is queerness's domain. Queerness is a structuring and educated mode of desiring that allows us to see and feel beyond the quagmire of the present.[46]

For Muñoz, queerness is potential energy, a force capable of shattering the present constraints of here and now, or present forms of embodiment. Queerness is a reaching, or a striving. The impetus for such movement depends on a deep level of dissatisfaction with the present—a feeling that there are other kinds of configurations, possibilities, and intimacies that can be yielded, or have not yet been wrought into existence. Muñoz's "ideality that can be distilled from the past" is put into praxis by thinkers such as Carolyn Dinshaw, Elizabeth Freeman, and Peter Coviello, among other scholars. Coviello, to extend the example of "earliness" cited before, speaks of the "erotic self in the twilit moment before the arrival or calcifying of the terms of sexual identity" and surmises that to live in this crepuscular moment "might also be to enjoy a special kind of freedom . . . whose fragile, uncollapsed spaces of illegibility or definitional ambiguity left precious room for much besides suffering and loneliness: for invention, say, or teasing obliquity, or coy solicitation, as well as evasion, improvisation, and all the other vectors of extravagant imagining."[47] Rather than render the past in purely nostalgic terms, Coviello and others see the past as containing fleeting, perhaps unrealized or unrecognizable forms of desire. *Queer Velocities* takes a similar approach by remaining theoretically imaginative yet historically grounded. A rejection of the coercive nature of "reproductive futurity" is necessary, but it must be done by drawing together Muñoz's utopic vision with a "special kind of freedom" afforded by early modern time.

And yet, I suggest that in queer theory's treatments of the relation between time and sexuality, the importance of *tempo*, *pace*, or *speed* has not yet been accounted for. Queer interventions have tended toward folding the linear trajectory back toward the past, or braking against a reproductive futurity, without ever calling the linearity itself into question. Such a queer rupture of time generally puts the present in relation to an imagined future or a reclaimed past. For example, Dinshaw's medieval writers feel that their "now" is not the now of the present, and such atemporal wrenching creates affective dissonance and imagined eroticized "touching" of long-gone pasts, but this "touching" still orients the past, present, and future like pearls on a string. "The most fundamental and consequential limitation of conceptions (and thus practices) of queer time to date is that they share with dominant, heteronormative temporalities the assumption that time is ultimately linear—indeed, that it is 'straight,'"[48] argues Tom Boellstorff, whose dissatisfaction I share. How might queer theory queer its own thinking about time, to amplify the aforementioned "chrono-mashups"? While many queer analyses point to the various ways that sexuality and temporality are linked, none offers a clear way to conceptualize the impact of *tempos*—of speeds and slownesses. *Queer Velocities*, then, sheds light on the blind spots of previous contributions to queer temporality and offers a new means of considering temporal intensities that are at odds with chrononormativity.

A queer approach to the study of neoclassical tragedy surely risks the charge of ahistoricism or anachronism. The subfield of early modern queer studies has responded to such charges in three distinct ways, and divergences between the historical and deconstructive approaches have ignited an intellectual debate within the field. Some, such as L. O. Aranye Fradenberg (*Premodern Sexualities*) or Dinshaw (*Getting Medieval*) have outright embraced anachronism, transforming what might be critiqued as an analytical weakness into a robust method that celebrates being out of sync, allowing for surprising affects and "touches" of history to bubble up when the past and the present are allowed to bump up against each other.[49] Others turn the question on its head, contending that the charge of anachronism itself belies an investment in chronology, which trades in the fixed and fixable categories of identity. Madhavi Menon's *Unhistorical Shakespeare* models this response, by advancing what she calls "homo-history" and sticking closely to rhetorical-deconstructive destabilizations of desire; in this vein, anachronism is itself queer, for it operates as a force that dissolves the fixity of identity categories and the rigidity of periodization that history itself depends on.[50] Freccero also argues against these strict categorizations, suggesting that "theoretically anything can queer something, and anything, given a certain odd twist, can become queer."[51] Critics have worried that a downside of these two approaches is that it risks advancing an overly expansive sense of queerness. When everything can be queered in the name of dissolving identity, queerness can lose its critical purchase or relation to embodiment or lived experience. Still others deny anachronism altogether by underscoring that queerness or antinormativity is itself part and parcel of the early modern sociosexual world: the unfamiliarity of the deep past is less foreign than we might think. Jonathan Goldberg's suggests this approach when he takes up the "void" of "sodometries" in Renaissance England, a capacious but historically specific category that indicated a range of acts, from adultery to buggery, which were deemed contrary to the social order—much like the critical ramifications of a contemporary sense of queerness that challenges the social order of a settled domain of normativity.[52]

My approach to queerness carefully balances both the historical and ahistorical approaches to the study of the queer early modern. Far from being anachronistic, queer velocity's particular strangeness is deeply embedded in the early modern world and intimately reflects the changing social and subjective experience of temporality, of a world in flux. I take a page from what Ari Friedlander calls the "historicist settlement," in which "scholars continue to ask pressing questions about the historical dimension of sexual experience even though the exact relationship between historical sameness and difference remains uncertain."[53] Friedlander builds on Valerie Traub's assertion that we can "assume neither that we will find in the past a mirror image of ourselves nor that the past is so utterly alien that we will find nothing useable in its fragmentary traces."[54] Chronometric innovations, development of theater rules, and even aurality of the French language all afford particular legibilities and illegibilities of historically situated queernesses of the seventeenth century. At the same time, it is within this historically situated matrix that anachronistic qualities like desire, fantasy, and affect emerge. And instead of treating this aporia of legibility as a deconstructive puzzle, we might understand it as an invitation to imagine unstable possibilities of feeling in the past.

Theater's Temporal Torsions

Dramatic literature in France underwent a highly contested refinement from the 1630s to the 1660s, moving toward the regularized disciplinary apparatus that absolutism wished it to become. The relationship between "proper" temporality and "appropriate" behaviors on stage was of utmost concern to both spectators and political leaders alike. Theater's relationship to time was not only limited to proclivities of aesthetic taste but also carried a concrete, moralizing function. To this end, Déborah Blocker explains that theater's form and presentation were engineered to elicit submission and docility. Actors were expected to refine their performance techniques into an art; authors were expected to adhere to rules of propriety derived from antiquity; and spectators were expected to defer to the "experts" in evaluating performances. In this way, for Blocker, "the practice of this entertainment would publicly provide the image of a collective submission to a superior rationality: the theater would therefore be likely to produce orderly behavior in the spectators, because it was itself the product of disciplined behavior."[55] Once a lowly practice associated with bawdiness, charlatans, or prostitution (performing a show for money), the theater underwent a radical change in status, elevated to the centerpiece of statecraft, thanks to a highly coordinated effort to reappropriate the medium for political ends.[56] In *Theatrical Legitimation*, Timothy Murray has highlighted the numerous strategies marshalled by writers, politicians, and playwrights alike to "legitimize" the theater, which in turn legitimized new modes of spectatorship and subjectivity.[57] To this end, Louis XIII's cultural minister Cardinal Richelieu organized a "Society of Five Authors," who were commissioned to write plays following (his) specific instructions and guidelines; Abbé d'Aubignac was even commissioned to write a type of manual cataloguing and standardizing the rules of theater "practice."

From theater critics to playwrights to state ministers, a wide range of professionals, politicians, and artists were all preoccupied with the seemingly simple question of the proper way to represent duration onstage. Two qualities governed most theater production: *vraisemblance* and *bienséance*. These oft-debated terms carried major theoretical and cultural significance during this period. Jacques Scherer offers a concise summary of these terms: vraisemblance, or verisimilitude, is an "intellectual exigency" that prohibits the absurd and the arbitrary, whereas bienséance, or the rule of propriety, is a "moral exigency" that forbids that which would shock taste, morals, and public prejudices.[58] Taken together, vraisemblance and bienséance meant that theatrical representation—in terms of both content and formal qualities—was heavily scrutinized, oriented toward an imagined public good, and charged with the duty of exemplifying intellectual and moral ideals. Therefore, standing at the intersection of knowledge and state power, the theater became increasingly conscripted as a machine apparatus, or as a form for "containing" and shaping affect and the normative experience of temporality. Giovanni Dotoli underscores that the initial relation between theater and the state was born from the necessity of governing unruly affects, desires, and even civil unrest, including the famous uprising of nobles the Fronde, (1648–53). In the earlier half of the century, the cultural minister Cardinal Richelieu thought it prudent to "push writers to create or recreate forms of sure thought, landmarks that could pilot the instinctive and the irrational."[59] Theater was initially designed to be a model of orderly propriety.

But one of the principles of bienséance held that explicit bodily representations (such as eating, death, sex, or pregnancy) had to be banished from the stage. This very foreclosure highlights the ways that a raw, inchoate, ungovernable sensuality or sexuality was always already designated as threatening to the pure, classical forms toward which absolutism was striving.[60] One could thereby say that the theater modeled proper sociosexual rhythms and intimacies by adhering to the Aristotelian unities of time, place, and action and by banishing obscene embodiment from the stage. But, on a deeper level, the theater itself became not only a vehicle of representation but also a terrain of engagement, a site where time—temporalities and chrononormativity—was not just conveyed but was, in fact, iteratively constituted through the very metatheatrical debates or the drama's own quibbles with representational duration. As I analyze in chapter 1, theater's treatment of theatrical time is not just the calcified product of the emergent "rules" of the era but, rather, can be seen instead as the very aesthetic emanation of an emergent chrononormativity.

All of these rules, debates, and initiatives toward sociopolitical order coalesced to render theater a rich site of inquiry. This book examines early modern theater's multiple capacities to generate surprising, forceful affects, grounded in temporal sensation. The queerness of the staged velocities I trace cannot be simply ascribed to resistance, hidden authorial intention, or surreptitious counterideological subversion. For theater to be successful, that is, to sway the audiences or move them to pleasure, tears, laughter, or sorrow, it had to be invested in the cultivation of affect, and oftentimes unruly, ungoverned, or even ungovernable affect. "La principale règle," Jean Racine writes in his preface to *Bérénice*, "est de plaire et de toucher" (The first rule [of theater] is to please and to move).[61] Theater, as I argued earlier, allowed for a new onto-epistemology of temporality. The tragedies I analyze all model, shape, and generate certain temporal feelings—surprising haste, aggravating delay—toward the goal of pleasing and moving the audience, not necessarily curating obedience or implementing biopolitical management. By sheer virtue of its primary orientation toward pleasure, the theater can be thought of as representing a spectrum of subversions of chrononormativity. Thus, the form that was intended for governance also affords its own troubling.

I use the rich strangenesses of the literature and culture of the seventeenth century, in a moment when bodies were being imprinted by a new kind of fragmented, measured temporality, to put pressure on the assumptions that we hold about what eroticism can look like and how time can feel today. Luciano points out that "feeling is not simply analogous to what Foucault identifies as sexuality but constitutes a crucial dimension of the *dispositif* of sexuality itself: the modern intensification of the body, its energies, and its meanings."[62] We can recall that for Foucault, biopower's relation to sexuality is not merely limited to blatantly sexual actions, desires, and embodiments. Sexuality as it is constituted, grasped, and produced by biopower can also include the range of sensations and pleasures that are reinforced by new sites of knowledge-power.

In the plays that I analyze, the pleasures afforded by the new kind of "temporal self-measurement" are intertwined with the experience of what Roland Racevskis calls an increasingly precise "micro-physics of power," drawing upon Foucault.[63] Landes points out that in the seventeenth century, the chamber clock or watch became an "ever visible, ever audible companion and monitor. A turning hand, specifically a minute hand . . . is a measure of time used, time spent, time wasted, time lost. As such it was prod and key to personal achievement and productivity."[64] This is an intensity that not only contributes to modern timework discipline but also generates new kinds of interiority and pleasure. Sherman notes that by the late seventeenth century, even technologies as minor as the clock dial or the minute hand "called attention away from endpoints and invested it in middles—of the current hour, of the ongoing life—that were sharply defined and indefinitely extended."[65] The new ticking second and minute hands furnished an unprecedented richness to an otherwise blandly indeterminate block of time; this focus on the *passing* of time (the "middles") relieved the weight and importance that we ascribe to the origins or the ends.

These are the "middles" that Iphis, in her overtures to Iante, seizes on to express a gender and sexual deviance. We can turn to Gilles Deleuze to consider how exactly velocity might signal resistance. Deleuze, building on Foucault, argues that since life is the ultimate prize at stake in the game of biopolitical discipline, life itself becomes a means of "hijacking" such monitoring: "Life becomes resistance to power when power takes life as its object . . . when power becomes bio-power, resistance becomes the power of life, a vital power that cannot be confined within species, environment or the paths of a particular diagram."[66] Deleuze's reading of biopolitics imagines redeploying the object of prey (life) as the very means of resistance. I apply this model to temporality, keeping in mind the particular temporal heart of biopolitics. When power takes the time of life as its object and objective, resistance becomes a matter of the time of living. We can divert disciplinary vigor into a countervitality that stems from velocity. If time is the object, then attention to temporalities—divergent tempos, swerving speeds—becomes critical. Deleuze's *pouvoir-vital* (vital power) becomes not a matter of life but a matter of speed.

Velocity, in a strange haste or slowness, allows a critical occupation of the "middles" of chronometry, a swerve away from the overriding importance of the ends, the appointment hours, the deadlines, or the beginnings. Velocity is the manifestation of a specific self-governance that heightens the attention to the middles of time and private experience; it reappropriates temporal discipline to let alternative forms of intimacy emerge. Therefore, the resistance that velocity proposes is not a dialectical pushback. Rather it is one of a queered "direction," declining to participate in the feedback loop of prohibition and repression. Velocity goes beyond the critique of the way one is oriented toward an optimistic future or a mourned for past. Instead of considering one's orientation to time (past, present, and future), velocity foregrounds the "extended middles." It is a vital dwelling within time.

Variations of Velocities

In the archive of French tragedies that I examine, each drama demonstrates a different kind of queer velocity, a different kind of troubling of temporal norms. While not exhaustive of the early modern concerns with temporality or queerness, the texts do share an interest in modeling chronormativities, such as the slowness of grief, the suddenness of religious conversion, or the speed of sovereign progress. But the dramas also highlight tempos whose speeds and directional "orientation" are strangely out of sync with normative expectations. Occasionally these velocities are remarked on diegetically in the text, such as Iphis pointing to her own slownesses. Because seventeenth-century French tragedy is written in rhymed verse of twelve syllable lines, called alexandrine verse, the aural or performed quality of velocity is made even more apparent. A multiplicity of vowel "elisions" may effectively sound a slower, stretched-out tempo (as I have analyzed elsewhere), or else when the normal rhythm of a full twelve syllables is splintered between characters, it can create a speedy stichomythic dialogue of two interrupting or interlocking voices.[67] The very structure of French neoclassical tragedy permits such temporal play. Velocities can also emerge in what J. K. Barret calls "microstructures," miniforms such as promise or rhyme that "entail a temporal component" or "future orientation, because they foreground anticipation and expectation."[68] Similar to the ways that Racevskis suggests that the fragmentation and subdivision of time elicited an understanding of the "microphysics" of power, some of my attention to velocities occurs at the microlevel of trope, for example, in the rushed nature of paranomasia, a pun that simultaneously strikes two different meanings within one, singular utterance. Parker also evocatively underscores the speed and directionality inherent in metaphor, a trope often imagined by early modern rhetoricians as a "figure of transport" insofar as a word is "wrested" from its originary locus and deployed in a new configuration. As she notes, in a description that interests this study of velocity: metaphor as that which "delay[s] the movement towards meaning or object." Parker writes: [Paul] Valéry [calls] metaphors "those stationary movements" ("ces mouvements stationnaires"), or "deviations that enrich" ("les écarts qui enrichissent"), creators of a space of "hésitation" distinct from the kind of language which disappears as soon as its "aim" has been reached, entirely replaced by its "meaning."[69] In Parker's analysis, metaphor can express both microtemporalities (of delay) as well as (stationary) movement or imagined directional errancy, all of which are captured in my concept of velocity.

The method that I bring to my study of queer velocities examines the proliferation of these "microtemporalities" in French early modern drama diegetically, performatively, and rhetorically. As an aside, I will signal to the reader that it is perhaps fitting for a book about detours and wayward rhythms that I make some substantial interventions and track some unruly trains of thought in this book's endnotes.

In chapter 1 I reconsider the notion of *bienséances* (rules of propriety), highlighting that they are not merely aesthetic guidelines intended to refine the theater, but also have a sociocultural component, which establishes and reinforces the "norm" and the proper tempos of behavior, desire, and love. I put pressure on the received notion of the theater's rules (including the "unity of time"); one commonplace derives from how the theater's imposition of order was a mirrored reflection of absolutist order. I swerve this conception toward the biopolitical, asserting that we must think of the "unity of time" and other theatrical rules as a form, which offers a range, or spectrum of affordances, some normative and some surprising. I ultimately suggest that one overlooked affordance of these neoclassical rules is the cultivation of what Foucault calls the "conduct of conducts" or the management of the possibilities of behavior and comportment itselfand the concomitant temporalities of the body.[70]

Perhaps no play better illustrates the anxieties and pleasures that surrounded the representation of time than Pierre Corneille's *Le Cid* (1637), which I analyze in chapter 1. At the end of the drama, the heroine Chimène is engaged to her beloved Rodrigue, who has just murdered her father. But because the action ostensibly takes place within twenty-four hours, the speeds of mourning, revenge, forgiveness, and sexual desire have all been frenetically compressed. This velocity, and its divergence from propriety and *vraisemblance* (verisimilitude), incited an early modern pamphlet war, generating more than several hundred pages of heated pamphlets and letters provoked by Chimène's "rushing" in defiance of the "laws of nature" (the expectations of feminine propriety)—but, despite breaking the rules of representation, the play was wildly popular. Chimène's resistance to the king governing her sexual subjectivity is, notably, expressed through time: her articulation of her own desires (to see Rodrigue, to hasten or delay justice) is expressed through odd rushing and clashing speeds. Velocity's pairing of speed and a directional "orientation" shows how sexual ends and tempos can sometimes queerly unravel each other.

I close this chapter by examining the sociopolitical impact of velocities through a close reading of selected letters and pamphlets of the "Querelle du *Cid*." The possibility of what Jacques Rancière might call the "emancipated spectator" was at stake, and the formation of this emancipation hinged precisely on the representation of time. Thus, this chapter ultimately highlights the doubled nature of theater as both normative and resistant; the Académie française wanted the theater to serve as a model of normative temporality, but *Le Cid*'s ability to incite such a powerful wave of affects, in both spectators and critics, confirmed the theater's crucial role as a means of cultivating new feelings in time.

The subsequent chapters of the book present case studies of velocity. In chapter 2 I investigate a queer velocity that is too slow—so slow that it appears inactive or indifferent. In Jean Racine's *Andromaque* (1667), the eponymous widow of Hector is faced with an impossible choice: either marry her captor Pyrrhus or allow her son to be executed. While most readings attribute Andromaque's hesitation to obsessive widowhood or bad motherhood, I read her delay as a competing velocity. Andromaque engages with the ashes of her dead husband in an active relationship (dialoguing with and calling out to them), which exceeds mere melancholy in the wake of her loss. Instead, the tempo of inaction permits a moment in which she can linger in another type of love, a queer desire. She valorizes ash *qua* ash, in its double status as *ruin* (testament to a loss) and as *remainder* (the persistent, material remains that enable memory to endure); deciding on the ultimatum would close off this affective ambiguity. Such an incomprehensible love generates friction against the expected, gender-normative velocities of action. This analysis also builds on queer theories of new materialism and object-oriented ontologies (e.g., Mel Chen and Jane Bennett) that expand the spectrum of what counts as love, erotics, or an appropriate object of desire.[71]

In chapter 3 I examine speeds that disrupt established temporalities associated with family, colonial governance, and marriage, and consider what it means for one to desire one's tempo to be exactly calibrated to another's. Set in AD 250, Corneille's *Polyeucte* (1643) depicts a crisis of Roman biopolitical management in colonial Armenia. The play depicts Polyeucte's conversion to the illegal religion of Christianity by his friend Néarque. The two men hasten toward their redemptive deaths, challenging the governor—the representative of the play's biopolitical force—who would otherwise wish to prolong, manage, and extend life. Polyeucte's loved ones are shocked not only by the conversion but also by the ways that Polyeucte desires his velocity to be matched exactly with his friend's: he ardently seeks martyrdom so that he can be reunited with the executed Néarque. The velocities associated with these literary figures not only communicate a nonnormative, socially transgressive desire (Christian, queer) but also challenge the acceptable rhythms and tempos associated with reproduction, genealogies, and marriage.

Chapter 4 addresses the temporality of polyamorous desire in Racine's *Bérénice* (1670). I read a queer triadic relationship between the Emperor Titus, his beloved Bérénice whom he must send away, and Antiochus, Titus's best friend who is secretly infatuated with Bérénice. Critics usually analyze the play in terms of pairs, of the pathos of the *invitus invitam* (despite him, despite her)—that Titus, to become emperor, must yield to Roman law and send away his beloved companion, the foreign queen Bérénice. This prioritizing of the male-female couple erases Antiochus's attachment to Titus and the plurality of desires and dependencies flowing between the three of them. In contrast to the speed of sovereignty, progress, and decision making, the eroticism undergirding the dynamics of this polyamorous triad relies on a temporality that is "dilated"—undecided and repetitive, yet full of possibilities. These erotic relationships are enabled by a repetitive temporality: "Depuis cinq ans entiers chaque jour je la vois,/ Et crois toujours la voir pour la première fois" (For five whole years, I've seen her every day, / And I always believe that I am seeing her for the first time [2.2.545–46]), says Titus.[72] Thus, a "circular" velocity that actively returns to the beginning offers a different vision of nonprogress than that of *Andromaque* and showcases the dilated temporality of sustaining multiple love relationships or intimate friendships simultaneously.

Finally, I consider in my conclusion how velocities can be used to leverage what Johannes Fabian has called the "denial of coevalness,"[73] or the presumed temporal "lag" between societies that have been othered as "unmodernized" and the West. I use Voltaire's tragedy *Zaïre (*1732*)*, set in the Jerusalem of the Crusades, to show how far from being primitive, this otherized space also allows for surprisingly complex intimacies forged within the harem or the prison. Although Enlightenment reason would seek to promote a sense of equality in which the Muslim sultan Orosmane and Christian French captive Zaïre could fall in love, such universality begins to crumble under the pressure of the sociosexual norms of Western monogamy, Christian intolerance, and more. The coexistence of radically different temporalities and velocities punctures a hole in the Enlightenment fantasies of equal ubiquity, for these universalizing, liberal beliefs fail to fully encompass certain troubling and queer attachments. I track how velocities, while not quite toppling the impoverished present, allow a fleeting "stepping out" of the dictates of rationality and a means of striving toward other tempos of being together, living with, and loving each other.

This book ultimately seeks to highlight the presence, in seventeenth-century French theater, of velocities—both slownesses and speeds—that diverge from reproductive ends or heteronormative expectations. Attending to these kinds of temporal intensities helps us see subtle, middle-ground moments that may not lead to any comprehensible outcomes or become phenomenologically legible sexual acts.

And yet, not only does queerness put pressure on the history of chronometry; the early modern particularities of timing and affect bear on queer theory itself. Accordingly, I have taken up Robyn Wiegman and Elizabeth Wilson's recent invitation to "think queer theory without assuming antinormativity from the outset"[74] through an oblique detour via an early modern moment when the notion of temporal normativity—and antinormativity, for that matter—was in the very process of coalescing. In the feedback loop between temporal norms and sexual norms, we find a snag at a point when time was neither always normative nor always timely (i.e., regulated, standardized, or precise). We cannot therefore assume the position of antinormativity without considering the churning process underfoot to render temporality "normative" in the first place. The incoherencies that queer theory has cherished become, interestingly enough, not the condition of marginalization but rather interwoven into the very fabric of the history of normative and nonnormative sexuality and time.

Eve Kosofsky Sedgwick once famously wondered about how to trace the "middle ranges" of agency, the middle zone between reifying a status quo or outright rejecting it. For Sedgwick, only such "middle ranges" could "offer space for effectual creativity and change."[75] In this book I suggest that such middle-range agency could be most clearly found in the middle ranges of time, in the opening of the middles of the moment, the temporal gaps and illogical fissures in the unity of time presented onstage. Chronobiopower seizes on the time of life as both the object of control and the apparatus of power. Queer velocities as staged in the early modern theater offer, in bursts of pouvoir-vital, a different kind of tarrying with time and biopolitical discipline and a different kind of erotics, as well as ever new middle sensations wrought from these fleeting and divergent tempos and temporalities of desire.

1

The Queer Disunity of Time, or The Affective Affordances of *Le Cid*

The Agitating Question of Temporality

"There has never been, in our times, a question more agitating than the one that I am about to discuss," writes François Hédelin, Abbé d'Aubignac; "Often the poets speak of it, and actors discuss it at every meeting, as do those who spend time in the theater; there is hardly a single salon in which women do not seek to educate themselves and others on the matter."[1] The "it" to which he refers is the so-called rule of twenty-four hours or the unity of time: a rule from the "ancients" of classical antiquity that limited the temporal frame of the tragedy to twenty-four hours, which, as d'Aubignac puts it, suggests that the action "should be enclosed within one turn of the sun."[2] The other two unities—place (that the drama had to take place within a single location) and action (that there be only a single motivating incident, sans subplots)—were all, effectively, derivatives of this temporal limitation, since space could only be traversed so far within one day, and too many threads of intrigue would be confusing if crammed into one twenty-four-hour period. One could surmise, then, that the unity of time was in many ways formative in both senses of the word: both giving form to and serving as a foundation for neoclassical tragedy.

D'Aubignac's rhetoric may seem exaggeratedly overwrought today, but it offers a snapshot of a particular cultural moment in the seventeenth century, when writers such as himself were called on by Cardinal Richelieu (Louis XIV's chief political adviser and cultural minister) to hone the theater into not only a respectable and respected institution (as Blocker has argued) but also a potential arm of the state to curate and cultivate orderly and adoring hearts and minds.[3] To this end, the theater had to be refined to become a refining cultural force, itself. A cornerstone of this institutionalization was d'Aubignac's *La pratique du théâtre* (1657), the first and most major volume in the seventeenth century to lay down dramaturgical principles and to explore theatricality as a metaconcept, according to Hélène Baby.[4] The book not only summarized diverse Aristotelian and neoclassical theories of proper dramatic writing and structure but also strove to establish itself as *the* definitive orthodoxy regarding the stage. And fittingly, the major playwrights of the seventeenth century—Molière, Racine, and Corneille—were all known to have read and consulted d'Aubignac's volume, along with the larger public.

I earlier proposed that developments in the technology of precise and portable timepieces catalyzed not only new ways of measuring and knowing time but also new *kinds* of temporal sensations and experiences—in short, *new onto-epistemologies of temporality.* As d'Aubignac's remark shows, time was of particular concern for the theater in the second half of the seventeenth century in France. But the rule he evokes does not merely interest actors and theatergoers. Temporality, in the world of the seventeenth century, was highly segmented and surveilled, from the limitations of the twenty-four hours of theatrical time to the daily tempos of Louis XIV's day. As Roland Racevskis has shown, Louis used temporal compartmentalization, down to fifteen-minute increments, to yield a sense of ritual and rhythm:

> The "premier gentilhomme" of the king's chambers would open the bed's curtains at a quarter past eight. After fifteen minutes of prayer, Louis XIV arose from his bed and put on his slippers and robe and, while being combed by the head barber, began to be clothed . . . Every gesture involved in the process of dressing Louis XIV was measured and repeated in the same way from day to day. A specific rhythm of daily experience structured mornings at Versailles, as anxious court members observed the proceedings and remained constantly aware of the moments at which they might speak to the king.[5]

In this minitheater of the king's daily embodiment, temporality was a crucial element in the display of control, power, and sovereignty—and not simply time itself, but a segmented, monitored, and maximized sense of timing.

In the theater, similar to this hypervigilant courtly life, this heightened sensibility to time was present onstage even during the earlier reign of Louis XIII. Authors often embedded allusions into the text to signal the passing of time. Jacques Scherer notes that "these allusions . . . show[ed] that one respected and valued the new rule. They did not have an aesthetic function."[6] But while Scherer insists that this is a way for the playwrights to signal their trendiness in adhering to the latest fashion, it also carries the additional impact of awakening the audience to the very passing of time, and the feelings associated with the delay or haste of events. Charles Sorel remarks, regarding the trend of highlighting the passing of time through theater decor and language: "It is almost surprising that they didn't also put a time-dial in the theater, to mark the hours one after the other, in order to better show the spectators that the play's length was within the twenty-four hour limit."[7] Sorel's tongue-in-cheek comment accurately reflected the ways that the performance of an aesthetic trend (obeying the classical rules) yielded new forms of social surveillance and new temporal sensibilities.

Therefore, on an aesthetic and political level, concerns about obeying the theatrical rule occupied a central place in the debates and discussions, from the women's salon circles to the grandeur of the stage. These effects of temporal fragmentation would eventually bloom in the mid-eighteenth century into structures that Foucault calls discipline and punishment. He examines a particular royal ordinance of 1766 that breaks down military guidelines for walking into multiple, micromanaged parts, including heel angle, leg motions, and movements. Whereas before, in the seventeenth century, military marching guidelines mostly urged unison. For Foucault:

> it is rather a collective and obligatory rhythm, imposed from the outside . . . We have passed from a form of injunction that measured or punctuated gestures to a web that constrains them or sustains them throughout their entire succession. A sort of anatomo-chronological schema of behavior is defined. The act is broken down into its elements; the position of the body, limbs, articulations is defined; to each movement are assigned a direction, an aptitude, a duration; their order of succession is prescribed. Time penetrates the body and with it all the meticulous controls of power.[8]

Although the theater and a handbook for military movement seem initially unrelated, in this chapter, I wish to elucidate what exactly was at stake in the lived experience of this new onto-epistemology of temporality, whether in the unity of time onstage or in the fragmentation of disciplinary time in the court of Versailles. I take up Foucault's suggestion that, with temporal segmentation and the management of properness, "time penetrates the body." Biet and Triau remind us that theatrical representation in particular requires a symbolic passage to another time—dramatic time—that requires not only the ritual of the "bells, announcements, trumpets and requests" but also the "synchronization of the spectators' movements [and] those of the actors and other practitioners (lighting technicians, machine operators, dressers, etc."[9] The movements of theatrical bodies—much like those in the military—are broken down and synchronized, not only to produce order or the aesthetic spectacle but also more specifically to produce *time itself*—the time of the theater.

Although Foucault suggests that penetration of power's grasp on the body is most apparent by the mid-eighteenth century, I contend that the seeds of this temporal control were planted earlier and most visibly in the debates over the *règles classiques* and the bienséances. The règles classiques (the classical rules of time, place, and action) contributed to yielding a verisimilar (*vraisemblable*) and proper representation and served as a foundational cornerstone of neoclassical theater. As I noted in the book's introduction, Jacques Scherer offers a concise summary of these terms: vraisemblance or verisimilitude, is an "intellectual exigency" that prohibits the absurd and the arbitrary, whereas bienséance, or the rule of propriety, is a "moral exigency" that forbids that which would shock taste, morals and public prejudices.[10] Taken together, vraisemblance and bienséance meant that theatrical representation—both in terms of content and in terms of its formal qualities—was heavily scrutinized, oriented towards an imagined public good, and charged with the duty of exemplifying intellectual and moral ideals.

Biet and Triau note that even though the rule of the unity of time was derided as *dirimante* (a constraining obstacle), another effect was that the temporal calibration allowed a flourishing of a different kind of aesthetic sensation. This happens in two ways: within the context of the play itself, and amongst the audience members. Within the frame of the twenty-four hours, "time remains plastic: it could accelerate, slow down, or be elided; narratives allow for jumps into the past; oracles could embody a jump into the future. In other words, discourse allows the twenty-four-hour principle to be exceeded."[11] The twenty-four-hour limit allows a different kind of creativity and cultivates a specific experience of theatrical time in which such temporal leaps and elisions stand out, magnified and highlighted more than they would be in a temporally "flexible" piece. Therefore, the audience experiences a different form of temporal sensation: "Inscribed into a politics of condensation, an economy of means, the concentration of emotions, this temporal plausibility was needed to better captivate the spectator, given her perception of time, and to make her attentive to the plot and story as much as to her own reactions, inasmuch as they were synchronized to those of the characters."[12] Biet and Triau's analysis of the unity of time and of temporal verisimilitude echoes my earlier point that we can consider seventeenth-century theater to convey new onto-epistemologies of temporality (new kinds of time represented on stage, as well as new ways of sensing and feeling time in the audience). The biopolitical and affective inflect back onto the sociopolitical and aesthetic aspects of theater and, inversely, the theater's aesthetic structure and form have biopolitical and affective consequences. In other words, the proliferation and management of these fleeting microtemporalities so necessary to biopolitical governance, as Foucault argued, also proliferated on stage. However, this control was not purely enacted through a top-down imposition of the aesthetic rule of the unity of time; rather, we must pay particular attention to the ways that affective sensations of the theater became harnessed to the velocities of temporal leaps or lags.

This chapter is in two parts. In the first part I reexamine the intense scholarly focus on the absolutist and literary effects of the delimitation of twenty-four hours of represented time on stage, shining a light on the biopolitical roots that were also being planted. This so-called unity of time has been previously analyzed as affording theatrical verisimilitude or providing political order. As we saw previously with d'Aubignac's writings, the règles classiques (classical rules) also served to garner respectability for theater as a proper institution, bolstering the "properness" of this institution against antitheatrical sentiment that would read the theater as the breeding ground for vice. By shifting the spotlight onto oft-ignored biopolitical valences of such contrived temporal rules, we can better understand why the question of the unity of time would become d'Aubignac's "most agitating question." What has not been fully analyzed is the affective level. The very nature of discussing the rules foments new zones of temporal awareness, or what I have argued are sites of new temporal onto-epistemologies, and that the rules themselves might have offered other kinds of productive possibilities than merely constraint, including fostering new kinds of relations, sensations, and generally other modes of being *with*. My book's larger argument around "queer velocities" can be sharpened against the backdrop of changing early modern aesthetic and social notions of taste, theatricality, and timing.

In the second part I examine the temporal torsions in Corneille's *Le Cid* to reconsider the relationship between disobedience (to the theatrical rules) and resistance (to orderliness and propriety) and the ways that both can offer a strategic grappling with the management of bodies and desires in time. Corneille's play was received with great public acclaim, but this very popularity gave cause for concern and for critique. For what kinds of theatrical pleasures were legitimate, and who had the authority to orchestrate pleasure? And how widely could the theater disseminate disorderly affects and desires? By the end of the year, the quarrel was finally quieted by the publication of *Sentiments de l'Académie française sur la tragi-comédie du Cid*, the first official instance of a governmental institution (the newly created Académie française) intervening in an aesthetic-literary debate, inaugurating for the first time the triangulated tensions between the public's desires and tastes, aesthetic freedom, and political control.[13] This triangulation would have as one of its flashpoints the growing concern with temporal control.

Bienséances and Temporal Propriety

Before I unravel these presumed ties, we should further consider what bienséances or the règles classiques meant in the first place. The bienséances are generally presented as a set of proscriptions that govern what can and cannot be staged that might "shock" the audience, such as the representation of quotidian life (eating), overt sensuality (kissing and sex), and extreme violence (such as duels or executions). The very notion itself of bienséance carried within it multiple and vague meanings. It is fitting that Jean-Yves Vialleton offers bienséance as a candidate for the 2018 special issue of *Littératures classiques* on the topic of "the untranslatable concepts of critical vocabulary." Vialleton says, "In seventeenth-century texts, the word 'bienséance' effectively has an expansive meaning of 'what suits' and a narrower sense of 'what is correct in discourse and comportment/behavior.'"[14] This suitedness was applicable in society and onstage. Vialleton summarizes that the word carried roughly three meanings in the seventeenth century: "1) the idea that there is a concordance between many things (harmony); 2) the idea of something fit to be used by someone (usability); 3) the idea of the properness of behavior according to social exigencies (correct comportment)."[15] But, even in these multiple definitions, we see a shared investment in attunement and calibration, with the repetition of the word *convenance* (roughly, to suit or to agree with someone or something). Overall, bienséance speaks to a fittingness and exerts what might be called a "norming effect"—the norm does not antedate the bienséances but is iteratively produced through repeated invocations of the rule.

Suitedness also takes on a moral quality for some seventeenth-century critics. John Lyons underscores that for La Mesnardière (the so-called godfather of bienséances) and other proponents of the bienséances, "goodness and appropriateness are mixed together."[16] Lyons cites an earlier 1606 Latin dictionary definition of bienséance to show that there is a "confusing double meaning of the word."[17] One is the term "*Convenientia rerum*" which he defines as the "fittingness of things." The second definition is "*Decentia*," or the "social and customary appropriateness of behavior that we call 'decency.'" He explains that taken together, "there is a dominant sense from which the other grows: *bienséance* refers to a framework within which each thing finds its place, within which a thing 'clicks' into its habitual association with things around it."[18] The confusion thus stems from whether bienséance refers to the normative, regulatory framework itself (norms of decency) or to the operations of "clicking" (to fit into place). The association of "clicking" into place underscores my earlier reflections about velocity as an imagined tempo oriented toward a proper telos or a direction. As I explained in the introduction, velocity can be thought of as a haste or delay with a directional component, and therefore the "directionality" may be the measure of where it does or does not match with an idealized telos or norm. When we consider the moral, decent qualities of bienséance, any deviation can be thought of as transgressive of the socially good. These are the very divergences and "unsuitedness" that queer velocity accounts for.

Corneille mentions bienséances twice in his *Examen du Cid* of 1660, in response to his critics, which I will return to shortly. Both of his admitted violations of bienséances refer to moments of possibly unseemly behavior. In *Le Cid*, Chimène and Rodrigue are set to be betrothed to one another, but their happy nuptials are delayed by a quarrel between Chimène's father, Don Gomès, and Rodrigue's father, Don Diègue. Fittingly, their argument concerns temporality at heart: who is truly worthy of educating the king's son or being the tutor-mentor of the future king. In the aftermath of a precipitous and ego-wounding slap, the elderly Don Diègue has his son Rodrigue duel in his place to rectify the blow to his honor. The result of this fateful matchup is that Chimène's own beloved fiancé Rodrigue ultimately kills Chimène's father Don Gomès during the duel. Chimène begs for revenge and Rodrigue, ridden with shame, begs for his own punishment.

Instead of responding to either claim, the king sends Rodrigue to fight the Moors; the young man subsequently earns the legendary title of "Le Cid," meaning "Lord" or "champion." By the final scene, Chimène is ordered to do exactly what she both longs for and dreads: she is commanded by the king to marry Rodrigue, meaning that her future husband is both her father's murderer and her dearest love. All this takes place, supposedly, within twenty-four hours.

Corneille's first mention of the bienséances regards the strange ending of the play in which the hero, Rodrigue, is somewhat forgiven for having murdered his beloved Chimène's father, but Chimène nevertheless finds herself rebetrothed to Rodrigue less than twenty-four hours after her father's death! "Il faut se contenter de tirer Rodrigue de péril, sans le pousser jusqu'à son mariage avec Chimène"[19] (we must be satisfied with rescuing Rodrigue from peril, without actually pushing him to marry Chimène), writes Corneille in his *Examen*, but he excuses himself for this somewhat inappropriate ending because his Spanish epic source text spans more than three years, whereas he, writing in the French context, is pressed for time. Furthermore, he barely conceals his disdain for the rules, saying that the drama (and especially the hasty marriage), "est Historique, et a plu en son temps; mais bien sûrement il déplairait au nôtre"[20] (is historical, and in its time was pleasing, but surely it is displeasing to our times). Corneille implicitly casts aspersions on the taste and critics of his own time by hinting that the current moment lacks the aesthetic sophistication of past eras. Finally, he acknowledges that it is only through "incertitude" (ambiguity) that "je pouvais accorder la bienséance du théâtre avec la vérité de l'événement"[21] (that I could harmonize the bienséance of the theater with the truthfulness of the story).

In Corneille's second mention of the bienséances, he agrees that he did violate the rules of propriety in act 3, by having Rodrigue come visit Chimène, his beloved, at her home immediately after the fateful duel with Chimène's father. But he does not apologize for or make excuses for Rodrigue's unseemly haste to see Chimène. To the contrary, he seems to relish the affective disruption that he has caused: "et j'ai remarqué aux premières représentations qu'alors que ce malheureux amant se présentait devant elle, il s'élevait un certain frémissement dans l'assemblée, qui marquait une curiosité merveilleuse, et un redoublement d'attention pour ce qu'ils avaient à se dire dans un état si pitoyable"[22] (and I have noted from the earliest performances that when this unhappy lover presented himself in front of Chimène, there arose a certain pleasurable shiver in the audience, signaling a marvelous curiosity, and intensified the attention to what the couple would say to one another under such pitiable circumstances). Here, Corneille grasps at what Elizabeth Freeman has called the "invention of the possibility of local assemblages, novel and contingent forms of belonging that neither required nor resulted in a subject";[23] Freeman rightly underscores that Foucault's work on biopolitics has generally been aimed at the level of the individual (what Racevskis analyzes as the Foucaultian "micro-physics of power") or at the level of the population.[24] Freeman argues instead for a methodology of "sense-methods [that] focuses on the embodiment of a relationality that does not always refer to or result in a stable social form but instead *moves*, with and against, dominant timings and times."[25] Sense-methods can help us understand the ways that the "dominant timings" of the bienséances produced modes of feeling in the audience that both go "with and against" the normative sentiments. Corneille highlights that the theater, and the use of a surprising velocity (Rodrigue's haste to see the daughter of his victim) yielded new kinds of wonderous sensations and a sharpened attention within and between audience members —the new onto-epistemologies of time that I alluded to earlier—instead of the expected reactions of horror and disgust.

Ultimately, Corneille treats the two principles of bienseances and the classical rules either as cumbersome constraints that force him to make ungraceful plot choices or as an "optional" code of conduct that he can choose to violate, in the name of giving the audience a frisson of pleasure. In both cases, the bienséances are depicted as inconveniences that must be either ignored, dispensed with, or otherwise flaunted. Corneille's *Examen* shows that his adherence to the unity of time provokes some ungainly authorial choices, which some of his critics were eager to label as a violation of the bienséances. Temporal properness could create sociosexual impropriety. Moreover, what Corneille implies is that watering down the plot for the sake of adhering to the rules of propriety would only yield a milquetoast spectacle. Sociosexual properness could yield aesthetic flatness. Ultimately, the orchestration of spectatorial pleasure, the timing (and speed) of such pleasure, and the line between literary freedom and public propriety were at stake.

"Conduct of Conducts" and Capillary Management

Theater critics such as d'Aubignac, La Mesnardière, and Jean Chapelain all imagined that the bienseances and the règles classiques, in the right proportion, could work together to produce a verisimilar (*vraisemblant*) and pleasing spectacle. While the rules were purportedly necessary to yield vraisemblance—meaning that the theater had to be believably realistic—these rules also carried a moral and political charge. Vialleton notes that in the eyes of eighteenth-century scholars such as Jean-François Marmontel, the quarrel of *Le Cid* marks a rough dividing line between a world where actions and words were hardly decent on stage and a period where writers, critics, and the public became increasingly sensitive to the rules in the name of taste. Vialleton summarizes that "[Marmontel saw in the rules] the effect of progress, not of 'mores' but of 'taste,' to the extent that the world enlightened and polished itself further."[26] In contrast to the contention that the concretization of rules was a sign of literary evolution, twentieth-century scholars such as Jacques Scherer, according to Vialleton, "saw in these rules a sort of moral censure amounting to the onstage suppression of a portion of the realities of life."[27] Vialleton thus puts his finger on another aspect of the "untranslatability" of the bienséances: that it could be viewed either as purifying society toward progress and refinement or as repressive and censorious. In either case, we can understand that the bienséances are particularly concerned with sexuality and sensuality insofar as most of the regulations govern the respectability and representability of bodily practices and corporeal intensification, whether kissing or dying (both proscribed from the stage).

Whether a sign of progress or prudish limitation, bienséance truly highlighted a sense of imagined propriety, but what this properness entailed was unclear. It still invites the question, how does the very norm (to which representation, behavior, or usage must suit) become, itself, established? How does one take the measure of that which does not *convenir*, or "click," into place, especially when the norm itself is in flux? And why was theater presumed to be the conveyor of such social discipline?

Scholars have long accepted a commonplace that the seventeenth-century investment in neoclassical theatrical rules (of the kind that d'Aubignac laid out in his manual and Corneille decried) is inscribed in a larger ideological strategy to link aesthetic order with political order. This is an assumption that I would like to examine closely, to reconsider the presumed and undertheorized equation between aesthetic rules and political control. Such considerations of the theater as an influential force on the body politic assume that the theater operates as a straightforward vehicle for corruption or for virtue. Therefore, the règles classiques are relegated to either a metaphor for political order or a technique for implementing said virtue. To give one example among many, René Bray summarizes that "the need for peace at the end of a long period of political trouble, the desire of some artisans for an authoritarian State, whose continuity of projects would ensure success, the institution of the Académie, the organ of authority in the kingdom of letters: these are all symptoms that denoted the irresistible tendency in seventeenth-century France to shift, in all domains, from confusion to order."[28] But even in Bray's language, the exact nature of this tendency is not fully explained. In his use of "besoin," "volonté" (need, desire, or will), and "irresistible," Bray underscores a kind of magnetizing desire for political and moral order, all the while implying some equivalence between the kingdom of letters and the kingdom of politics. Similarly, Mitchell Greenberg argues that, for both Cardinal Richelieu and Louis XIV, "in some ambiguous way the theater represents the state, that it [the theater] can stand in for the Prince who is its privileged spectator and for whom it is the privileged spectacle";[29] this is a commonplace within seventeenth-century French scholarship, but the "ambiguous way" remains to be fully unpacked. Moreover, this imagined function of the theater must be contextualized in its historical function: Déborah Blocker underscores that the theater wasn't "viewed as a fiction, in the contemporary sense of the term . . . because a play was perceived . . . as an intervention fully capable of influencing the body politic through its representations."[30] Once one assumes the direct cause and effect between theatrical representation and public influence, such a connection would necessitate a clear articulation of the rules of the theater for seventeenth-century artists and theatergoers, and the development of the theater as a disciplinary tool. Given the turmoil in France during the Fronde—the civil revolt of the nobles between 1648 and 1653—scholars tend to retroactively justify the rules, situating the mid-century imposition of political and aesthetic theatrical order as a balm for the previous years of disorder, or in a rearview mirror perspective, positing the rules as the founding catalyst for aesthetic production. But, the mechanics of this causal relationship has not yet been fully unpacked.

By assuming the natural link between literary and political authority, we do not allow ourselves to interrogate the mechanisms or means by which absolutist authority seamlessly sutures two different kinds of discourses: its own spectacular political power and the language of the stage itself. All these interpretations, however, might be grouped under what I call a "vehicular" understanding of the rules. In other words, the theatrical rules are assumed to be the medium or technique for conveying political power, authority, order, or more. But considering theater as a medium of politics—a mediating force and a media that conveys—does not fully explain the heightened scrutiny of the unity of time in the règles classiques and the unity of absolutism.[31]

How can we understand the tie between the "ambiguous way" that the theater and politics were intertwined? In *Absolutist Attachments*, Chloe Hogg detours the focus away from the unquestioned, dazzling body of the king, to focus on the "nonhegemonic affections and sensorial or taste experiences" that she groups under the term "absolutism's alternative affects."[32] In a similar vein, I veer away from the insistence on the spectacle of ideology and its bodily control on the magnitude of the subject and instead turn to the biopolitical dimension that management embodiment and desire on a capillary level. Instead of only producing flashy operations of ideological control, the *querelle* (quarrel) and the development of the bienséances and the règles classiques also reveal and foment the subtle temporal control of bodies, desires, and life. The velocities allowed by the rules of the theater and of propriety may be counted among what Freeman calls "small-scale techniques that might be conceptualized as coming between anatomo-politics and biopolitics; that may be aimed at subjectification but may produce a small-scale collective consciousness instead of an individual, interiorized subjectivity."[33]

Biopolitics, as I argued in the introduction, takes the cultivation of life itself as its object and objective. One element that clearly runs through Foucault's vision of biopolitical governance is the fragmentation of totalizing sovereign power into more capillary management, and for our purposes, it is essential to underscore that this control occurs at the level of the body. I will cite at length Foucault's famed *conduire des conduites* ("conduct of conducts") to unpack what I hope to indicate: "To 'conduct' is at the same to 'lead' others (according to mechanisms of coercion that are, to varying degrees, strict) and a way of behaving within and more or less open field of possibilities. The exercise of power is a 'conduct of conducts' and a management of possibilities."[34]

Threaded throughout Foucault's definition of conduct is a repeated insistence on the *possible*, *probable*, and *eventual*. It is a governance not concerned with disciplining past errors, nor with extracting firm promises and contracts, but rather with foreclosing and opening a delimited range of possibilities. Conduct governs temporalities. He continues,

> To govern, in this sense is to structure the possible field of action of others. The relationship proper would therefore be sought not on the side of violence or of struggle, nor on that of voluntary contracts (all of which can, at best, only be the instruments of power), but, rather, in the area of that singular mode of action, neither warlike nor juridical, which is government.[35]

What Foucault underscores here is that grappling with power does not happen on a spectacular, violent level, but rather on the subtle, relational level. A second aspect that we can deduct from Foucault's reasoning is that biopolitics exerts its power precisely through the control and calibration of time; it crafts those kinds of relation, as well as the modes of being that happen, *in time*. When the field of action is delimited or expanded by a certain range of possibilities, governance is able to manage temporality and the conditions of possibility.

Therefore, I argue that it is impossible to only consider the concerns of the règles classiques and the bienséances as a tool of aesthetic-political order; we must see it *also* as a biopolitical tool of governance, operating on the intimate level of the anatomopolitics of the body as well as at the midlevel of the theater public. Certainly, Corneille's attention to the bienséances served to defend his aesthetic choices considering the pamphlets and quarrel attacks. And yet, in his description of the hasty meeting between the guilty Rodrigue and the still-grieving Chimène, the power of the audience's frisson was unmistakable. We might imagine that it was not only a shiver of pleasure but also an affective reaction embedded in and reacting to temporality. The audience becomes more intensely aware that speeds and timings themselves offer a range of feelings. There is an awakened understanding of properness, as well as appropriate and inappropriate paces and rhythms. This knowledge itself shapes the eventual "field of action" to which Foucault refers.

Present in d'Aubignac's earlier "agitating questions" over the revalorization of temporality is an intensification of time. "The more time is broken down," Foucault argues, "the more its subdivisions multiply, the better one disarticulates it by deploying its internal elements under a gaze that supervises them, the more one can accelerate an operation, or at least regulate it according to an optimum speed."[36] The represented duration of two hours, for example, could no longer be simply a neutral passing of time. Rather, it could be understood by the spectators as two precious hours of the twenty-four allotted, or it could be debated afterward as an insufficient imagined cushion of time between a character's murder of his fiancée's father and his appearance at her house (as it was in *Le Cid*). The temporal duration becomes charged, intensified, and valued in new ways, yielding new affordances—a concept that I will return to shortly.

To be clear, I am not arguing that Corneille and other dramatists strategically manipulated the bienséances to craft the theater as a biopolitical tool. The impact and the implementation are more subtle and perhaps more insidious than the ideological equation (between absolutist unity and theatrical unities) would allow. Ultimately, if we remain in thrall to the "vehicular" acceptance of the rule, we retain our focus on that which is being conveyed, without questioning the very means of conveyance. The very nature of an ideal properness, and a restraining action that curtailed or guided behavior, brings us, however, to reconsider discipline and capillary management. In *Discipline and Punish*, Foucault draws on the panopticon to suggest a model of self-perpetuating disciplinary power. The panopticon is an architectural figure for a prison in which the cells are arranged in a circle around a protruding watchtower in the center. It does not matter if the tower is actually inhabited; the function is "to induce in the inmate a state of conscious and permanent visibility that assures the automatic functioning of power."[37] This sensation of "permanent visibility" has the effect of eliciting a type of self-subjugation: "He who is subjected to a field of visibility, and who knows it, assumes responsibility for the constraints of power; he makes them play spontaneously upon himself; he inscribes in himself the power relation in which he simultaneously plays both roles; he becomes the principle of his own subjection."[38]

One might imagine, following Hélène Merlin-Kajman, that the birth of the literary public in the wake of the *querelle du* Cid (hereafter *querelle*) allows for a type of panoptic scrutiny of others. Even in the experience of attending the theater, not only does one take in the events of the spectacle but also one becomes aware of the frisson of enjoyments, pleasure, or fear shared between all of spectators. Yet, what most interests this study is the automatization of submission to the rule; regardless of the networks of intrasurveillance or presumed scrutiny, a strange internalization exists vis-à-vis the rules that takes place. Bray writes that the rules were so seamlessly installed because of this internalized submission:

> They (the authors) did not have to bend themselves to fit; the rule already suited them. They could call themselves free, free to behave, much like a well-mannered child to whom the thought of wrongdoing would never arrive. It is because they perceived,

> within the form of the rule, the essence that would make it valuable, the reason that dictated conduct and legitimized it. The seventeenth century veered towards the rule because it needed to submit; once subjugated, it legitimized its own obedience through its cult of reason.[39]

Bray's analysis of the submission to the règles classiques renders the subjected writer "liberated" in his submission to the rule. The writer, believing in the rule's value and the "cult of reason," continues to submit his own writing, thoughts, and literary tastes to such a rule. Bray shows how neoclassical writers flipped the narrative of submission and constraint; one cannot be constrained by that which one willingly submits to, much like Foucault's prisoners who offer themselves up for their own surveillance and submission. Therefore, the rule has already shaped the conduct of conducts, not through a top-down imposition but rather by restructuring the field of possibilities. One can indeed be "free" within a delimited field of action as long as behavior does not itself challenge how and why the field became delimited in the first place.

The conduct of conducts is performatively produced through an iterative insistence on qualities like the *bienséant* (the good, or the decent). The social norm, and the epistemological field, are produced through a repeated recourse to the "framework" to which things can be fitted or not fitted (*convenientia rerum*). The existence of bienséances themselves means that the terms of the debate are limited to considering whether an action, a being, or a desire is fitting or unfitting. But, as John Lyons highlights, flipping the commonplace assumption, "verisimilitude was not the dramatist's *goal* but rather the *means* of obtaining the complete adhesion of the public."[40] Because the principles of vraisemblance and, I would add, the bienséances, are the twin apparatuses of public shaping, discipline, and adherence, they become a mode of capillary management and thus evades an ontological sedimentation that one could rail against or disrupt. In fact, any debate over the bienséant itself obscures its constitutive conditions of emergence, for the epistemological field (and the legible field) is already predetermined by the very notion of fittingness or unfittingness, without any challenge to the very conditions of possibility under which things can emerge as fit or unfit. If the theater principles of bienséances and vraisemblance were truly restrictive, these could be decried as unreasonable constraints on art. The operations of the bienséances and criteria of verisimilitude were thought to be the end goal, the very *ideal* of theatrical representation, but they are actually a vehicular *medium* whose true objective is the "conduct of conducts."

Affordances of the Unity of Time in *Le Cid*

When we equate aesthetic order with political order, as a by-product of this perspective, the disruption of aesthetic order is treated as resistance, or as a calculated troubling of political order. In my examination of *Le Cid* in this second part, I look at the ways that temporal disruption challenges governance of the time of life not through outright resistance but rather through a proliferation of varieties of sensations (of haste and slowness), a multiplicity that "queers" the norms of tempos of feeling, loving, and desiring. To tarry with temporality, in this instance, might be akin to Deleuze's idea of the *pouvoir-vital* that I mentioned in the introduction—to proliferate possibilities of life, and the time of life, in response to the increased scrutiny and management of time.

In contrast to seeing the disruption and violation of bienséances as resistance, I draw on Caroline Levine's description of the affordances of forms in my thinking about the règles classiques. Levine suggests that forms might be thought of not only in their organizing and structuring (restraining) iterations but also through their affordances, a concept she borrows from design theory to consider the functionality and effects of forms. A given object or form (a doorknob, a staircase) may have perceived range of possible, intended affordances as well as a set of latent, unintended affordances. Levine writes that, by considering the range of affordances of a form, forms' capacities are expanded, swerved from traditional uses, opening the possibility of reappropriation or misuse. She points out that a doorknob, for example, "affords pushing and pulling" but also "hanging clothes."[41] Levine says of the clashing of forms:

> New encounters may activate latent affordances or foreclose otherwise dominant ones. Forms *will often fail to impose their order* when they run up against other forms that disrupt their logic and frustrate their organizing ends, producing aleatory and sometimes contradictory effects. We can understand forms as abstract and portable organizing principles, then, but we also need to attend to the specificity of particular historical situations to understand the range of ways in which forms overlap and collide.[42] (emphasis mine)

Thus, when considering the relationship between affordance and form, an unexpected affordance that hijacks the form does not necessarily "resist" or overturn the form itself; it is a swerving *within* and *of* the form's inherent capacities. Moreover, there is an interactive, co-creative (almost interpellative) relationship between forms and users. The form itself can be designed in such a way as to invite the user to imagine other, alternative affordances, or the user may be hindered by false affordances (a light switch that is unconnected to any lamp) or perplexed by an unclear range of the form's possibilities.

In early modern French theater, we find an equivalent "form" in the unity of time. Its limitation to "one turn of the sun" affords constraint, but it also allows tarrying, play, and temporal intensification.[43] The unity of time, on a biopolitical level, may also make possible capillary management and multiple points of intensification, surveillance, and self-monitoring. Indeed, it is the very production of such variation and diversity of temporality that allows the management of bodies and tempos to flourish. As Biet and Triau suggested earlier, the unity of time allowed the "seizing" of the spectator and the heightening of his or her attention: "this temporal plausibility was needed to better captivate the spectator."[44] Corneille presented the unity of time not just as a constraint but also as a structure that could be inhabited and detoured to suit his own authorial will. "I cannot deny that the rule of twenty-four hours hastens the events of this play too much,"[45] writes Corneille in his *Examen*, admitting that the play's events (a romantic engagement, a murderous duel, two appeals for vengeful execution, a heroic war battle, a false duel, and a possible reconciliation) all within twenty-four hours is a bit preposterous. Corneille once again blames the rule itself, in terms that render the rule as the *agent* of this hastening or constraint.

> This same rule forces Chimène to ask the king for justice a second time. She had already beseeched the king the night before and had no reason to return the next morning to importune the king, of whom she had no grounds for complaint, for she could not yet say that the king had failed to uphold his promise. A novel would have given her seven or eight days of patience before she urged the king again, but the twenty and four hours *would not permit her this*; this is the inconvenience of the rule. (my emphasis)[46]

In his second complaint Corneille only addresses the impropriety of Chimène's behavior. Although she has just seen her father die at the hand of her beloved Rodrigue, Chimène, in her grief, seeks Rodrigue's death as just retribution for this murder. Corneille seeks to excuse Chimène for her rudeness in bothering the king a second time for vengeance even though a full day hasn't yet passed. The form of the rule affords "incommodité" (inconvenience), but the very same window of time also offers Chimène the possibility of outspoken hastiness: daring to beseech the king twice within one day, taking matters of revenge into her own hands, and brazenly displaying her grief in such a public manner that she flaunts norms of propriety. Therefore, while the same twenty-four-hour window yields awkward haste, it also allows for the eruption of a variety of other sensations. Variation, and varying temporal intensities, are all afforded by the same rule and are part of fostering a rich theatrical experience (not necessarily reinforcing or subverting the unity of time). In *Le Cid*, we can find spectrums of haste and slowness—queer velocities—veering towards nonnormative and feminist ends that proliferate *within* the obedience to the rule itself.

Resistance to such capillary management of the bienséances and vraisemblance does not look like outright opposition. Regarding resistance, Judith Butler suggests that it can only occur at the level of the stylization of the self at the limits of (and exposing the limits of) the epistemological field. Building on Foucault, she writes, "critique will not be a single act, nor will it belong exclusively to a subjective domain, for it will be the stylized relation to the demand upon it. And the style will be critical to the extent that, as style, it is not fully determined in advance, it incorporates a contingency over time that marks the limits to the ordering capacity of the field in question."[47] Stylization's temporality is important, because it is not necessarily a future-anticipated action (of resistance, of pushback, or of refusal to fit or comply). The very contingency of the stylized critique takes aim at the weakness of the conduct of conducts: that it operates at the level of what Foucault calls "aménager la probabilité" (managing probability). To enact the improbable or the unexpected is not to outright destroy this governance's grasp on probability. Rather, it more subtly offers critique by calling into question the legitimacy and authority of governance to "structure the possible field of action of others," as Foucault puts it.[48] Stylization shines a light on how the careful management of probability permits another affordance of an otherwise oppressive or constrictive form.

Stylization might take the form of play, as in Butler's notion of parody and drag, but it also might look like tarrying, excessive affect, or unexpected elaborations. Or, to tie in my earlier assertion, stylization might appear as a detoured affordance: a creative, unexpected use of a form (the unity of time, the règles classiques) that was not necessarily forbidden, but not its intended use either. In short, it might look like queer velocities, which expose the possibilities and limits of such "rules" as the unity of time and the bienséances, but do not outright overturn them. The queerness of velocity becomes not only an "unfitting" but also an uncontainable, contingent, and improbable stylization, an alternative affordance of time.

The debate around the play, called the *querelle du Cid*, was significant insofar as it was the first literary quarrel of its magnitude, prompting the general theater public, politicians, and scholars alike to seize their pens. Jean-Marc Civardi's annotated volume of pamphlets and letters from the quarrel stands at nearly one thousand two hundred pages. Even with the additional annotations, it is still impressive to consider that, in roughly a year's worth of time, there was such an outpouring of public opinion. In the *Sentiments de l'Académie française*, the state verdict on the matter penned primarily by the poet and critic Jean Chapelain, the Académie condemned several of Corneille's faults in the play, from the accusation of plagiarizing a Spanish epic to the crime of Corneille's overweening ego. One main critique they levied at him was the divergence from temporal norms, which is a violation that is depicted as both unnatural and unseemly: "The poet, wanting this Poem to end happily, to follow the rules of Tragicomedy here has Chimène trample on all of the rules that Nature has established, an act of disdain and transgression that ought to horrify the ignorant as well as the skilled."[49] The disruption of order might stimulate affects of disgust (or, worse, interest and pleasure taken in something that ought to be horrifying). Therefore, to revisit the notion of affordances, we might understand the publication of the *Sentiments* as not only dampening a nascent republicanism but also shutting down debate that could question the biopolitical conduct of conducts. Allison Stedman has noted that Cardinal Richelieu's directive to the newly founded Académie to produce an official decision was not primarily intended to minimize chaos but rather to quell public discussion itself. As Stedman argues, the very existence of the debate itself revealed that the classical rules were debatable and a nascent republicanism was inherent in the existence of the quarrel: "The longer the quarrel continued, the more of a threat its very existence posted to monarchical authority because it illustrated that individuals had the capacity both to launch and to endorse new ideas in the context of an open public forum."[50] The quarrel contested that kinds of feelings and sensations ought to be experienced and ought to elicit shock and disgust. But the more that the play was discussed, the more attention and interest was drawn to the aberrancies, and the very possibility of aberrancy, as a critical stylization of form.

Perhaps the strangest temporal moment in the play comes at the supposedly happy final betrothal scene, which Corneille acknowledged as weak yet attempted to defend in his own *Examen* through the language of "incertitude" (ambiguity).[51] The king, Don Fernand, suggests to Chimène that she wait a year before finalizing her marriage to Rodrigue: "Prends un an, si tu veux, pour essuyer tes larmes" (Take, if you wish, a year to dry your tears [5.7.1821]).[52] The reasoning behind this delay is that "Le temps assez souvent a rendu légitime / Ce qui semblait d'abord ne se pouvoir sans crime . . . Cet hymen différé ne rompt point une loi / Qui, sans marquer de temps, lui destine ta foi" (Time has often made legitimate / That which seemed, at first, to be a crime . . . This delayed marriage does not break any laws / And without marking time, it secures your betrothal [5.7.1813–14; 5.7.1819–20]). Thus, even the "traditional" wedding or engagement that would close a comedy or tragicomedy here is swerved, delayed, and queered. The *hymen différé* (delayed marriage) was characterized by the antagonists in the *querelle* as an aberrant rush and an unsatisfying stalling. The hybrid time that the Académie diagnoses as distasteful ("doivent donner de l'horreur"; ought to provoke shock)[53] actually adequately maps the mixed emotions that Chimène might feel: the revulsion to be wedded to her father's murderer, the still-lingering sentiments of love, the erotics of Rodrigue's valorous exploits to win her hand, and the temporality of mourning and loss.

Here delay is presented as a smoothing force, erasing criminal or egregious behavior, a palliative to the painful losses from the past. This unresolved ending has provoked a wealth of scholarship on *Le Cid*. Paul Scott interprets the delay not as indicative of a weakly indecisive monarch but rather as reassuring moderation, a sign of the king's "instinctive and pedestrian personality,"[54] whereas Christopher Braider reads the "hymen différé" (deferred marriage) as a moment of Derridean *différance*, a productive differing and deferral that inscribes, in the indeterminate nature of royal authority, an amplification of the author's agency.[55] This delay, in M. J. Muratore's analysis, allows Corneille to bolster Chimène's position as almost a heroic obstinance: steadfastly committed to her family values and not yet yielding to the temptation of love.[56] And yet, on a more metalevel, we might also understand this moment of delay as a temporal form in and of itself, which can allow other possibilities. The staging of the delay and the diegetic reference to time's passing and the unfitting ending provides a metatheatrical awareness of time, a sensation of what time should look like or feel like. The bienséances become a means instead of an end.

In fact, the strange ending is but one moment in the play's rich fabric of temporal experience that I suggest is the key to understanding both the popular outcry and the biopolitical operations of temporal management. Not only does the end of the play fail to adhere to the arc of a traditionally sovereign resolution but also the play itself is characterized by a plurality of queer velocities that trouble the tempo of progress and order. To return to my earlier point, these types of temporal deviations afford what Butler might term a stylization at the limits of governance. Chimène's slowing and hastening is a way of underscoring a clash between the temporality of sovereign decision making and capillary management of life. Don Fernand the king (the first king of Castile) is not fully able to execute the decisive temporality of "let live and make die" that Foucault associates with the sovereign, as Don Fernand retracts, feigns, and rescinds his orders. Hélène Bilis has analyzed the critique of Don Fernand as a weak sovereign,[57] and many of these critiques align with the vision of the negative image of the indecisive king. Yet, instead of sovereign weakness as catalyzing chaos, as one might expect, the lack of a strong authoritative hand means that the spotlight is centered on other modes of control. Biopolitical, capillary control moves to the foreground.

Although a close analysis of the entire play is not the aim of this chapter, I do want to underscore that *Le Cid* is not just an example of too many "events" crammed into one twenty-four-hour period. Instead, the play is full of what Cymene Howe calls "chrono-mashups" that are deployed to particularly feminist ends. Chimène's manipulation of velocities is precisely what allows her an expression of power in a social situation that should have reduced her to powerlessness—without a father to guide her or her husband to defend her. Mitchell Greenberg has suggested that "her grief and mourning enclose Chimène in an obsessive stance that refuses time . . . Not able to accept either a past or a future, she lives only in a present which finds her bereft."[58] This is a refusal of time that is interpreted as a rejection of what Greenberg calls the "male order," a heterosexual investment in "genealogy-history."[59] Greenberg cites Chimène's distressed cry: "Le passé me tourmente, et je crains l'avenir" (The past torments me, and I fear the future [2.3.480]), as an example of Chimène's miredness in the present.

In addition to rejecting the norms of "genealogy-history," Chimène and others perform a subtle but significant strategic tarrying with the rates and paces of mourning, love, and vengeance. In other words, if Don Fernand suggests the delayed marriage is a solution "sans marquer de temps" (without marking time [5.7.1820]), Chimène's pushback is to, in fact, mark time, to show time's force (Deleuze's pouvoir-vital) through these velocities. She highlights that the simple elision of time cannot be commanded, since time is imbricated with lived embodied intensities.

Even in the throes of grief, Chimène uses speeds and slownesses to her advantage. It falls to Chimène to describe her father's death to the king, Don Fernand, complete with a quite graphic description of her father's blood spurting out onto the ground: "mes yeux ont vu son sang / Couler à gros bouillons de son généreux flanc" (my eyes have seen his blood / gush from his great, noble-hearted side [2.8.659–60]). Felled by grief, she explains that she can no longer continue describing the gory scene: "Excusez ma douleur, / Sire, la voix me manque à ce récit funeste" (Sire, forgive my grief. / My voice fails as I tell this fearful tale [2.8.668]). Despite Chimène's excessive sorrow, the king forces her to narrate the horrific story again, a repetition that seems inexplicable, even to Chimène. "Je vous l'ai déjà dit," says Chimène, "je l'ai trouvé sans vie" (I already told you, I found him lifeless [2.8.674]). When Chimène begins to recount the horrific scene again to the king, even after she has asked for a reprieve, her language in the second telling is characterized by dynamism and haste. Her father's spurting blood "écrivait mon devoir" (wrote my duty) and her father's valor "me parlait par sa plaie, et hâtait ma poursuite" (spoke to me through his wound, hastening the call for revenge [2.8.676; 2.8.678]). By using active commands to the king, Chimène demonstrates what this haste ought to look like: "Ne souffrez pas que sous votre puissance / Règne devant vos yeux une telle licence" (Do not tolerate that under your watch / Such lawnessness should reign [2.8.681–82]) and "Vengez-la [mort] par une autre, et le sang par le sang. / Immolez, non à moi, mais à votre couronne" (Avenge this [death] by another, blood for blood / Sacrifice, not for me, but for your crown [2.8.692]). Her language is urgent, commanding, and even bloodthirsty. In response to this impassioned plea, the king urges Chimène to pause and go home: "Prends du repos, ma fille, et calme tes douleurs" (Get some rest, my daughter, and calm your grief [2.8.739]), issuing a command to wait and ignoring her directives to act. This is a period of stasis that Chimène bristles against: "M'ordonner du repos, c'est croître mes malheurs" (Commanding me to rest only augments my woes [2.8.740]). Don Fernand's and Chimène's temporal positions are thus continually clashing:

while Chimène asks for a break, to be excused from speaking further, the king insists on a second telling and a further description of the action. Later, after Chimène takes up the banner for a hasty tempo of revenge, the king orders an intermission and a rest. Effectively, this is governance through dictating the spectrum of possibilities; power is at play here, through the manipulation of Chimène's time. If, diegetically, the calibration of the affective tempos is the sovereign attempt to instill order, on the metatheatrical plane we can see that Corneille enacts different kinds of affordances within the unity of time to create different velocities, simultaneously stalling and speeding the pace of action.

At her home, time and, specifically, tempos are at stake, when Don Sanche gallantly offers his hand to Chimène to exact revenge by killing Rodrigue. At first, Chimène demurs, saying, "J'offenserais le roi, qui m'a promis justice" (I would offend the king, who has promised me justice [3.2.782]). Don Sanche's retort not only criticizes the speed of sovereign resolution but also describes his sword as the more attractive option precisely because of its haste:

> Vous savez qu'elle [la justice] marche avec tant de langueur,
> Qu'assez souvent le crime échappe à sa longueur;
> Son cours lent et douteux fait trop perdre de larmes.
> Souffrez qu'un cavalier vous venge par les armes:
> La voie en est plus sûre, et plus prompte à punir. (3.2.784–87)
>
> (You know that justice marches along with such languidness
> That often enough the crime slips away in the wait;
> Justice's slow and doubtful pace has spilled too many tears.
> Accept that a knight avenge you by his sword:
> This solution is the surest, and quicker to punish.)

The king's "langueur" (languidness) is implied to be almost like a second crime, which allows the initial offence to go unpunished. Don Sanche's language also contrasts the official temporality of sovereign justice with the hasty, affective reaction of a suitor's vengeful sword. After his entreaties, Chimène responds, "C'est le dernier remède" (It's the last resort [3.2.788]), effectively buying herself more time by deferring the decision to choose between Don Sanche's rapid resolution and the delay of sovereign justice that would preserve her love for Rodrigue—a love that would have space to fully blossom with the time of *longueur* (lengthy wait). Yet this is the opposite reaction to her earlier plea to the king for hasty justice.

When her governess Elvire urges Chimène to rest, Chimène reacts in a torrent of emotion: how unfitting rest feels at that moment! In her complaint, she brings up a different emotion in nearly every line:

> Ah! que mal à propos
> Dans un *malheur* si grand tu parles de *repos*!
> Par où sera jamais ma *douleur* apaisée,
> Si je ne puis *haïr* la main qui l'a causée?
> Et que dois-je *espérer* qu'un tourment éternel,
> Si je poursuis un crime, *aimant* le criminel? (3.3.803–8, emphasis mine)
>
> (Oh, how inappropriate
> During such great *sorrow*, you speak of *rest*!
> By what means will my *pain* ever be appeased,
> If I cannot *hate* the hand who caused it?
> And what can I *hope* for but eternal torment,
> If I avenge a crime, *loving* the criminal?)

From rest to peace, from hate to hope, from torment to love, perhaps the one thing that is consistent throughout these lines and these scenes is Chimène's inconsistent tempos and emotions. Her speech reveals the incompatibility between the multiple temporal systems tugging on her: the pace of courtship (the would-be engagement), justice, and grief. In other words, the *very divergence of her velocity* is the measure of the magnitude of her feeling. Regarding the bienséant (the decent or the good), it is appropriate that nothing feels like it is it "clicking" into place.

Following Chimène's plea for justice and her admission that she still loves Rodrigue, none other than Rodrigue himself appears at her home, still bearing the murder weapon. He begs her to kill him as just retribution for his murder. Rodrigue's intrusion in Chimène's private space of grief thus hastens an intervention—a distraction of grief—insofar as he is her desired beloved, but simultaneously augments grief itself as he is in fact the very source of her woes. This convergence is performed, in the play, through zeugma. Zeugma, a figure of speech commonly called a "yoking" term, occurs when a single verb is applied to two phrases that follow (e.g., "he took his hat and his leave"). Zeugma might be considered a figure of speed, for the governing verb's repeated distribution across its objects is eliminated, collapsed (instead of the lengthier "he took his hat as well as taking his leave"). Chimène says, upon seeing Rodrigue: "Ah! Quelle cruauté, qui tout en un jour tue / Le père par le fer, la fille par la vue!" (Oh, what cruelty, which all in one day / Kills the father by the sword and the daughter by sight [3.4.865–66]). Just as the structure of the line and the play of syllables and elisions created a sense of slowness in Benserade's *Iphis et Iante*, the structure of zeugma and rhyme here in *Le Cid* also enacts a kind of temporal collapse. This haste is remarked on by Chimène herself, who underscores the unbelievable fact that all these events have happened "all in one day." The rhyme of alexandrine verse gives the lines a regular structure and tempo: listening to "tue" (kill) would normally invite the anticipation of the "vue" (sight), creating a temporality of waiting and satisfaction bridging the normal span of two alexandrine lines. But in this couplet a multiplicity of other pleasing rhymes and consonances are crammed in between the "tue" and "vue," such as the repetition of "f" and "p" and the interior rhyme of "père" and "fer" (father and sword, respectively). These interior repetitions create their own microrhythms and temporalities, diverting from the traditional pace of "tue" reaching toward "vue" and the regular meter of the twelve-syllable alexandrines. Chimène's couplet, in the rushed yoking of zeugma or in the proliferation of consonant sounds, stages a plurality of temporalities and pleasures that are more than the traditional twelve-syllable–rhymed rhythm.

Chimène's recourse to her own temporal management of her grief is not embedded in a "present" immediacy and uncoupled from what might be considered "normative" time: the tempo of national wars against the Moors (in which Rodrigue fights heroically) or the time of sovereign decisions of justice. Specifically, we can understand that she does not urge haste and delay merely to "refuse time," as Greenberg suggested.[60] She is not isolated from the sovereign "langueur" of justice or the speed encouraged by Don Sanche. Rather, her use of velocities highlights a range of affects and allows her to regain control of situations: startled by Rodrigue's too-soon appearance, she counters with her own rush of zeugma; courted by Don Sanche's haste, she generates deferral and delay.

This is the crucial scene that raised the hackles of the public and theatre critics: the meeting of Chimène and Rodrigue after the fateful murder. This same scene occasioned Corneille's self-congratulation as generating the greatest frisson of pleasure or fear in the audience. *Les Sentiments de l'Académie française* flagged this moment as violating the bienséances of propriety. In my feminist analysis of tempos, I want to underscore that most of their complaints hone in on gendered concerns.

Chapelain writes: "the *bienséance* of the mores of a girl introduced as virtuous is not maintained by the poet when she resolves to marry the person who killed her father."[61] The language of the *Sentiments* specifically faults only Chimène for her mixed emotions. The main error, in the Académie's eyes, is that, after making a public declaration of revenge and a plea for justice, she still accepts Rodrigue in her abode: "as soon as Rodrigue presents himself in front of her, although stained by the blood of her father, she tolerates him in her house and even in her room . . . confesses to him that despite everything she does not cease loving him . . . this too clearly betrays her natural obligations in favor of her passion; it is too openly seeking a cover for her desires."[62] Although the *Sentiments* note that it may be reasonable to expect that Chimène could still love Rodrigue, a gendered normativity and a temporal normativity are at hand. The *Sentiments* underscore the "unnatural" fault: Chimène yields too easily ("si tost") to feelings of love over her daughterly duty. It would have been "more understandable to attribute this fault to Rodrigue than to Chimène," because Rodrigue is a man, "and his sex, which has the trait of closing one's eyes to all considerations in order to satisfy oneself in matters of love, would have rendered his actions less strange and less intolerable."[63] In other words, the haste of Chimène's yielding to love, as well as the spectacle of a woman—not a man—openly ("trop ouvertement") expressing her desires, shocks the Académie and merits her actions being labeled "intolerable" or "against nature." The temporal propriety (vraisemblance) of the play's action and its moral propriety (bienséances) are at odds here, and the incongruity is amplified by gender.

But how can we understand the targeted attack on the bienséances associated with sexuality? Foucault underscores that in a previous "society of blood . . . power spoke through blood: the honor of war, the fear of famine, the triumph of death, the sovereign with his sword, executioners, and tortures; blood was a reality with a symbolic function."[64] We see that the society of blood—whether in the blood that "ecrivait [son] devoir" (wrote out her duty [2.8.676]) or the bloodshed that redeems Rodrigue as Le Cid is present—governs the logic of retribution and honorable lineage that characterizes much of the violence of the drama. Yet, on the actual level of jurisprudence and governance, there is, according to Foucault, a competing "society of sex: the mechanisms of power are addressed to the body, to life, to what causes it to proliferate, to what reinforces the species, its stamina, its ability to dominate, or its capacity for being used."[65] Chimène heightens the contradictory affects and emotions generated from these chrono-mashups.

Her use of speeds allows her to contest or control otherwise hegemonic tempos such as the unseemly nature of a woman too quickly yielding to love or stalling the speed of vengeance.

Chimène's temporal violations, rather than solely conveying a lack of female virtue, may also afford a type of virtuous critique. Butler suggests that "certain kinds of practices which are designed to handle certain kinds of problems produce, over time, a settled domain of ontology as their consequence, and this ontological domain, in turn, constrains our understanding of what is possible."[66] One way to push back, or critique such a limited notion of ontology, Butler contends, is not to outright shatter it but to "stylize" it. Or put in a more precise way, the self, incorporating the rules of conduct that represent the virtue of austerity, creates itself as a specific kind of subject. This self-production is what Foucault calls "the elaboration and stylization of an activity in the exercise of its power and the practice of its liberty."[67]

Rules and the Spectator

I have suggested that the technological innovations of the seventeenth century, as well as an attention to the representation of time passing onstage, offered not only a new way of knowing time but also new ontologies of temporality itself; the polemical debates around the theater yielded a "settled domain" of normative tempos and speeds. Thus, instead of looking for resistance as temporal disruption against the constraint of the règles classiques, perhaps we can more precisely find tarrying in the "stylization of an activity" of Chimène's use of temporality. These come to the fore when we are attentive to the multiple and unexpected velocities within the play that offer a certain creativity and elaboration of the agency of the subject. Velocities, however, also have an impact on the spectator, and allow a spectatorial "stylization" of the rules.

The unity of time provides not only a verisimilar representation onstage but also a subtle, yet critical conduct of conducts. One angle of this shaping force is visible in the ways that the unity of time fostered or foreclosed the agency of the spectator regarding imagination. Joseph Harris notes that the debates surrounding the unity of time illuminated opposing views on the importance and role of the spectator.[68] For Chapelain, the unity of time played a vital role in sustaining the vraisemblance of any spectacle: "in the sole intention of removing from the spectators any opportunity to reflect on what they were seeing and thereby doubting its reality."[69] Any fissures in the illusion would alert the spectators that they were, in fact, watching a play and thus shatter the suspension of disbelief. Chapelain's justification rests in his belief that "the eye . . . is a limited organ" (l'œil . . . est un organe fini");[70] the fragile eye cannot be overloaded with too many events. Chapelain's delicate spectator risked being overburdened with too many things to remember or to string together mentally if the time span represented in the play were to extend too far.

For Chapelain, the "regularity" of time onstage not only governs the streamlined aesthetics of play but also produces correct and incorrect pleasure. A kind of Bourdieusian association of taste and status emerges, wherein one's class status is affirmed and performend by one's aesthetics tastes and pleasures, and vice versa.[71] Civardi summarizes Chapelain's viewpoint: "The theater ought to remain useful and pleasing, and the rule of twenty-four hours allows the separation of . . . false pleasures from true ones . . . Indeed, the people ('idiots' and 'riffraff') are satisfied with cumbersome plots, farces, 'rustic pleasures' and therefore with vice."[72] The unity of time helped create the vraisemblance necessary to enthrall spectators, but it also allowed a winnowing function, to distinguish intellectual pleasure from "vice" or baser pleasures. Moreover, Chapelain's comment reveals that the unity of time was never simply about guidelines for stagecraft; it underscores the importance of temporal regularity to the very governance of pleasure and, implicitly, ties the control of time to the conduct of conducts.

In contrast to Chapelain's upholding of the rules, Harris analyzes how critic Jean-Gilbert Durval instead focuses on the spectator. For Durval, this restriction shortchanges the spectator of creative imagination[73] and he warns against too much handholding on the part of the "regular" dramaturge—a term for the writer who respects the classical rules—as he or she endeavors to smooth over any snags in the representation that could alert the spectator to the fact of the illusion. Strict obedience to the temporal rule eliminates any participatory or creative spectatorship: Harris contends that for Durval, "what the 'regular' spectator lacks above all is imagination—that mental agility required to lend credence to the performance even when it lacks perfect mimetic exactitude."[74] The divergence from the unity of time permits and encourages the spectator's imaginative engagement. Ultimately, both theories of theatrical representation vied for acceptance in the seventeenth century, which may also further explain d'Aubignac's quip regarding the "most agitating question" over the representation of theatrical time.[75]

Imaginative spectatorship, in this light, generates the possibility of critique. Harris contends that for Chapelain, in contrast to Durval, imagination is what must be "tricked" for the spectacle's effect to hold: imagination is that "critical impulse that must be stilled if the play is to succeed."[76] Judgment, as Harris reminds us, was viewed "almost exclusively in a negative way . . . aesthetic judgment is passed only when the play fails to maintain the illusion."[77] We can surmise that a unique critical position emerges from the interplay between the dulled and the active imagination, between the pleasure of the "perfected" vraisemblance of the show and the momentary temporal snags that require the supplement of an audience's creative reshuffling.

Between Chapelain's and Durval's senses of theatrical time, we find the potential for the type of emancipated spectator position that Jacques Rancière has advanced. Rancière explains that the emancipated spectator "composes her own poem with the elements of the poem before her"[78] that is, she hijacks the energy of the performance, not experienced as a top-down flow of knowledge pinning her to her seat but rather as a spectrum of offerings that can be recomposed, refashioned, and interwoven with one's own personal experiences and desires. Part of this emancipation, then, rests in the possibility of critique or at least the possibility of the middle zone between the complacent pleasure and the jarring temporal irregularity.

In the top-down imaginary of how theater operated as a tool of biopolitical discipline, the spectator, according to Rancière, is "held before an appearance in a state of ignorance about the production of this appearance and the reality it conceals" and thus doubly passive, not only ignorant but also "immobile in her seat" in contrast to the action on stage.[79] In the early modern context, Blocker notes, spectators' discipline was to be elicited due to the fact that the theater presented itself as a disciplined and organized institution.[80] Durval's comments regarding the impact of the temporal irregularity on spectatorship hint at the possibility of a subtle kind of spectatorial resistance, one that stood in opposition to the disciplined subject's quieted imagination. Durval's spectator could not only lose herself in the pleasures of theatrical representation but also, given the "irregular" time of the drama, hone her apparatus of judgment and calibration of pleasure. Thus, the description of the public and widespread nature of the debates regarding the unity of time to which d'Aubignac refers is not so surprising after all. As the pamphlet writers of the *querelle* contend, respecting or violating the unity of time becomes a critical means of either generating the lulled complacency of a perfected illusion or of fissuring the illusion and stimulating doubts. Imagination and the possibility of fantasy are thus rooted in the experience of temporal snags, of queer velocities onstage, in the ephemeral speeds and intensities that interrupt the temporal conditioning so crucial to chronobiopolitical management.

Scholarship has generally tended to consider why and how the *querelle* contributed to the formation of a literary public sphere, and the importance of this literary public to statecraft or female public salon culture. Yet, I would go one step further to underscore that this public sphere hinged on the formation of ideal spectators, namely, those primed to enjoy temporal regularity. Such disciplined, temporally "regular" spectators are thus essential to forming chronobiopolitics—not just the literary public—and securing theater's role as an apparatus of chronobiopolitical discipline.

The theater debates also elicited a sense of shared, communal pleasure. The *querelle* has been cited by literary historians as the inception of not only a literary public but also the public sphere itself. Hélène Merlin-Kajman builds on Jürgen Habermas's notion of the "bourgeois public sphere," to suggest that coterminous with centralization of power in the seventeenth century was the proliferation of a whole host of institutions of power, a "depersonalization" of power that unknotted older ties of obedience based on interpersonal fidelity and instead saw increased institutes and rules.[81] For civil society, according to Merlin-Kajman, "Encumbered in this initiative by the powers of the State, society took on another organ of pressure: public opinion. It is thanks to this public opinion that the bourgeois public sphere could be properly constructed."[82] In this light, public opinion and the stoking of discourse was essential to the founding of such a public sphere or a zone of shared enjoyment. Also, the *querelle* yielded affective supplements of pleasure. Chapelain, one of the main authors of the *Sentiments de l'Académie français sur Le Cid* noted that literary debates, while often bitter and polemical, produced more supplementary affects and pleasures than the content of the debate at hand. Thus, infused into the debates over literary regulations was an investment in creating a site of discourse, not only to regulate the pleasure of the theater but also to situate a larger arena in which the "search for a shared pleasure" could be undertaken. But it is significant to note that staging of "differends" (disagreements) in terms of divergent literary opinions or sociopolitical ideals is crucial to generate the pleasure of arriving at a shared consensus.[83]

The theater was marked by a proliferation of knowledge—by the codification of rules that accompanied the transformation of the theater into an "art," as d'Aubignac undertook. The coalescing knowledge and practices that organized and produced temporal norms also brought to the fore new matrices of visibility—new ways that timing, tempos, and velocities could be discerned, named, and felt. For Foucault, "there is no power relation without the correlative constitution of a field of knowledge, nor any knowledge that does not presuppose and constitute at the same time, power relations."[84] Therefore, the knowledge circulating around the theater in debates, published rules, and performances alike, rendered the theater a site of power, a site of chronobiopower: the disciplining of the rhythms of desiring, living, and loving. All these temporalities presented on stage, from Chimène's strategically deployed delay to Rodrigue's hasty redemption, interweave to code time and specifically the time of life. The *querelle* revealed a constellation of anxieties: about the potentially nefarious effect of "bad examples," what correct and incorrect tempos looked like, what kinds of spectators ought to be watching the plays, and what kind of pleasures ought to be prioritized. One of the commonplaces about seventeenth-century theater is its relationship to constraint and limitation. On the one hand, the historical-cultural context of the bienséances and its seventeenth-century acceptance of multiple senses of properness or "fittingness" allows us to better understand the "clicking into place" or "directionality" harbored in the concept of queer velocity. On the other hand, I sought to put pressure on the very notion of the norm (or fittingness) by disentangling the sleight of hand that linked the imposition of aesthetic order to sociopolitical order. In this chapter I demonstrated that the stories that we tend to tell about neoclassical theater and the règles classiques overemphasizes the ideological dimension at the expense of overlooking the affective and biopolitical dimension. When the focus shifts to the fact that the bienséances and the vraisemblances are a means instead of an end, we can understand the rules not as an imposition of power or an arbitrary constraint, but rather as a *dispositif* with multiple affordances. Temporal regularity and regimentation can be understood as not only allied to an ideological investment in patriarchal sovereignty, but also as biopolitical management that fosters affective intensities, that changes the sensation of time passing, and that—unregulated –may provoke the imagination of spectators. As the règles classiques became deployed as part of the conduct of conducts, resistance began to look less and less like outright violations of the rule, and instead more similar to the "stylization" or tarrying with tempos that Chimène enacts in *Le Cid*.

2

Animate Ashes

The Time of Ruins and Remains in *Andromaque*

"Hélas! Il mourra donc."

"Hélas! Il mourra donc." *Alas, he'll die then.* In the 2010 staging of Jean Racine's *Andromaque* (1667) at the Comédie-Française, Cécile Brune as Andromaque delivers this line regarding her son's impending death in a low, emotionless monotone.[1] The flatness of her affect is further echoed by the actors' gray, diaphanous costumes. Everything appears dismal and muted.

This flat affect is even more striking given the crisis point of the intrigue onstage. In the aftermath of the Trojan War, the widowed Andromaque and her infant son Astyanax have been taken captive by Pyrrhus, king of Epirus. Yet, it is the captor, Pyrrhus, who is the real prisoner, hopelessly shackled to his unrequited love for Andromaque. Tired of waiting, Pyrrhus threatens Andromaque with a terrible ultimatum: either marry him or he will surrender her child to Oreste and the Greeks, who demand that the infant be killed, for fear that the boy will grow up to become like his warrior father Hector, raise another Troy, and avenge his father's and the Trojans' defeat. Andromaque responds to this ultimatum by refusing to make a choice. She merely sighs.

Racine's play was initially staged in 1667 in Queen Marie-Thérèse's private apartments and was met with resounding critical success. The tragedy's popularity secured the renown of the then twenty-seven-year-old as one of the most brilliant playwrights of his generation. In comparison to Corneille, whose tragedies often elicited criticism for stuffing too many events within the presumed "un tour de soleil" (one turn of the sun), Racine effortlessly adhered to the règles classiques: the unities of time, place, and action. Temporal-spatial constraint paradoxically enables, rather than limits, Racine's poetry.

Because of Racine's adherence to the unity of time, Andromaque's delay in deciding the fate of herself and her child, extending over three acts of the play, becomes even more significant and has posed a puzzle that has long intrigued scholars. Roland Barthes criticizes this stalling, pointing out that a "good" mother would never have hesitated: "Faced with the contradiction of her duty, it is not to her maternity that Andromache refers (and if she had done so, would she have hesitated a moment?"[2] Brune's flat interpretation of Andromaque and her emotionless response to Pyrrhus's threat confirms this heartless diagnosis, a sentiment that characterizes a Barthesian approach to Racine's play: Andromaque presents a troubling vision of motherhood, because she is so overcommitted to her dead husband's memory that she cannot take action to save her son in the present. Her delay signals her deviance from the behavior of a "normal" mother, who would immediately jump at any opportunity to save her child. For other scholars this delay, however, is not indifferent, but rather strategic, and offers cause to celebrate her as a nationalistic or selfless Trojan heroine, or even a devoted widow committed to "performing" the past.[3] But these have been symptomatic readings of the delay, insofar as they interpret the time of inaction as either an inner moral failure or a strategic virtue. Thanks to this delay, *Andromaque* risks violating the *bienséances* (rules of propriety). Yet, unlike Corneille's treatment of *Le Cid*, as analyzed in chapter 1, Racine's tragedies do not cram together too many plot points, nor are there strategic disruptions of temporal propriety akin to Chimène's feminist management of speeds. Indeed, the near-perfect fit of events to the twenty-four-hour frame affords a clearer view of Andromaque's inexplicable slowness, as well as the ways that these tempos gesture toward alternate possibilities and worlds made otherwise.

Rather than seizing on delay as symptomatic, what would it require to take Andromaque at her word? In other words, how can we bracket the traditional "ends" associated with maternity or national progress? In the suspension that such bracketing permits, the delay—the time of inaction—emerges as an end in and of itself. Stuart Sherman notes that, by the late seventeenth century, even technologies as minor as the clock dial or the minute hand "called attention away from end-points and invested it in middles—of the current hour, of the ongoing life—that were sharply defined and indefinitely extended."[4] Sherman suggests that these technological innovations revolutionized the experience of the *passing* of time (the "middles"), relieving the weight and importance that we ascribe to the origins or the ends. Andromaque's delay may thus also be read as a breath, a pause against other exigencies of action, a slowness or drag that does not necessarily seek to obtain the "ends" so privileged by motherhood and widowhood, but perhaps points to other, queerer investments.

In the "inaction" of this drama, not one but two scales of inaction or delay are at hand. On the diegetic level, there is Andromaque's perplexing lack of responsiveness, intoning in a low monotone, instead of jumping readily to save her son. But what is permitted or enhanced by "delay" itself? Andromaque repeatedly cries out to Hector's ashes (*cendres*)—not only invoking his memory but also speaking to his material remains. Hector's ashes, in fact, intrude as an active agent at various key points of the play. As Peggy McCracken and Basil DuFallo write in their introduction to *Dead Lovers*, "the continuing possession of the lover's dead body, in whatever form, suggests a reluctance to acknowledge loss but is also the assertion of a singular identity—the living lover of a dead lover—whose *claims must be reckoned with* rather than simply rejected."[5] Therefore, we must grapple with Andromaque's attachment to ash, and the temporal liminality that it conveys, as signaling a specific, queer type of claim.

The second form of delay takes place on the mythopoetic scale: the play itself is self-reflexively concerned with its status as a lull point. This is because the ending is so victoriously framed as a future, not only for Astyanax and Andromaque, as Leo Bersani has noted, but also for the French nation. In Andromaque's last staged scene, we find that she decides to marry Pyrrhus (securing Astyanax's safety) and then immediately kill herself, or what she calls an "innocent stratagème" (innocent strategy [4.1.1097]) that allows her to preserve both her child and her virtuous widow's vow to Hector. But before this suicidal strategy can take place, the people of Epirus rise in revolt, and in a maddened fury, kill Pyrrhus and crown Andromaque queen. Significantly, this surprise twist feeds into French nationalist mythologies of past and future that were prevalent in the seventeenth century. Tiphaine Karsenti suggests that "from the seventh century on, indeed, several chroniclers related how the Franks—and after them other European peoples—descended from Trojan survivors who, much like Aeneas, had fled from Troy in flames and settled in Western Europe."[6] More specifically, the imagined genealogies linking the ancient Franks to the French nation, via the Trojan survivors, "offered a set of convenient qualities for a nation eager to found and then legitimize its own existence, but also to justify its desire for military and cultural domination over other nations."[7] Karsenti notes that by the seventeenth century the myth was commonly understood to be just that— a myth— but this imagined story still loomed large in the cultural imaginary. However, the narrative itself was predicated on a simple fact: Astyanax's survival.[8] Racine, cognizant of this fantasy-generating myth, signals even in his second preface that "j'ai été oblige de faire vivre Astyanax un peu plus qu'il n'a vécu"[9] (I was obliged to make Astyanax live for a bit longer than he actually did). His language couches survival as excess life ("un peu plus"). Even in Andromaque's last staged speech in act 4, by the time she has vowed to undertake the "innocent strategy" her language is imbued with the rhetoric of survival and duty, echoed by numerous future verb tenses: "Je vais donc . . . Assurer à Pyrrhus la reste de ma vie / Je vais . . . L'engager à mon fils par des noeuds immortels" (I will thus . . . secure the rest of my life to Pyrrhus / I will . . . tie him to my son through immortal knots [4.1.1089–92]). But her main emphasis is not on bio-life but rather on the survival of the narrative: "qu'on parle de moi," "fais-lui valoir," "dis-lui," and "fais connaître," ("that one speaks of me," "make him value," "tell him," and "make known," respectively [4.1.1089–92]), she says, urging her friend Céphise to continue to tell her story. The teleological arc of the *story's* longevity (and the glorious future it portends) papers over the significance of delay itself.

We have then two kinds of delay: one that takes place in the time of the play (within, we recall, the "unité de jour"), a delay in which Andromaque sighs in lieu of making a choice. The second kind of delay takes place on a national-historical scale: the lull before the glorious accomplishment of French destiny. Delay can only be understood as such against the backdrop of expectations of action, that is, it can only appear within the frame of a specifically organized, normative tempo. Such ideologies, Elizabeth Freeman reminds us, are constructed to appear naturalized: "Chrononormativity is a mode of implantation, a technique by which institutional forces come to seem like somatic facts . . . manipulations of time convert historically specific regimes of asymmetrical power into seemingly ordinary bodily tempos and routines, which in turn organize the value and meaning of time."[10] Some of these ordinary tempos—ones that go unquestioned—include the speedy protection of a mother, or the temporality of survival and national progress. But the same (in)action that can be denigrated as a failure of speed can also be read as a radical opening of Sherman's "middles."

The question of choosing life or choosing death is not only at stake. In other words, the focus has been on analyzing the dramatic reluctance or rush to choose Astyanax's life or Andromaque's strategic suicidal death, instead of thinking about the structures that govern microtempos, of decision making and gestures of intimacy and, conversely, the pleasures and erotics that these temporal deviations and dilations can elicit. For example, Andromaque's first lines of the drama points to a peculiarity of lived time that she has been experiencing:

> Puisqu'une fois le jour vous souffrez que je voie
> Le seul bien qui me reste, et d'Hector et de Troie,
> J'allais, Seigneur, pleurer un moment avec lui,
> Je ne l'ai point encore embrassé d'aujourd'hui. (1.4.261–64)
>
> (Because once a day you begrudge me the sight
> Of the sole good that remains to me of both Hector and of Troy
> I was going, Sir, to cry a moment with him
> I have not yet embraced him today.)

Although she is using this phrase to sidestep Pyrrhus's amorous advances—"Me cherchiez-vous, Madame?" (Are you seeking me, Madame? [1.4.258])—it is noteworthy that Andromaque insists on her spatial and emotional captivity though references to the ways that her *temporality* is regulated: that "une fois le jour" (once a day) she is permitted to see her son, an exceptional time that she has not yet enjoyed. During this time, we know, she will indulge in a quasi-incestuous, strange embrace of Astyanax, kissing and calling him by her dead husband's name.[11] But more than indicating temporal governance, she *uses* this temporal calibration as a shield and cover, excusing herself from Pyrrhus's embrace and claiming her own kind of rhythm that defines and conditions her quotidian life: the unhindered tempo of Pyrrhus's day permits the possibility of seeking his captive (the agency of an expression of love), whereas Andromaque's daily rhythm is split binaristically between waiting and embrace. The differences between the captor's and captive's abilities to live time (to experience or endure waiting, anticipation, pleasure, dread) highlight the divergences in the general capacities to live and love. Her language points to an awareness of temporal constraint and the larger game of manipulation at hand, thus revealing that Andromaque is far from oblivious to the impact of the time of inaction. Foucault's attention to capillary biopolitical control not only conditions the speeds of action (such as Chimène's calibrated speeds of justice, as we saw in the previous chapter) but also colors the time of *not doing anything at all*. Given the chronobiopolitical management of temporality, whether it's the time of waiting for her daily visit to her son or the time of indecision, Andromaque's time of waiting is far from being homogenous and empty—to borrow a term from Walter Benjamin—and she strategically opens these "middles" toward queer ends.[12]

Furthermore, previous scholarship treating Andromaque's delay is grounded in assumptions about what counts as life. This chapter unearths unexpected attachments that trouble the inanimate-animate divide, yielding a lingering with an expanded sense of *bios* in chronobiopolitics that complicates the nature of temporal management of such biolife. As we saw in the previous chapter, reading the "ends" of sexuality and the paces of desire together—the queerness of velocities—allowed us to see how the pace can generate different erotic possibilities, such as the opening of the "middles" for Iphis in *Iphis et Iante*. Conversely, wrenching the action toward certain ends (a heteronormative marriage) can produce a rushed effect, as in *Le Cid*. Directional ends and speeds unravel each other; thus, an attention to velocities permit a richer understanding of the ways that ends and tempos interact. And certainly, when bios or the spectrum of what counts as life changes, the ends alter as well. The two kinds of delay—diegetic and mythohistorical—will be treated separately in this chapter, and both shed light on different meanings of Andromaque's attachment to ashes.

Animate Ashes

Andromaque's friend and confidante Céphise scolds what she perceives as Andromaque's excessive hesitancy, saying, "Madame, à votre époux c'est être assez fidèle: / Trop de vertu pourrait vous rendre criminelle" (Madam, you've been faithful enough to your spouse / Too much virtue could render you a criminal [3.8.981–82]). As the minutes tick away, Céphise urges Andromaque to decide if she will give herself to Pyrrhus to save her son. Andromaque answers in neither the affirmative nor the negative, instead plaintively exclaiming, "Ô cendres d'un époux! Ô Troyens! Ô mon père! / Ô mon fils, que tes jours coûtent cher à ta mère" (Oh, the ashes of my husband! Oh Trojans! Oh my father / Oh my child, how your days cost your mother dearly [3.8.1045–46]). While the list of people she invokes is not strange, in this list, instead of sighing for Hector, she specifically apostrophizes his *ashes*. But "criminelle," in Céphise's indictment, can point not only to Andromaque's contribution to Astyanax's impending death but also to the offense of an unseemly and deviant attachment to these ashes. When Céphise presses her again as to what she will choose, Andromaque replies, "Allons sur son tombeau consulter mon époux" (We shall go consult my husband at his tomb [3.8.1048]). By insisting that they go to the tomb, Andromaque reveals a particular investment in the matter and material surrounding Hector's death.

Much like Antigone, Andromaque chooses the tomb over the bridal chamber, saying, "Ma flamme par Hector fut jadis allumée; / Avec lui dans la tombe elle s'est enfermée" (Although my love for Hector was once aflame, now, it is enclosed in the tomb with his remains [3.4.865–66]). And yet, there is something more than the death drive at hand here. Judith Butler's analysis of Antigone in *Antigone's Claim* provides an analogous model for reading Andromaque's choice toward nonreproductivity:

> Certainly, [Antigone] does not achieve another sexuality, one that is not heterosexuality, but she does seem to deinstitute heterosexuality by refusing to do what is necessary to stay alive for Haemon, by refusing to become a mother and a wife, . . . by embracing death as her bridal chamber and identifying her tomb as a "deep dug home" (*kataskaphes oikesis*).[13]

Without directly equating the nonreproductive position with a queer one, we should keep in mind the force of a critical stance that "deinstitutes" certain forms of intimacy and desire, as exemplified by Andromaque and Antigone. In other words, instead of understanding the delay in the negative—as a widow's refusal to move on or to remarry or a mother's refusal to save her son—we must notice how the space of delay offers, instead, the possibility for something positive: an active engagement with ashes as its own queer mode of love and attachment.

The widow (and especially the royal widow) was judged by a range of heteronormative and gendered criteria, ones that were particularly temporally inflicted. Carla Freccero in *Queer/Early/Modern* remarks on the "double bind that Christiane Klapisch-Zuber has named 'the cruel mother' syndrome: on the one hand, it is a young widow's duty (to her family of birth) to remarry and thus to put her wealth back into circulation: on the other, it is a sign of devotion to her family of marriage that she does not, retaining wealth for the male heir of that family (her son)."[14] While Racine's Andromaque is not necessarily concerned with putting "wealth" into circulation, effectively her love and fidelity become themselves a type of capital, which the other characters are eager to seize. The Greeks assume and fear a type of maternal love from her, a nurturing love that would fertilize the young Astyanax's development into a second Hector. Pyrrhus seeks to stoke the embers of Andromaque's "flamme" from one of anger against him and his people to one of amorous passion as his future queen. But, despite all these groups' claims on Andromaque's affection and desire, her affected energies are instead intensely noncirculated, deeply and resolutely entrenched toward *another* form of attachment—namely, one to ash.

On the surface, the "fidelity" that Céphise decries as an excessive attachment to the dead Hector follows an established classical paradigm of the devoted widow. Harriet Stone, for example, argues that "Racine depicts a widow's efforts to keep alive the hero's values through her own fidelity and her veneration of his name . . . the re-presentation of Hector in Épire which constitutes Andromaque's performance, this imitation of history, is the life principle through which Troy extends itself over time."[15] But even in light of this accepted mourning paradigm, Andromaque's affective *excess* is plainly visible, as a "trop" in Céphise's "trop de vertu" (excess of virtue).

Certainly, on the rhetorical scale, a classical precedent exists for Andromaque to transpose and to "faire vivre" (make live) Hector's remains, as Racine alluded to in his preface. Georges Forestier reads this gesture in the light of the Ovidian tradition of a plaintive heroine:

> It is in the style of Ovid's *Héroïdes*, that Andromaque, in the middle of a tirade directed at Pyrrhus, begins to speak directly to [Hector] whom she has never ceased to mourn . . . [This is] the poetic transfiguration of one of the basic rhetorical training exerçises, the *ethopoeia*. To make a character, generally taken from mythology, speak within a tragic context, considering the parameters established by past literature . . . such are the rules of *ethopoeia*.[16]

Yet in Forestier's analysis of Racine's language, the invocation to "faire parler" Hector is minimized to an example of a rhetorical training exercise, and Forestier declines to explore what this animation through rhetoric might portend.

There is also a sociocultural precedent for this type of attachment to ash and the performance of delay. For Christian Biet, Andromaque represents a virtuous type of widow using this temporal management to her advantage:

> a symbol of conjugal virtue in perfect harmony with what both moralists and the representatives of religion and of Canonical law affirm. It is true that Andromaque is still prey to a morbid passion, except that this passion is consistent with the dominant discourse on marriage and remarriage, and that it acquires legitimacy in the face of the tyrannical use of power[17]

Hers is an intimacy with Hector and with the past that employs and is obfuscated by this visible screen of virtue. What appears to be a lingering attachment to a virtuous marriage vow can conceal, in the very same "open" language and orientation, a perverse attachment to the traumatic loss, and the material marker of such loss. But, while this "morbid passion" is able to hijack social and temporal norms to cover over the intensity of her attachment, we might be able to penetrate this screen of virtue when we take Andromaque *at her word*, when we examine her commitment not to Hector or to his memory, but to his actual ashes.

In Biet's, Forestier's, and Stone's analyses, Andromaque's invocation of ash is grounded in rhetorical strategies that allow for a certain veneration of the past and an extension of the future, but at an arm's length distance of pure figure, or rhetorical play, instead of literalized attachment. For these scholars, a figurative treatment of ash renders it as a metaphor or metonym for Hector, a placeholder for the past.[18] By suspending these established rhetorical and sociocultural norms of attachment, we can find that ash is syntactically and dynamically positioned as something encompassed in the spectrum of the animate. In his preface Racine cites an excerpt of the *Aeneid* in which Andromaque is depicted as immersed in the throes of attending to funereal rites for Hector's ashes: "At this moment a solemn sacrifice and funereal libations were offered by Andromaque, to Hector's ashes."[19] In Racine's French translation of the Latin, the ashes receive the focus of care and attention, rendered even more "active" by the passive-voice construction of the line.

Another royal widow, the Spanish queen Juana "la Loca" (1479–1555) provides another historical counterpart that models what Andromaque's "morbid passion" accomplishes. Juana repeatedly ordered that her husband's cadaver be disinterred, kissing the body and displaying it ceremoniously in a procession across Castile. As Samuel Sanchez y Sanchez analyzes, such a gesture of love stood as a calculated means of shoring up political power: "if by remaining unburied Philip's dead body hovered over the border between two states—life and death—so did Juana's matrimonial identity oscillate between widowhood and wedlock . . . this control [over the mortal remains] allowed her to guard her widowhood, prevent the sexual appropriation of her own body and by extension protect the patrimonial body of her kingdom."[20] Similarly, for Andromaque, her love for Hector's ash *as* ash ultimately answers the puzzle that her inexplicable delay poses. Love for ash requires and elicits a suspended temporality, one hovering between life and death, ruin and remainder, past and future. The "delay" that Andromaque enacts is the time of this love for ash.

I take up Jane Bennett's challenge to "take seriously the vitality of (nonhuman) bodies . . . the capacity of things—edibles, commodities, storms, metals—not only to impede or block the will and designs of humans but also to act as quasi agents with trajectories, propensities, or tendencies of their own."[21] In the drama the ashes are depicted as conveying such vibrancy, and this dynamism twists Andromaque's attachment from a widow's traditional, mourned for love to a different kind of desire, a queer love that engages actively with ash. Such an attachment to what Bennett might call "vibrant matter" places Andromaque aslant of the prescriptive ideals of motherhood and heteronormative desire.

The animate capaciousness of ashes situates the very material of ash in a temporality that exceeds the static time of a merely passive object. My contention is that ashes, in this light, emerge as a paradoxical figure of both *ruin* (a testament to the past) and *remainder* (that which remains past the point of destruction, enduring into the future). Loving an inhuman object changes the nature and importance of time. This paradoxical past-future (ruin and remainder) temporality of ashes is redoubled by the tragedy's diegetic time of postwar survival and the time of trauma. Against other, established temporal metrics, Andromaque's delay is categorized as a failure to accomplish or to perform a certain kind of action, or as a successful strategy (a gesture of nationalistic heroism or of a widow's fidelity). But within the context of the temporality of ashes, delay swerves from the domain of legible actions and offers a liminal suspension in which an ash-oriented love can flourish. Just as we noted earlier that the ends and speeds can queerly unravel each other, so, too, do the queer "ends" of an attachment to ashes change what the temporalities of delay and of progress-oriented love should look like.

In this attachment to ashes, I am considering Andromaque's desire as exceeding a mere fetish. In the psychodynamics of fetishism, Freud defines the fetish object as a substitute for the missing maternal phallus. Here, I am interested not in the substitutive but rather the literal relation to the material of ash itself. In "Objects of Desire," Amber Jamilla Musser explores a new category of queer sexuality, *objectum sexuality*. For objectum sexuals, the object "and nothing else— is the desired sexual partner, and all sexual fantasies and emotions are focused on it"[22] Musser writes: "Erika introduces herself by saying, 'I'm a person who's in love, very much in love. I just happen to be in love with an object' . . . hearing her words juxtaposed against an image of her standing alone caressing the Berlin Wall still has an impact. These words alter our image of the Berlin Wall and open an array of possible ways to relate to it."[23] Although Musser uses objectum sexuality as a means of exploring the ethics of sameness (the feeling of becoming object, instead of the rendering subject of the inanimate thing), I am equally compelled by Musser's suggestion that a love relation changes our notion of not only the thing but also the modes of orientation and relation to it. Anachronistically cross-applying these categories to *Andromaque* brings to light that some inhuman objects—such as ash—take on the qualities of animacy and thus elicit and condition erotic behavior.

Mel Chen's *Animacies* allows a reconsideration of object attachments similar to Andromaque's interaction with ash. Chen centers on affect as a prime means of rethinking objects, defining affect as "something not necessarily corporeal in that it potentially engages many bodies at once."[24] Once we accept that affect is not necessarily an emotion housed in one individual, but rather a flow of forces that mark the "capacity to affect and be affected" then we might think of "animacy hierarchies" as structures that predetermine our understanding of what kinds of things can or cannot affect, touch, and move other things as well as what types of objects are even worthy of such affect.[25] In other words, how can we tell what counts and what matters as an acceptable object of love? Can there be a range, or gradations, of "living matter" instead of a binary opposition between the living and the inanimate?

In Andromaque's rhetorical questions, served as ripostes to those who urge her to act, she frames her responses not in terms of passivity but rather as a presently experienced and active engagement: "Aux cendres d'un époux doit-elle enfin sa flamme?" (Do her husband's ashes demand her flame still? [1.4.358]), or "Est-ce là l'ardeur tant promise à sa cendre?" (Is this the ardor so promised to his ashes? [4.1.1081]). To take "Est-ce là l'ardeur tant promise à sa cendre?" the question situates the "cendres" as anchoring the promise, demanding ardor, and more. Chen, a linguist, explains the syntactical structures that undergird such animacy: while "stones" are typically used as an example of an inappropriate verbal subject, in keeping with linguistic norms, the phrase "the hikers that rocks crush" is a grammatical phrase that is not necessarily *wrong*, nor bereft of meaning, we see that it is propelled by strange valences of agency and animacy.[26] The stone begins to operate as a grammatical, quasi-real subject just as the ash in *Andromaque* becomes endowed with animate sensibilities. In Chen's vision of animacy, rocks contain some, however minimal, capacity to act and to be affected, and thus can no longer be treated as the absolute binary opposite of animatedness. By taking up Chen's animacy seriously, we can consider ash to hold a "scalar position" on the animacy scale as well: not necessarily "active" but not without affect either. Accordingly, Andromaque's desire for Hector's ashes *qua* ash (and not merely as a placeholder for the dead husband) can be analyzed as an alternative form of erotic attachment. Ash hungers for flame, demands promises. Rather than an affinity for ash as marking an excess in mourning, or stagnation, ash can signal different arrangement of animate love.

This alternative, animating love has contagious effects, expanding the realm of Andromaque's attachments, as well as impacting the nature of time. Just as Pyrrhus seems ready to deliver Astyanax to the Greeks, Andromaque makes one last emboldened plea, but it is not a plea for life. Rather, she apostrophizes Hector, animating him by invoking ash:

> Ah! S'il l'était assez pour nous laisser du moins
> Au tombeau qu'à ta cendre ont élevé mes soins,
> Et que, finissant là sa haine et nos misères,
> Il ne séparât point des dépouilles si chères!" (3.6.943–46)
>
> (Oh, if he were [magnanimous] enough to simply leave us
> At the tomb I have erected in caring for your ashes
> And that, ending there his hatred and our misery
> He did not separate such dear remains.)

"Cendre," in her plea, is ensconced in the center of the alexandrine line, much like the tomb built around the ash; the line's syntax heightens the sense of care and investment in ash. Andromaque engages the ashes in conversation and effectively closes off the dialogue with Pyrrhus as interlocutor. Her pleas for the tomb and for ashes, however, elicit a curious reaction from Pyrrhus: a detour from the forward-moving logic of his plan, a questioning of his right as sovereign to decide. He opts instead, for further waiting, deferral, and demurral, telling his friend, Phoenix, "Va m'attendre, Phoenix" (Wait for me, Phoenix [3.6.947]), as he reconsiders his decision.

Pyrrhus also uses the language of ash but in an opposite way: to propel the action forward. All the other characters attempt repeatedly to orchestrate some sort of forward-moving action—rebuilding the city, renewing allegiances, upholding promises. Pyrrhus needs the literal image of ash to mark the finality of the war at the moment when he refuses to hand over Astyanax to Oreste and the Greeks. He paints a picture of the war's destruction in order to put the past behind them, and move on.

> Je regarde enfin
> Quel fut le sort de Troie, et quel est son destin.
> Je ne vois que des tours que la cendre a couvertes,
> Un fleuve teint de sang, des campagnes désertes,
> Un enfant dans les fers; et je ne puis songer
> Que Troie en cet état aspire à se venger (1.2.199–204)
>
> (I finally envision
> What Troy's fate was, and what is her destiny
> But I can only see ash-blanketed towers
> A river stained with blood, deserted fields
> And a child, held captive; I cannot make myself believe
> That Troy, in this state, would aspire to vengeance.)

Ashes temporally follow flames; they mark the quieting of destructive flame. To this end, the active verb "entreprendre" (undertake) is crucially paired with "cendre" (ash) to emphasize the possibility of progress. In this way, ash represents, for Pyrrhus, a type of futurity in which renewal is possible, the past is forgiven, and his burning desires have been satiated; he is able to extend promises of love and of rebuilding entire cities and only awaits Andromaque's affirmation. For Pyrrhus, the forward movement of promises and action he requires is remedy to the pain of the past.

In response, Andromaque draws on an animated rhetoric, flipping the language of fire and ash back on Pyrrhus and invoking the image of "cendres" in response:

> Et pourquoi vos soupirs seraient-ils repoussés?
> Aurait-elle oublié vos services passés?
> Troie, Hector, contre vous révoltent-ils son âme?

Aux cendres d'un époux doit-elle enfin sa flamme?
Et quel époux encore! Ah! Souvenir cruel!
Sa mort seule a rendu votre père immortel. (1.4.355–60)

(And why would all your advances be repulsed?
Has Andromaque forgotten everything you've done?
Do Troy and Hector harden her heart against you?
Do her husband's ashes still demand her love?
And what a husband! Oh! Cruel memory!
His death alone has given your father fame.)

Andromaque's memorialization of the past prevents Pyrrhus's "clean slate" of the future. At the same time, in a reversal of cause and effect, "cendres" is what incites or demands "flamme." We might productively think of this destabilizing gesture, of Andromaque's invocation of animate ashes, as an instance of what Patricia Parker describes as the preposterous, a "disruptive inverse of the proper and the natural."[27] For Parker, "*Preposterous*—from *posterus* (after or behind) and *prae* (in front or before) connotates a reversal of 'post' for 'pre,' behind for before, back for front, second for first, end or sequel for beginning . . . it involves not just verbal but also social or hierarchical reversal."[28] The productive disorderliness of this rhetorical figure has been traced by Parker, Jeffrey Masten, and Jonathan Goldberg, in the early modern English context of the term "as the marker of the unnatural as well as the reversed, it therefore stands as the inverse of orders claimed to be 'naturall & necessary.'"[29] Scholars of early modern queer studies have also emphasized the "sodomitical" connotations of "arsie-versie"; generally, the term was applied when the effect comes before the cause. Certainly not every pre-posterous turn is inherently queer, but in Andromaque's particular deployment of the figure, this reversal of cause and effect—ashes demanding flame, the lost husband demanding love, care (*soins*) invested in the object—shows how Andromaque's attachments to ash queers temporality, not through outright resistance to Pyrrhus's sovereign decisions but rather through oblique actions and rhetoric.

While Chen's analysis of animacy hinges on the syntactical reversals that allow for an expansion of the affective dimension, and Bennett urges the reader to "direct sensory, linguistic and imaginative attention toward a material vitality,"[30] this attention to animate matter is not new. It can be traced back to Lucretius, a first-century BCE philosopher, whose poem *De rerum natura* (On the Nature of Things) was "rediscovered" in fifteenth-century Renaissance Europe. Stephen Greenblatt notes that Lucretius's main concept, the clinamen, contained both terrifying and awe-inspiring qualities: "the stuff of the universe . . . is an infinite under of atoms moving randomly through space, like dust motes in a sunbeam, colliding, hooking together, forming complex structures, breaking apart again, in a ceaseless process of creation and destruction."[31] Similarly, Bennett takes up the Lucretian clinamen to transform it into a new way of considering objects and inanimate matter: "A primordial swerve says that the world is not determined, that an element of chanciness resides at the heart of things, but it also affirms that so-called inanimate things have a life, that deep within is an inexplicable vitality or energy, a moment of independence from and resistance to us and other bodies: a kind of thing-power."[32] Ellen McClure has analyzed Racine's correspondence, tracing the presence of puns and jibes based on Lucretius's phrasing to demonstrate that he was indeed aware of Epicurian philosophy.[33] Given the context of his basic familiarity with Lucretian-Epicurian thought, Racine's animatedness of the ash may also reflect a subtle but fleeting vision of this microscopic, imagined thing-power. Ash's animacy as depicted in *Andromaque* challenges the scope of the "bio" in chronobiopower, allowing us to think of not only the "sexual disciplining of the time of life"[34] but also the sexual disciplining of the time of a spectrum of animacies. An expanded sense of the animate also critically enriches our consideration of chronobiopolitics, or the disciplinary force of time's hold on "life." An "animate" sense of ash and its very persistent materiality alter what we can assume about the capacities of chronobiopower to discipline and choreograph temporality and sexuality. The more animate the ashes, the more undisciplined the realm of bios and intimacy. This new terrain of the animately inanimate veers away from norms of chonobiopolitical temporal governance.

Time of Trauma

The second type of delay to which I alluded—the snag in the smoothly progressing national history—can be found in the ways that the temporality of survival and trauma is tarried with. As evidenced by the proliferation of ambivalent locutions on the rhetorical plane, all the characters struggle in various ways with the nature of traumatic time. When Pyrrhus seems at the peak of his ire, saying "Je n'épargnerai rien dans ma juste colère" (I will spare nothing, in my justified rage [1.4.369]), Andromaque responds, perhaps provoked by his unironic invocation of "just," with radical passivity and a disinterested relation to the time of life, as well as indifference to the death of her son:

> Et peut-être après tout, dans l'état où je suis
> Sa mort avancera la fin de mes ennuis.
> Je prolongeais pour lui ma vie, et ma misère.
> Mais enfin sur ses pas j'irai revoir son père. (1.4.375–78)
>
> (And perhaps after everything, in the state that I am in
> [Astyanax's] death will hasten the end to my woes.
> I extended, for him, my life and my sorrow
> But finally, following his footsteps, I can rejoin his father.)

Claude Saint-Girons calls this response a "a burst of self-centeredness that horrifies even Pyrrhus himself."[35] But rather than dismissing her plaint as pure selfishness, an answer to this puzzling outburst may lie in paying due attention to Andromaque's own indication of what might be called trauma, in her evocation of "l'état où je suis" (the state that I am in) referring to both her condition of imprisonment and her status as a survivor of the Trojan War. Andromaque's temporality of prolonging highlights the negative, affective implications of a heightened temporal sensorium.

In the play's postwar context, the ashes of families and lovers lie among the burnt remains of the incinerated city. The Trojan War's survivors—the children of the Homeric heroes—struggle to make sense of the possibilities to love and live. As Cathy Caruth has noted, trauma imposes a duality of impossible situations, the event and its survival, which encompass "a double telling, the oscillation between a *crisis of death* and the correlative *crisis of life*: between the story of the unbearable nature of an event and the story of the unbearable nature of its survival."[36] Both these conditions of "unbearability" radically alter possibilities of articulation, narration, and speech. In a similar vein, Mitchell Greenberg has described the characters of *Andromaque* as the "walking wounded, the traumatized survivors of a war" mired in "a harrowing muddle of slaying, rape, and arson."[37] The importance of the traumatic context elevates Andromaque's attachment to ashes from a widow's rhetorical plaint to one capable of testifying to loss.

Her language does not merely represent a straightforward death drive oriented toward the tomb. This repeated invocation of loss, death, ruins, and remains also actively engages in an ethics of testimony in the present. As long as Andromaque continues to love and desire ashes, to dialogue with them and to consult them, then the memory of the trauma and her loss can live on, similar to Queen Juana's situation. The twinned terms of "ruin" and "remainder" that ash spans become key here. Hector is dead, and ashes are his ruins. But more than mere loss, ash is the only matter that literally "remains" past the point of destruction. Diegetically, as we have seen, this lingering materiality is endowed with animate qualities—dialogue-worthy, advice-giving, memorializing. Therefore, his "cendres," as both ruin and reminder, figure a material, persistent marker of loss *and* a remains more "animate" than grayish powder.

These redoubled temporalities of ash allow Andromaque to both linger in a memorialization of the past and cling to the remaining, enduring matter in the present. This relationship to ash and to temporality is slightly, but significantly, askew from other understandings of Andromaque's attachment to ash. The same word figures a whole host of affects and situations that lack a proper term: ungrievable loss, persistent remains, affectively charged ruins, beloved husband. Thus, when Andromaque says, "Est-ce là l'ardeur tant promise à sa cendre?" (Is this the love that I so promised his ashes? [4.1.1081]), or "Aux cendres d'un époux doit-elle enfin sa flamme?" (Do her husband's ashes demand her love still? [1.4.358]), she employs rhetorical questions as well as the specific invocation of ashes to deflect Pyrrhus's advances. She rhetorically pushes back against Pyrrhus's use of "juste colère" by reminding him that if he is the one to bring up the question of justness or justice, the wrongs he has enacted outweigh any measurable retribution. As Stéphane Natan notes, "her accusing and tactical questions aim to shift the situation in her favor, and they reveal a combative Andromaque who has no intention of losing the war [*guerre*]."[38] Natan's use of the word "guerre" (war) alludes to both the commonplace seventeenth-century term for literary quarrels as well as the literal, diegetic aftermath of the Trojan war.[39] In this strategic recourse to cendres and in Natan's fitting metaphor of a "guerre" that has become rhetorical, her use of cendres underscores the brutal reality of Hector's death, as well as the queerly latent possibility that the ashes actually can be the object of ardor or the "flamme" of passion. But on the scale of language, we find that the literalization of ash itself not only alters action (as in Pyrrhus's "va m'attendre") but also the domain of expression.

Racine's use of metaphor has been oft-discussed, insofar as Racine's choice of metaphoricity and literalization are not just fanciful poetic devices, but often drive the very action of the drama. Robert Hartle, to cite one perspective, proposes: "What is important to notice is the frequency with which Racine uses a dead metaphor [euphemism] to express the moral problem in a place, and then suddenly in the final scenes of the play he uses that metaphor quite literally and quite concretely as the instrument of catastrophe."[40] For Hartle, this movement occurs in *Andromaque* around the cluster of "furie, furieux" around Oreste, in which the passions expressed in Hermione's urgings become literalized as the imagined, haunting Furies that pursue him at the end of the play. But, instead of a simple transition from euphemism to literal agent of destruction, I read the reverse: language's poetic elevation or gallant distancing against a literal deployment in the play are the very actions of the "guerre" that has become rhetorical.

A brief detour to consider "flamme" (a mirror counterpart to "cendres," in a sense) will illustrate this rhetorical "guerre" and clarify the strategic force of a literalized, concretely animate ash. In act 1 Oreste first presses Pyrrhus to give up Astyanax by reminding Pyrrhus of Hector's violent past, a past that threatens to haunt the Greeks' and Astyanax's future. He chooses an appropriately fire-filled moment to insist on the risk:

> Et qui sait ce qu'un jour ce fils peut entreprendre?
> Peut-être dans nos ports nous le verrons descendre
> Tel qu'on a vu son père, embraser nos vaisseaux
> Et, la flamme à la main, les suivre sur les eaux. (1.2.161–64)
>
> (And who knows what this son may undertake one day?
> Perhaps we'll see him fall upon our ports
> Just as his father set our ships on fire,
> And, torch in hand, follow them out to sea.)

On one level, this is a cunning diplomatic gesture, in line with Timothy Hampton and Ellen McClure's understanding of Oreste as a diplomatic representative of the Greeks.[41] As Hampton notes, "The action of embassy *simultaneously* projects a new political order and enables the destruction of its own projection. It imagines a world beyond aristocratic blood lines and obsessive love, but by its very effect as a plot device—the movement of Orestes through space in the service of the state—it revives the passions that hinder the emergence of that world."[42]

Oreste invokes a commonly held vision of the traumatic past to woo Pyrrhus to yield. Destructive Hector is visible and lit only by the torch in his hand, the very fire that destroyed the Greek ships. This very same fire, Oreste insists, may be taken up by Hector's son; the uncertain future is illuminated only by the flickering destructive fires of the past. Thus, on another level, in Oreste's use of "flamme" is not just invoking the past flames but points to a future path. He underscores his own embeddedness in a temporality of inescapable repetition. Notably, this is a repetition that he both fears and desires, as he later urges Hermione that they could in fact retrace their parents' Trojan war exploits: "Mettons encore un coup toute la Grèce en flamme" (Let us once again alight all of Greece aflame [4.3.1159]).

The specters of the threatening fire and the cooled ash, as we saw earlier, are figural footholds for Pyrrhus and Oreste to approach the trauma of the past and orientation to the future. As Louise Horowitz underscores, "Envisioning liberation through a seemingly contradictory expression of reenactment and replication, [Pyrrhus] proposes to Andromaque a *reborn* Troy."[43] This temporality of "moving on" hinges on "returning" to do the past over again properly. It is also a "contradictory" time that requires rhetoric—and, specifically, the interplay between the metaphoric and the literal—to do the heavy lifting of erasing the traumatic past and forging the future. Alain Viala notes that part of the emotional energy of the play derives from the demetaphorization of language.

> The words, paraphrases and gallant metaphors that abound in *Andromaque* take on a new force because they are re-invested with their literal meanings. For example, there is nothing more clichéd than to speak of "fires" and "flames" of love, or even to depict the would-be-suitor as a slave of the beloved woman. But when Pyrrhus calls himself, before Andromaque, "conquered, burdened with chains, consumed by regrets / Burnt by more fires than [he] ever had lit" he equates these banal metaphors with a referent that has nothing metaphoric about it: the fire that destroyed Troy. In so taking these gallant terms literally, he authorizes himself to treat his suffering and that of his victim (Andromaque) equally. His speech thus loses its gallantness because the metaphorical aspect dissolves."[44]

By the word *galant*, Viala is referring to a complex French sociocultural concept in the seventeenth century, a type of comportment that mixed courtly courtesy with a discreet, genteel notion of male (heterosexual) seduction. Pyrrhus's usage of "feu" and "flamme," at first glance, is a simple translation of traumatic flames to unsatiated fires of desire. The excess of fires "que je n'en allumai" (than [he] had ever lit [1.4.320]) becomes the gnawing burning of guilt: "Je souffre tous les maux que j'ai faits devant Troie" (I suffer all the sorrows I inflicted on Troy [1.4.318]). His unabsolved remorse that doggedly plagues him is transformed, through a metonymic fire-figured chain, into burning, persistent, unrequited lust and love: "Tant d'ardeurs inquiètes / fus-je jamais si cruel que vous l'êtes?" ("So many anguished desires / Was I ever as cruel as you are?" [1.4.321–22]). Pyrrhus's self-pitying and manipulative language wrenches "flammes" from its signaling of the traumatic past to the future-oriented possibility of love. He promises Andromaque that ash need not be limited to destruction; it can also stand for a new beginning: "Votre Illion encore peut sortir de sa cendre" (Your Troy still can rise from its ash [1.4.330]). The problem is that a lightly *galant* use of "flamme" is impossible, given the realities of the Trojan War. At the same time, a wholly literal use of "flamme" (signaling the past destruction) is impeded by Pyrrhus's desire for a future-oriented love, his hope to move on neatly from these losses.

Building on Viala and Horowitz, I propose that Pyrrhus performs an "equalizing" move between his suffering and that of the Trojans. In addition, recurring throughout the play is a restaged fallenness: the very distance between metaphoric-poetic language (e.g., "flammes" of passion) and the literal referent (fire and ash) is itself to be interrogated. A rhetorical "war" is staged by toying with this divide between the poetic, euphemistic, and literal. Andromaque uses "flamme," like her use of ash, specifically to counteract Pyrrhus through rhetoric. This is a significant gesture, insofar as she reveals her mastery of the "guerre" of rhetoric and, more particularly, the very temporal conditionings that his deployment of fire invokes.

In the famous incantatory summoning of a key traumatic moment, Andromaque's vision of the horrors of war is illuminated by the very fires that annihilate her city and her loved ones. Thus, paradoxically, the possibility of the memory (and the very material of ash) is indebted to the agent of destruction. During this nighttime pillage of her city, she can only see by and through the light of the burning flames:

> Songe, songe, Céphise, à cette nuit cruelle
> Qui fut pour tout un peuple une nuit éternelle.
> Figure-toi Pyrrhus, les yeux étincelants,
> Entrant à la lueur de nos palais brûlants,
> Sur tous mes frères morts se faisant un passage,
> Et de sang tout couvert échauffant le carnage.

Songe aux cris des vainqueurs, songe aux cris des mourants,
Dans la flamme étouffés, sous le fer expirants.
Peins-toi dans ces horreurs Andromaque éperdue:
Voilà comme Pyrrhus vint s'offrir à ma vue. (3.8.997–1006)

(Think, think, Céphise, of that cruel night
That was for a whole nation, an eternal night
Imagine Pyrrhus, with glittering eyes,
Entering by the gleam of our burning palaces,
Carving his passage over my dead kin,
All covered in blood, inciting the heat of carnage.
Think of the victor's cries, think of the cries of the dying,
Choked by the flames or perishing under the sword
See Andromache distraught amongst the horror:
This is how Pyrrhus first appeared in my sight.)

This fire-illuminated vision stands as a counterpoint to Oreste's earlier invocation of Hector's "flamme à la main." In both instances, fire becomes both the source of obliteration *and* the condition of possibility to remember; memories are only illuminated, seen, and reenvisioned by the light of fiery destruction. But here is an ethical dimension to refuse the gallant metaphoricity of "flamme." Whereas Oreste's memory of fire catalyzes his action to redo the fires of the past, for Andromaque, the flames of war, which were the bursting apotheosis of her trauma narrative, transform through her rhetoric into flames of testimonial vision. Thus, fire, like the dual properties of ash, also takes on the position of *ruin* (the actual agent of ruin) and *remainder* (the illuminating light that allows for the visibility of memory).

In fact, in Andromaque's telling of trauma, fire takes on something of an animacy or agency of its own, exceeding the possibilities of human operators' redoing or remaking. Fire gradually grows and dominates the whole narrative: the destructive spark in Pyrrhus's "glittering eyes" bursts into a figured flame that consumes "our burning palaces"; the intensity of the fiery heat escalates, echoed in the increasing violence ("inciting the heat of carnage") until ultimately all perish in incendiary annihilation: "Choked by the flames or perishing under the sword." This fire-laced story culminates in the most traumatic image for Andromaque: "Voilà comme Pyrrhus vint s'offrir à ma vue" (This is how Pyrrhus first appeared in my sight [3.8.1006]).

With Andromaque's insistence on the immediate haste of traumatic vision, her invocation of fire as animate, literal, and testimonial stands as a rhetorical challenge to Oreste's redoing or Pyrrhus's gallant metaphoricity. The more that she makes present the fire—both in the painted presence of ekphrastic invocation and in the presentness of the relived trauma—she strategically insists on a certain fallenness of language. "Flamme" can no longer be purely gallant, and, similarly, *ashes* are actively animate, not a mere stand-in for ethopoeiac address.

If Andromaque's language refuses Pyrrhus's distanced elevation of gallant metaphoricity, how might we then understand the poetics of her own rhetoric? In the *Institutes of Oratory* (CE 95) Quintilian defines catachresis as a type of trope "which we properly call *abusio*, and which adapts, to whatever has no proper term, the term which is nearest . . . catachresis is used where a term is wanting; metaphor, for where another term is in use" (8.6.34).[45] Unlike metaphor, catachresis does not replace; it is the poetic figure that wrenches a word from its traditional deployment out of necessity. The most common example of catachresis, the "legs of a table," highlights catachresis's closeness to metaphor. "Legs" seem initially to be metaphoric or figural: the table shape might loosely resemble a horse or a dog on all fours, and "legs" offer support and standing just as physical legs do. But if the legs of a table were not called as such, how might we term them? Posts? Stands? "Legs of a table," while initially conveying a "dead" metaphoricity or banality, is a figural term that fills a need: what to call the four things on which a table stands.

This tension between choice and need, or artistic freedom and linguistic necessity, threads through the discussion of metaphor and catachresis in most ancient and early modern manuals of rhetoric, as Parker has analyzed. By analyzing rhetoricians from Cicero through Pierre Fontanier, Parker traces the anxiety over the porosity between metaphoricity and catachrestic usage. One recurring classification is the "naturalness" of metaphor, as opposed to the "forced" usage of catachresis.[46] In Andromaque's case, the deployment of euphemism or a gallant metaphor of fire is unacceptable to Andromaque; a similar refusal of metaphoricity is revealed in her use of ash. There is no playful poesis or choice, since "ash" is the nearest, properly improper term that she uses to highlight the past trauma, the enduring, animate matter and her husband's remains. Catachresis is wrought from trauma.

Considering "cendres" as catachresis shines a light on the workings of metaphor. Instead of functioning as a smoothly natural, gallant distancing or euphemism (as in "flamme"), the strangeness of animate ash points to its own figural force. In its "abusive" misplaced figuration, catachresis simultaneously marks and unmarks—it reaches toward figuration, but in its improperness also traces figure's "failure" or inadequacy. Gerald Poselt explains:

> Catachresis is marked by a lack or a lexical lacuna, but at the same time it opens up new possibilities of usage, resignifications and speaking otherwise . . . whereas metaphor is fundamentally related to substitution, in the case of catachresis no substitution takes place. Thus, catachresis is neither truly proper nor literal, nor metaphorical or figurative; and yet it has something of both. It is neither a proper denomination, because it signifies by a metaphorical transference of a word, nor is it a figurative expression, because it merely signifies by the extension of a given term.[47]

Ash, as catachresis, makes a proper thing of something that ought to have been only figurative, (ash as the material eliciting love questions and demands), as well as highlights the figured quality of something that would normally be proper (Hector's literal ashes also stand metonymically for the ruin of Troy, and the "reste" that remains). Therefore, to extend d'Aubignac's famous maxim regarding the theater: "là, parler, c'est agir"[48] (there [onstage], to speak is to act), catachrestic speech, in Andromaque's usage, enacts a specific, strategic kind of action in such a rhetorical war.

Contingent Time and Queer Temporality

Andromaque's traumatic context illuminates the ethics of loving animate ash, as a testament to the ruin and an extension of the remainder. But perhaps the most poignant figure of trauma and its impossible temporality is offered not by Andromaque but Oreste in the first scene of the play. Upon his return to Epirus, he tells his friend Pylade: "Tu vis mon désespoir, et tu m'as vu depuis / Trainer de mers en mers ma chaîne et mes ennuis" (You witnessed my despair, and you've seen me since / Dragging this chain and my woes from sea to sea [1.1.43–44]). Here the "désespoir" (despair) refers most immediately to his hopelessness in seeing his beloved Hermione betrothed to Pyrrhus, but we may also imagine the word referring in a larger sense to trauma of loss and war. "Depuis" and "ennuis" become a matched rhyming couplet, paired not only phonically but also thematically, as they mutually engender one another; "depuis" stands for both the temporal marker of "after" as well as the notion of a possible aftermath itself. The tragedy of the situation for Oreste (as well as for the other characters) is that there *is* a "living on," or a time "depuis" (after) enduring after the rupturing break, much like the general structure of trauma itself, which signals a "rupture" in normal, fluidly progressing time. Oreste's metaphoric "chaîne" is particularly apt: it is a chain anchoring him nowhere yet weighing on him constantly during his voyages "de mers en mers," the heaviness imprisoning him only to the brokenness of the past.

Even in his name, the word "reste" (remains) lingers as an echo, a remainder. In many respects, all the characters in the play are somehow "out of time": they are all latecomers and view themselves as secondary enactors of the cataclysmic event that has already happened. As Oreste tries to convince Hermione to leave with him, he urges: "Mettons encore un coup toute la Grèce en flamme; / Prenons, en signalant mon bras et votre nom, / Vous, la place d'Hélène, et moi, d'Agamemnon" (Let's set all of Greece aflame again/ Let us retake, boasting of my strength and your name / You, Helen's place and I, Agamemnon's [4.3.1158–60]). For Oreste, no anxiety of influence exists here. He does not want to outdo his ancestors but hopes to reenact the scenes from his parents' past to the letter. Oreste's desire to take the place of his forefathers signals stagnation; these survivors eschew making their own histories in favor of drawing on preestablished pasts as templates for their future. Roland Racevskis, among others, has suggested that *Andromaque* stages a crisis of a generational transition in the throes of change regarding a past that has both traumatized the characters (in the war) and overdetermined them (though their parents' famed legacies).[49] What Racevskis calls a "parasitically referential relationship"[50] is one that not only folds temporal progress back on itself but also, in my view, ignites the possibility for a queer, contingent temporality, which I will elaborate shortly.

The second generation's desire for duplication is echoed in epithetical names: Pyrrhus is called "fils d'Achille" (son of Achilles), Hermione is the "fille d'Hélène" (daughter of Helen), and Oreste is the "fils d'Agamemnon" (son of Agamemnon); and Astyanax is called "fils d'Hector" (son of Hector) no fewer than six times in the play. This generational naming has the effect of representing the child as both the product of and the justification for the progress-oriented linearity of "straight time." In contrast, Andromaque is the only character not attached to the preceding generation via epithet. Instead, her appellation is the "veuve d'Hector" (the widow of Hector), a type of naming that appears as a type of a synchronic swerving against the force of the diachronic generational trajectories.

This synchronic swerving can be thought of as contingent, a notion that I borrow from Carolyn Dinshaw. Andromaque's out-of-timeliness is analogous to one that Dinshaw analyzes in a study of the medieval pilgrim Margery Kempe. During her travels, Kempe weeps and sobs hysterically, irking the other parishioners around her. A priest approaches her and tries to calm her down, reasoning that "Jesus is long since dead." Kempe replies: "Sir, hys deth is as fresch to me as he had deyd this same day."[51] Dinshaw takes up this temporal irrationality, writing: "Her response is ethical and moral, focused in the now and distanced neither by institutional structures nor by the chronological time they seek to control. Her time, her present, her now, is defined by its being invaded or infused by the other."[52] The incomprehensibility surrounding Kempe's excessive behavior stems from the fact that *her* temporality—a particular temporality of fresh and presently felt mourning—does not match that of her peers or her priest. Dinshaw suggests that we can think of Kempe's temporality as queer insofar as she is propelled by and committed to forms of love that do not make sense according to other, legible forms of devotion and intimacy. The intensity of this attachment stems from the "freshness" of the distant past erupting into her lived present, experienced as raw emotion. Similarly, we can think of Andromaque's obstinate attachment to ashes as generating a different velocity, an incomprehensible slowness to those around her (e.g., Céphise and Pyrrhus). Dinshaw's analysis thus illuminates the ethical dimension of Andromaque's rejection of the norms of progress: it permits an expression of a contingent, undecidable temporality that "touches on" the temporality of the narration, but still progresses at its own speed, undetermined by the exigencies of politics or of maternity.

The concepts of "coincidental time" and contingent temporal speeds illuminate Andromaque's velocity. A friction is created when Andromaque's "queer time" (animated, delayed, trauma-inflected) contingently touches and falls on "straight time." In the contingent point in mathematics, when a line touches a circle, the point of contact, however slight, is a point shared by *both* the line and curve. This investment in ash can be thought of as contingent since it participates in established paradigms of veneration and memory, as well as veers off toward queer object sexuality. In both the queer animated attachments and the traditional mourning, Andromaque appears to be expressing an orientation to ash (the shared, contingent point). But instead of following the point along its trajectory of the straight line, the affects and dynamics of ash generate the "curve" of a contingent, other time.

Andromaque draws on an established, virtuous screen of widowhood (as Biet pointed out)[53] specifically to counter the progress-oriented temporality of reproductive futurity, a type of positivist possibility that was famously presented by Leo Bersani's vision of Astyanax:

> *Andromaque* gives us Racine's purest image of the liberating betrayal of the past; but the play brings us only to the threshold of a new order for which no content is imagined . . . Pyrrhus and Andromaque finally identify themselves unreservedly with Astyanax's safety . . . he is the child, the future, the blank page of the play, the invisible character who finally replaces the oppressive Hector as the absent dominating force of the other characters' lives. Astyanax is nothing less and nothing more than the value of *pure possibility*.[54]

Bersani upholds Astyanax as a figure for the future and of radical newness, but his use of "unreservedly" merits closer examination. If Astyanax is upheld as a "blank slate" betokening a promising future replete with "pure possibility," then Andromaque's resigned sigh, "Alas! He'll die, then," may not necessarily indicate maternal indifference but a critical stance against the idealistic vision of progress-ridden narratives that Bersani offers. In other words, Bersani wishes to capitalize on the optimism of Astyanax's survival, without interrogating the microdisciplinary chronobiopolitical forces that condition us to desire survival itself. Biopolitics trains us to invest in life and to veer away from life's diminishing. The shining example of Bersani's Astyanax eclipses other kinds of subtle, ash-driven desires or trauma-inflected temporalities that do not feed into this temporality of living on.

A belief in the future as something "liberating," such as Bersani's optimistic figuration of Astyanax, can ultimately be toxic, as Lee Edelman argues in his polemic *No Future*. Edelman suggests that "reproductive futurity" can be understood as an unquestioned privileging of the future as a marker of social good, and the site of the fantasy of "meaning's eventual realization."[55] Elsewhere Edelman has critiqued a sense of "normative" temporality as defined, condensed in, and predicated on the trope of the child. This valorization of the "after" of futurity is sustained through two ways: first, by "privileging reproduction as the after-event of sex [that] imbues straight sex with its meaning as the agent of historical continuity," and secondly a privileging of "forms of historical knowing whose authority depends on the fetishistic prestige of origin, genealogy, telos."[56] Therefore, the unquestioned good that is reproduction becomes not only the end result, but also the retroactively applied justification of sexuality, effectively tying heteronormative sex into a tautologically closed loop. The good of reproduction and its forward movement shapes the ways that we think of temporal progress, continuity, and history.

This temporality that undergirds "the child, the future, the blank page" is precisely what Edelman wishes to critique. One must only think of how "protecting our children" serves as justification for a range of social, sexual, and political discourses. The child becomes both the justifying cause *and* the produced effect of all kinds of capillary behavior monitoring and conditioning, established to maintain a certain kind of "good life"—from concerns about the environment for future generations to homophobic opposition to gay adoption. Just as Edelman refuses reproductive futurity, Andromaque refuses to buy into the unquestioned good of the "after," rejecting such a fantasy of future investment.

Both Bersani's and Edelman's analyses of temporality are overdetermined by endpoints of futurity, whether upheld or repudiated. In the play, even though Racine extends Astyanax's life, the future for Astyanax is one that is generated despite Andromaque's hesitations, whether in her actions, or words. Bersani's vision of the future is overly revolutionary and optimistic; Edelman's model is limited to a type of negative refusal to engage with the heteronormative social world and with the futurity of the "good life." In this context, a queer stand against the incessantly positive temporal norms can only emerge via one of two options: clinging to the past, like Biet's "morbid passion,"[57] a force of love that obscures any kind of maternal investment in the future of Andromaque's child; or else outright rejecting any type of action that produces this "blank page," or other teleologies of progress.

Andromaque's contingent temporality offers a third way of considering both past and future. Ash is deployed by Pyrrhus to mark the possibility of renewal, to represent the forward thrust of rising out of ash (no less metaphorized in the figure of his friend Phoenix).[58] In contrast, Andromaque's temporality is neither maternal indifference nor a complete investment in a future securing the safety of Astyanax. Rather, what appears as "delay" is the space carved out for a presently felt, active attachment to these animate ashes that testifies to loss while braking against progress. Here, the paradoxical and dual temporality of ash is key to intervene in this sexual-temporal normativity. The ash's "past" temporality acknowledges the trauma and violence of the event, while the enduring nature of ash's "remainder" allows Andromaque a different experience of extension through time that is not intertwined with reproductive futurity.

This contingent temporal clashing is grammatically presented in the first scene of act 4. Céphise, Andromaque's confidante, is relieved and elated that, apparently, Andromaque has acquiesced to marry Pyrrhus, thus securing the structure of heteronormative marriage ties, royal lineage, and the future of the child. Céphise says:

> Ah! Je n'en doute point; c'est votre époux, Madame,
> C'est Hector qui produit ce miracle en votre âme.
> Il veut que Troie encor se puisse relever
> Avec cet heureux fils qu'il vous fait conserver.
> Pyrrhus vous l'a promis. Vous venez de l'entendre
> Madame: il n'attendait qu'un mot pour vous le rendre. (1.4.1049–54)
>
> (I have no doubt, it's your husband, Madame,
> It is Hector who produces this miracle in your soul
> He wants that Troy be able to rise up again
> With this lucky son that he has helped you save
> Pyrrhus promised it to you. You have just heard it
> Madame: he only is waiting for your word to give [Astyanax] back to you.)

Céphise's speech opens with a flurry of cataphoric deixis: "c'est votre époux," "c'est Hector," "ce miracle," the deictic "ce" announcing the husband, the husband's role, and the miracle yet to be explained. Cataphoric deixis, defined as a "forward pointing," indicates a type of presentness and immediacy that is still to be announced within the context of the phrase. For example, when Céphise says "ce miracle" it creates a tension between the extremely present-oriented indicative of "ce" ("this") and the anticipatory promise of fulfilling this knowledge gap ("what is 'this' miracle?"). Céphise uses the grammatical mood elicited by such forward pointing to hold up the future-oriented values of production ("produit"), saving the child ("cet heureux fils . . . conserver"), and moving on ("relever"). She even enthuses later: "Quel plaisir d'élever un enfant qu'on voit craître, / Non plus comme un esclave élevé pour son maître, / Mais pour voir avec lui renaître tant de rois !" (What joy to raise a child who will be brought up/ Not as a slave but as a master/ But to see reborn through him so many kings! [4.1.1069–71]).

Against this optimistic futurity performed affectively and grammatically by Cephise's discourse, Andromaque's "innocent strategy" is her plan to marry Pyrrhus to secure Astyanax's future and then to immediately kill herself.

> Quoi donc? as-tu pensé qu'Andromaque infidèle
> Pût trahir un époux qui croit revivre en elle;
> Et que, de tant de morts réveillant la douleur
> Le soin de mon repos me fît troubler le leur?
> Est-ce là cette ardeur tant promise à sa cendre? (4.1.1077–81)
>
> (What now? Did you think that an unfaithful Andromaque
> Could betray a trusting spouse who thought to live on in her
> And stirring up the pain of countless dead,
> I'd take care of my peace by troubling theirs?
> Is this the ardor so promised to his ash?)

This strategy is illegible and incomprehensible within the context of Céphise's future-oriented vision. Andromaque's decision is intensely informed by her attachment to this other mode of temporality. Just as "cendre" appeared at a key moment to thwart Pyrrhus's forward-moving plan, the invocation of "cendre" here points away from an optimistic futurity. This contingent temporality enabled by animate ashes—ashes that could demand an upheld promise—allows her to testify to loss and to mark queer modes of attachment.

Perhaps the most telling component of Andromaque's contingent time is that she simply disappears from the stage after she announces her "innocent strategy." Ultimately, we find out that the people of Epirus have murdered Pyrrhus in a maddened fury and have crowned Andromaque queen. This narrative, however, is only recounted through others' words. This disappearance must be read as such. Insofar as she continues to haunt the time of the play but ceases to be a physical, speaking being on stage, she signals a contingent otherness—a swerve away from the legible or representable domain of action and narrative.[59]

Addressing the pluralities of temporality may necessitate a torsion within time's trajectory, a twist that arrests the insistent forward flow to bring to the fore the value of inanimate, strange attachments. Shifting away from previous critics' focus on Andromaque's contentious actions as a mother and widow allows another vibrant and animate kind of attachment to come to the fore. As she clings to ashes, not only as a reminder of Hector's death, but also as a queerly animate remainder, Andromaque prolongs a catachrestically inflicted testimony to the ruin of her city, family, and past. Andromaque faces a multitude of demands: Troy's survivors ought to take a stand against the Greeks; a mother ought to save her son; and a widow ought to cherish her dead husband. These very demands are founded on and produce what might be considered a normative temporality. In the play's "war" that has become more rhetorical than literal, Andromaque takes a stand against these types of imperatives to "act"—injunctions wrought from norms of sexuality, survivorhood, and more. Ashes become a tool for declining participation in the political chess game or amorous blackmail she faces, for ashes swerve contingently askew. The paradoxical nature of "cendres" as both ruin and remainder, animate and inert, makes them the ideal figure of a different type of love and a different type of contingent temporality.

The time and temporality of life is altered by trauma. Indeed, we have seen how trauma and grief shift language and even wider conceptions of animacy or appropriate object attachments. I suggested earlier that chronobiopower seizes on the "middles" of time, mapping and choreographing presumed norms of living, or tempos oriented toward certain kinds of futurities. But, as *Andromaque* demonstrates, this hold on lived time is subtly but strategically undone when the scale of "bios" is expanded to encompass inanimate matter such as "ash." Loving ash, as a testimony to the past, as a rhetorical riposte against gallant rhetoric, creates and requires a moment in time—a swerving of the "middles" toward other ends—that signals so much more than mere delay.

3

Polyeucte and the Speeds of Sects (Sex)

Polyeucte and Fanaticism

Fanatic. Terrorist. Martyr. These words are often splashed across the news headlines, pinning the violence of crimes to the overabundance of religious zeal. Such stories blur together to create an archetype: an impressionable young man, seduced to convert to another religion by an older friend whom he admires (and loves) deeply, becomes radicalized by his passion for his newfound religion, and seeks to change the corruption and the idolatry that he perceives around him. The two men turn to violence, destroying sites of idolatrous worship and announcing their faith publicly. The convert seeks to follow his friend to the end and die a martyr's death.

Rather than a modern-day headline, the tale depicted in Corneille's *Polyeucte* (1643) is a martyrological tragedy and presents an unsettling resonance to this contemporary moment—a resonance that is apparent in Brigitte Jaques-Wajeman's 2017 staging of Corneille's play, which casts Polyeucte as a religious terrorist.[1] In Corneille's original tragedy, set in colonially occupied Armenia in AD 250, the eponymous Polyeucte is drawn to the Christian faith by his dear friend and fellow Armenian, Néarque. The two men, spurred by their religious passion, rush into the Roman temple and smash the idols of the pagan gods, and then are promptly condemned to death for such a blasphemous transgression against the state.

Some critics have insisted that the conflation between contemporary trends of religiously motivated violence and the role of religion in the play is not a productive one. In the French Wars of Religion (1562–98) that predated the play and in contemporary shootings and bombings in synagogues, temples, and churches around the world, the violence is inflicted on *other* bodies, on the elimination of the worshippers of a competing faith. In contrast, as Barbara Selmeci Castioni notes, Polyeucte only dreams of inflicting violence on himself and not on others per se (only the idols of the pagan temple are demolished).[2] Critics of Jaques-Wajeman's staging insist on this difference: Polyeucte, as a martyr, cannot be read in a genealogy of fanaticism.

But I agree with Ross Lerner that early modern considerations of fanaticism are not so far from our contemporary moment, especially if we consider not the object of fanatical violence but rather the ways that fanaticism itself is used to rhetorically winnow out worthy lives from expendable ones as wells as the temporalities of fanaticism. Lerner contends that

> Reformation condemnations of fanaticism, usually meant to justify state violence, live on in systemic strategies of racialized neocolonial brutality that rely on terms such as "terrorist" and "fundamentalist" to vindicate war, indefinite detention, torture, murder, dispossession, and economic immiseration—in short, to make many lives, especially in the so-called Greater Middle East, "ungrievable."[3]

Polyeucte, too, asks whose lives are expendable and whose lives are grievable, a question that resonates with the governance of the time of life.

As a Roman colony, Armenia is managed by Félix, a Roman governor appointed by Emperor Décie. In the play, the emperor himself never makes an appearance. Félix is unsure of his decisions and unsteady in his grasp on power but clings adamantly to the goal of protecting valuable life, sometimes at the cost of executing perceived contaminants (fanatics). To secure his foothold in the region, Félix has married his daughter Pauline to an Armenian noble, Polyeucte, despite Pauline's heart truly belonging to Sévère, a war hero and favorite of the emperor. Even Félix says, "Polyeucte est ici l'appui de ma famille" (Polyeucte is the support of my family here [3.5.1053]),[4] heightening how Polyeucte's Armenian heritage allows Félix a certain kind of authority as the outsider, the Roman governor of Armenia. This is why Polyeucte and Néarque's conversion is "n'est nullement un délit privé"[5] (hardly a private crime), as Serge Doubrovsky insists, but also a political one. Their affinity stands as an affront to both the pagan Roman religion and the colonial purchase on the territory. The Armenian Néarque is executed quickly, but Polyeucte's life—as an anchor to the colony and as a relative of the governor—hangs in the balance. The plot centers on the attempts made by Pauline and Félix to dissuade Polyeucte from following through with his fanatical demise. Polyeucte, in return, parries this management of his own life, in large part because of his deep attachment to the executed Néarque. A particularly queer version of Christian passion emerges: a type of ardor that is difficult to distinguish from their mutual love for one another, a love that provokes the two men to stray from and to disrupt the normative colonial, religious, and political management of heteroreproductive life.

This chapter explores *Polyeucte*'s destabilization of temporality on two levels: the intimate scale of relationships and identity—the nature of converting one's religion and one's identification through *seduction*—as well as the larger political and biopolitical scale. The fanatic presents a governmental crisis in managing the time of life and thus serves as an apt illustration of the quandary: if biopower hinges on the augmentation of the value of life, what happens considering the martyr's (or the fanatic's) drive toward death, a loosening of the life-oriented grasp of the biopolitical?

Analyzing *Polyeucte* through the angle of fanaticism allows us a deeper investigation into the ways that the play overturns temporal norms. By this, I rely on Lerner's definition of early modern fanatics (following Edmund Spenser) as "'organs' of divine might who undergo a self-loss so total that they can become purely passive instruments of God."[6] The very nature of the fanatic as organ forebodes the possible emptying of identity. Indeed, conversion and fanaticism imply that one *can* shift identities and affinities. Temporally sedimented identifying markers, such as genealogy, family, or nobility, are eschewed in favor of the contingencies of the affective, seductive, and amorous—emotions that might sway conversion. *Polyeucte* can thus be considered in dialogue with contemporary (and past) anxieties about conversion—or what today's media might call "radicalization." After discovering the sad truth that his beloved Pauline has married Polyeucte, Sévère reflects on Polyeucte's previous status: "Polyeucte a du nom, et sort du sang des rois" (Polyeucte has a renowned name, and descends from the blood of kings [2.1.420]). The suddenness of Polyeucte's religious conversion shatters the primacy of genealogy, blood, and tradition that others venerate—identities that hinge on a temporal sedimentation. Doubrovsky has argued, "As the head of the Armenian nobility, descended from the blood of kings and as a Christian adherent, Polyeucte reverses order and hierarchy, destroying the empire proclaimed by Tully and founded by Augustus. The revolt against the pagan gods is also a rebellion against the legitimate source of power and the decrees of Décie."[7] These temporally inflected structures of identification—nobility and kingly blood—no longer have the same potency. Polyeucte repeatedly declares the unsuturing of the sedimented legal and sexual ties that had bound him to his previous subject position, and gestures toward a type of subject position founded on contingencies: affinity, attunement, and desire. He becomes an emptied-out organ. Polyeucte's previous temporally charged status and identity is constantly lauded and reinterpreted by others not only to remind him of what he risks leaving behind with his death but also to reinforce the normativity of the very structures within which identity can even be articulated and legitimized. To convert, here, is not necessarily a "religious" gesture but rather inscribes a specific type of political upheaval, or a strong, radical break with one kind of temporal timeline (of genealogy and blood), thus inaugurating a new network of liaisons and a new queer time.

A second queerness implicitly opposes the natural temporality of heteroreproduction (e.g., marriage and children) with the unnatural reproduction as instigated by Sévère. In the play, Stratonice, Pauline's friend, suggests that Néarque ripped Polyeucte from Pauline's arms. She describes Pauline's husband's conversion explicitly as a seduction:

> Néarque l'a séduit:
> De leur vieille amitié c'est là l'indigne fruit.
> Ce perfide tantôt, en dépit de lui-même,
> L'arrachant de vos bras, le traînait au baptême.
> Voilà ce grand secret et si mystérieux
> Que n'en pouvait tirer votre amour curieux. (3.2.807–12)

> (Néarque seduced him
> This is the disgraceful fruit of their old friendship
> This traitor, earlier, despite himself
> Tore Polyeucte from your arms, drove him to baptism.
> Behold this secret, so mysterious
> That even your inquiring love could not draw from him.)

In her discourse, the Roman Stratonice's hatred of Christians is apparent. She directly counteropposes the married, heterosexual love that Pauline can provide ("de vos bras") with another type of generative love ("amitié") that Néarque's seduction is founded on. Painted as such, the conversion does not merely enact a change in religious comportment or social status, but explicitly swaps out marital love for the "disgraceful fruit" begotten of same-sex friendships. We might also recall that Polyeucte and Pauline are newly married and do not have children. Therefore, Stratonice's discourse highlights the queer time of seduction, especially transgressive seduction: an attachment between men that risks yielding shameful fruit. Ibbett reminds us that in this play "maternity is constantly present as potential," alluding to Corneille's dedication to Anne of Austria as "'having given birth to miracles,' a discreet nod not just to her patronage or religious devotion but also to the great relief brought about by the birth of the long-hoped-for future Louis XIV, the year before the play appeared."[8] Polyeucte's conversion is transgressive not because of the "birth" of a new Christian thanks to his tender same-sex friendship with Néarque, but because of its queer reappropriation of maternity-as-potential. Since maternity-as-potential can be thought of as a temporal not yet, this engendering force is unsutured from heteroreproductive or genealogical relations: Polyeucte's conversion as "indigne fruit" shows that maternity as potential might also derive from "une vielle amitié" (an old friendship).

In Stratonice's eyes, Polyeucte does *not* embody the fanatic, or the "epistemological mystery of individuals who annihilate themselves to becomes instruments of divine violence."[9] That is, the anti-Christian sentiment cannot accept that Polyeucte has emptied himself to be a vessel of God; rather, they presume that he is a vessel of Néarque's manipulation, that he is emptied only to receive seductive love from his friend, a connection that posits a queer origin to Polyeucte's conversion. This bodily emptying and engendering, which might even be thought of as a type of queer progeniture, is apparent in the source text. For John Boswell, noted historian of gay sexuality, the historical Polyeuct-Nearchos couple (from one of the source texts that inspired Corneille) stands as one of three key early Christian queer martyr pairs. Drawing on Benjamin Aubé's account in *Polyeucte dans l'histoire*, Boswell reminds us that "St. Polyeuct and Nearchos . . . were described in their fourth-century biography as 'brothers, not by birth, but by affection.'"[10] They enjoyed "the closest possible friendship, being both comrades and fellow-soldiers."[11] More than merely fraternal affection, however, Boswell, citing Aubé, recounts an episode in which the historical Nearchos and Polyeuct learn that all Christians are to be executed for their faith. Polyeuct attempts to comfort his friend in the face of imminent death, but Nearchos has other worries:

> "But this, dearest (φίλτατε) is precisely what weighs on my soul. There is something worse than the death of humans: the separation that I fear might take place . . . for I had feared that I would lose you from my love (φιλίας) and that we would lose the unity of our soul (συνειδήσεως)" . . . Polyeuct then roused within himself

> the organ of his soul, and reaching for Nearchos with his bodily eyes, took his hand and asked, "Is this then what you feared, Nearchos, and was this your suspicion about us from the beginning? Did you realize this about the bodily part of our love?"[12]

The phrase "organ of the soul," as Lerner reminds us, was a frequent term that Renaissance English readers would have recognized as linked to fanaticism. Theologians such as John Calvin, Lerner suggests, "referred to prophets as 'organs' (organa, organes) of the Spirit, and related terms (such as versions of the words 'instrument' and 'vessel') can be found throughout his work."[13] Seventeenth-century French contemporaries would have understood "organe" to also evoke one person being used by another entity as a conduit. "Des personnes dont le Prince se sert pour declarer ses volontez, De ceux par l'entremise & par le moyen desquels on fait quelque chose," (Those persons whom the Prince uses to declare His will, those by whose intermediary and by means of which one does something) as indicated in the 1694 *Dictionnaire de l'Académie française*.[14] The fanatical organ becomes, in Stratonice's paranoia, akin to a womb or a matrix, a site of male-male progeniture of "disgraceful fruit."

Polyeucte in Corneille's version, however, is depicted as a type of fanatic who is both an organ and embodied—paradoxically emptied out *and* made vibrantly fleshly at the same time. According to Aubé and Boswell, the strength of this "bodily" love and the fear of being separated from one another propels Polyeucte to convert; thanks to this same forceful attachment they also pursue the adamant destruction of the temple, as we shall see. In the source text, a fleshliness is present, a repetition of the word "bodies," "eyes," and "roused," which intimates a richly corporeal bond rather than a purely metaphysical conversion. With the specter of such corporeality at its origin, Néarque and Polyeucte's love is not merely "an old friendship" but a deeply felt, physical, and sensuous attachment to one another.

Fleshliness, then, introduces a doubly transgressive stuckness: it is that which needed to be superseded or transcended to obtain a martyred death, but it is also that which founds and fuels queer attachment between Polyeucte and Néarque, a source that generates affection and pleasure. Flesh catalyzes not only Polyeucte's desire for conversion but also the desire to not be separated from his beloved friend. In this regard, flesh is the troubling bit that remains, as Eric Santner puts it.[15] Polyeucte, facing his pending execution, while eager for his execution and to obtain his heavenly rewards, remarks on the difficulty of leaving behind attachments to the flesh: "Honteux attachements de la *chair* et du monde, / Que ne me quittez-vous, quand je vous ai quittés?" (Shameful attachments of the *flesh* and of the world, / Why do you not leave me, when I have left you? [4.2.1107–8], emphasis mine). Despite his desire to leave the temporal domain, it is not so easy to free oneself from the anatomopolitical injunction, because we are so trained to believe in the ultimate good of cultivating more life, attached to the promise of always extending the quality and temporality of life itself. In the source text, Polyeucte's flesh, we must recall, is also the site of desire and longing, the site of being "roused" with "bodily eyes": the remnant of his love for Néarque. Taking into account the temporality of the martyr and the temporality of queer same-sex friendship, the velocity at hand in this chapter is one of passionate attunement: temporal intensities and hastenings that are aligned perfectly with that of one's beloved. This queer velocity, however, veers directionally away from the normative trajectories of marriage, lineage, and empire.

The Temporality of the Flesh

Starobinski insisted on the political implications of Polyeucte's conversion and martyred death, and in this colonial-governmental terrain, two competing political temporalities are at stake. Sovereign decision making needs to happen almost instantaneously, since deciding on the exception, as Carl Schmitt has suggested, occurs with a nearly deictic immediacy. That is to say, the determining of the state of exception deciding that which is exceptional) happens in the "now" insofar as "the precise details of an emergency cannot be anticipated, nor can one spell out [in advance] what may take place in such a case."[16] The exception is autoreferentially deictic: he who can determine the state of exception is the sovereign, and the very moment of determining enacts or performs a sovereignty. This transformation, Schmitt says, is akin to the miracle in theology; the instantaneous and exceptional event that suspends the norms (of law or of the natural world) and thereby inaugurates faith in the system.[17] In contrast to the immediate deixis of sovereignty stands the longer-term biopolitical investment that seeks to conserve life. In Corneille's play there is a background anxiety over to augmenting, conditioning, and orienting life toward an imagined reproductive, future good.[18] The state is thus poised between haste and extension. As Foucault has demonstrated, under sovereignty, "power was essentially a right of seizure: of things, time, bodies, and ultimately of life itself; it culminated in the privilege to seize hold of life in order to suppress it,"[19] that is, power's ultimate privilege under sovereign rule was its destructive capacity. Instead of the deductive power of sovereignty, the diffusive force of biopower, incites and invests in the body—in bodily capaciousness, vitalities, and intensities. The flesh, and particularly the martyred flesh, highlights a temporal paradox that is compounded by the colonial setting. "If the martyr's desire to die reveals a desire to stage an ending and to decide on questions of duration that are usually imagined to be beyond human control," suggests Katherine Ibbett, "a similar but contradictory desire to manage life is also evident in the projects of reason of state."[20] Using examples from Jean-Baptiste du Tertre's *Histoire générale des Antilles* (1667), Ibbett shows how the colonial context of *Polyeucte* offers this paradoxical time: the French colonial project in New France and the Antilles was a charged site for both political expansion (possibly destroying conquered life) and terrain for cultivating and conserving sustained settler-colonial life. As *Polyeucte* is set in the Roman colony of Armenia, the time of life in the context of the play is similarly both shortened and lengthened in one colonial thrust, a thrust that has a winnowing function that decides between valuable and inviable lives.

In *Polyeucte* the sovereign's deductive capacity—swiftly executing the transgressive Néarque, for example—is enacted through an instantaneous temporality, one that can be thought of as "digital" (a decisive, binaristic temporality), whereas biopower's incitement occurs though "analogic," or gradual processes of extending and prolonging. The power of the aforementioned sovereign exception rests with the governor, Félix, who must decide if he will execute the rebellious Polyeucte, or if he will continue to invest in life. Sustaining the settler colony in Armenia and prolonging his precious foothold in the region hinges on fostering the chronobiopolitical management of the time of life. At heart, both sovereignty and biopolitics are invested in stabilizing life vis-à-vis a proper, imagined *end*; biopolitics purports to be a system that holds death in abeyance (extending life), while sovereignty wields the threat of an accelerated, untimely end to yield submission and obedience.

I take as a point of departure, following Santer, that biopolitics is a complex, messy, and intricate form of power and knowledge, and it does not neatly supersede sovereign forms of governing life; nor are its workings without points of weakness. Foucault contends that biopolitics is implemented through a microphysics of power, a "physics of a relational and multiple power, which has its maximum intensity not in the person of the king, but in the bodies that can be individualized by these relations."[21] Santner suggests that

> We could say that the precariousness, the fragility—the "nudity"—of biological life becomes potentiated, amplified, by way of exposure to the radical contingency of the forms of life that constitute the space of meaning within which human life unfolds, and that it is only through such "potentiation" that we take on the flesh of creaturely life. Creatureliness is thus a dimension not so much of biological as of ontological vulnerability, a vulnerability that permeates human being as that being whose essence it is to exist in forms of life that are, in turn, contingent, fragile, susceptible to breakdown.[22]

To cross apply Santner's analysis, the problem of the fleshliness in *Polyeucte* is grounded in the martyr's desire to be released from the biopolitical cultivation of more life *and* to remain unstymied by (even eagerly coveting) the sovereign threat of death. By actively inviting the sovereign threat of execution, the martyr then may possibly detour or hijack one of sovereignty's main sources of power, but the question still remains: to how to dispense with or to dissolve a remaining attachment to the flesh.[23] The martyr is both dead and alive—proleptically dead, because he or she undertakes actions that hasten the punishment of death, but also stubbornly alive—the martyr must be a priori alive and possess the valuable, vulnerable "creatureliness" of life to become a "nude" subject that can be seized and killed.

Similar to *Andromaque*'s oblique relationship to the cultivation and preservation of life as analyzed in chapter 2, *Polyeucte* does not merely hold up a death drive as a facile oppositional block to the "conservationist" tendencies of biopower or to the sovereign decision (as if he were to say, "I strip you of the power over my life or death by actively seeking my own sacred death"). Polyeucte represents both preservable, manageable life and the potential pathogen—the enemy within (the community). In tension with the sovereign and biopolitical temporal thrusts, the martyrological drive inaugurates, or founds, something else: a temporality of fleshliness that is both forestalled and hastened. In other words, the presence of the flesh and the fleshly desire in *Polyeucte* trouble the neat tale of a fanatical martyr who would race to his death. The queer velocity is elicited through his lingering, troubling attachment to the flesh and to Néarque ("Shameful attachments of the flesh and of the world" [4.2.1107]) that causes Polyeucte to parry the temporal forces that would seek to seize and manage his own life (whether in the biopolitical extension of life or the sovereign threat of death).

Polyeucte and Saint Paul's *Katechon*

Corneille himself admits that there is a troubling hastiness in *Polyeucte*. In his *Examen* he signals that the pacing of the events of the drama does not quite fit with the conventions of the unity of time: "Doubtlessly, if we hold the poem up to our standards, the sacrifice takes place too soon after the arrival of Sévère, and consequently this event will diverge from verisimilitude due to the necessity of obeying the rule."[24] Corneille conveniently places the blame on the "rules" and on "custom." Despite the deference Corneille feigns to pay to the rules, Jacques Scherer notes that, instead of working within the unity of time, Corneille simply skirts this constraint: "Corneille's solution was simply to evade the problem itself: it would suffice not to mention the length of time assigned to the action."[25] Corneille's ignoring the temporal frame, however, yields more problems than solutions. The crush of events violates the aesthetic tenets of staged action, but the haste of Polyeucte's desired martyrdom also risks defying Church doctrine. Speed becomes reinterpreted as a sign of fanatical excess. André Georges dissects whether such an excessive display of zeal would be acceptable: "Saint Cyprien, bishop of Carthage proclaims: 'Everyone,' he would say, 'should be ready to confess one's faith but no one should race to meet one's martyrdom.'"[26] Therefore, speed itself becomes an evaluative tool, to diagnose the aptness of Polyeucte's conversion and the appropriate tempo of racing toward desired death.

I read *Polyeucte* as being in dialogue with another conversion, that of Saint Paul, a former Jew and Roman persecutor of Christians. Paul's "miraculous" conversion to Christianity, subsequent apostleship, and writings to early Christian churches offers fertile ground for thinking of political theology and Pauline philosophy regarding the body of the church. I take a cue from Julia Reinhard Lupton who, reading Shakespeare, argues for an understanding of "Paul as a fellow traveler of inter-communal negotiation and epochal transformation."[27] Although Corneille does not directly cite Pauline epistles (beyond the nominal reference to the character of Pauline), like Shakespeare, Corneille was navigating questions related to the presence of religious tradition in the face of immense change. *Polyeucte*, Ibbett reminds us, "represents the late Empire and early Church to a seventeenth-century audience themselves imagining, in the first decades after Edict of Nantes, just how divine law and political expediency might be made to work together."[28] Corneille's play implicitly asked the unresolved question of how those of differing faiths—Protestant and Catholic—could coexist harmoniously in the name of civic unity.[29] Thus, while Corneille's use of Paul might be more speculative than evident, the context is similar and resonant between the playwright and the saint: both Paul and Corneille highlight the "epoch-making 'forcing' of change that is far from a simple step outside the inherited tradition in question."[30]

Pauline philosophies of time help underscore the queerness of Polyeucte's own velocities and thus necessitate a slight digression to unpack Paul's temporal positions. Paul, in his second letter to the Thessalonians, ominously signals that the end of time will only occur once the "falling away" has taken place and the "man of sin" is revealed.[31] Paul writes: "And now you know what is holding him back, so that he may be revealed at the proper time. For the secret power of lawlessness is already at work; but the one who now holds it back (*katechon*), will continue to do so till he is taken out of the way. And then the lawless one will be revealed, whom the Lord Jesus will overthrow with the breath of his mouth and destroy by the splendor of his coming" (2 Thess. 2:6–8). Marc De Wilde wryly points out that though Paul assures us "and now you know," many scholars, commentators, and even Church Fathers did not, in fact, *know*; all were relatively perplexed over what the "restraining" or "delaying" force, or katechon, could be.

Paul signals that the katechon is what delays a certain falling away or revelation. But is such a force positive or negative, and what constitutes the force itself? The katechon could signal a means of holding at bay, forestalling the coming of the Antichrist (the "man of sin") and the end of times. This would bolster what De Wilde calls the "state-affirming tradition"[32] in Pauline philosophy, a mode of interpreting the katechon as necessitating the state's orderly force of justice, holding the apocalypse at bay. In this light "the sovereign thereby acquired a theological legitimacy, justifying state violence as a necessary means to prevent worse, namely the 'falling away' and the revelation of the Antichrist."[33] Within the play, the state-affirming tradition of the katechon is most clearly presented by Félix who paints himself a representative of order to extend life, restraining the "chaos" of Polyeucte's conversion: "Je flattais ta manie, afin de t'arracher / Du honteux précipice où tu vas trébucher; / Je voulais gagner temps, pour ménager ta vie" (I indulged your madness in order to drag you / From the shameful abyss into which you will stumble / I wanted to buy time, to spare your life [5.2.1573–75]). Even with the words "arracher" or "précipice," Félix signals his "holding back" of an imminent collapse, reinforcing his position as a state-affirming restrainer of disorder.[34]

For Schmitt, the katechon was the key to understanding the necessary function of the sovereign, De Wilde suggests, noting: "The sovereign has to protect the existing order and suppress lawlessness at all costs, even if it requires violating the laws."[35] Such a move invokes a state of exception that elevates the ruling power's reaction to crisis into a "powerful myth that supports his claims to power: the myth of the divine right of kings."[36] Therefore, as long as the sovereign both curates the threat of pending end times and establishes himself as the katechonic force forestalling the end, he can hone power within "a type of interregnum situated between redemption and fall."[37] In other words, temporal experience is simultaneously the keystone of sovereign power *and* the product of such sovereign, katechonic forestalling. The state *makes time*—by holding in abeyance the end.

Problematically, because the katechon is a temporal paradox, the inverse reading is also true; the katechonic restraint could in fact signal a "state-critical" tradition if the restraining force were viewed as an "obstacle to eternity."[38] In other words, the opposite reading would hold that the orderliness of the state, which holds the apocalypse at bay, is actually the "sinful one" that delays the bliss of the hereafter. In opposition to the "state-affirming" tradition, the "state-critical" reading of the katechon would celebrate Polyeucte's haste in breaking the Roman pagan idols and rushing to his reward. Polyeucte's vision of himself aligns with "revolutionaries in whose anarchistic violence [Benjamin] recognizes traces of a divine law-destroying violence."[39] Such foundational violence pushes past the obstructionist techniques of the state, a life-preserving state that would endeavor to forestall the end. The play transforms the same violence that would be a "lawmaking" violence (the death of a rebellious transgressor) into a Benjaminian "law-annihilating violence" (the death of the martyrs that shatter the law in order to catalyze a new kind of interest, community and identity).[40]

After Polyeucte has converted, he urges Néarque to "come out" as a Christian, repeating the word "allons" (let's go) multiple times to urge him to hasten: "allons aux yeux des hommes / Braver l'idolâtrie, et montrer qui nous sommes" (Let us go before the eyes of men / Stand up to idolatry and show who we are [2.6.645–46]). Néarque responds in horror: "Mais dans ce temple enfin la mort est assurée," while Polyeucte retorts: "Mais dans le ciel déjà la palme est préparée" (But in the temple death is assured in the end / But in heaven the reward is already prepared [2.6.661–62]), opposing the finitude of "enfin" against the eager anticipation of "déjà." Polyeucte chides Néarque, "Mais loin de me presser, il faut que je vous presse!" (But far from pushing myself, I must press you to hasten [2.6.682]). In this tension between delaying or hastening the end, the katechon is a force that will either preserve or complete the order of things. What is essential to remember here is that Corneille's play collapses the two figures of the katechon, showing that sovereign power is always tenuous or incomplete (failing to hold back the end) and that revolutionary power—especially revolutionary power founded on deep, fleshly, affective attachments—is likely to undermine itself, as it might hesitate to bring about the end.

Like many other neoclassical tragedies that begin with a missing center of sovereign gravity—consider Racine's *Phèdre* or *Iphigénie*—in Corneille's *Polyeucte* the authoritative voice is present but is founded on shaky ground: the distant emperor's desires are transmitted through the representative, Félix, who himself is unsure, paranoid, and vacillating. When Pauline comes to beg her father to free her husband Polyeucte, she has to remind him that he is, in fact, acting in the stead of the emperor: "Au nom de l'empereur dont vous tenez la place" (in the name of the Emperor, in whose stead you stand [3.3.918]). But she is unable to complete her plea because Félix interrupts her to underscore that he is just the representative, the prosthetic tool of the emperor. "J'ai son pouvoir en main; mais s'il me l'a commis, / C'est pour le déployer contre ses ennemis" (I have his power in hand; but if he granted it to me / It's to deploy it against his enemies [3.3.919–20]). Félix merely wields power "in hand," but this power is not total; it is only invoked in certain particular instances or states of exception against "enemies" or transgression. We are thus faced with a question of Polyeucte's martyrizable, vulnerable flesh: is it a valuable life or an enemy contagion?

There is a clumsy instrumentality with which Félix invokes the necessary violence of capital punishment. He only has power "in hand" since he is not the sovereign himself. Benjamin explains this clumsiness or roughness in the exercise of capital punishment by suggesting that it reveals "a kind of lawlessness at work in the legal order, an immediate violence that escapes attempts at legal regulation. Confronted with this violence, the laws prove to be powerless and fragile, incapable of checking the excess on which their applicability seems to depend."[41] And indeed, Félix's muddling indecision sets him to be a prime candidate for Benjamin's vision, set forth in the *Origin of German Tragic Drama*, of what De Wilde calls the "tragic image of a sovereign who is faced with a permanent catastrophe and proves unequal to his task . . . falling victim to doubt and despair instead."[42]

Félix's failure to stand in for the emperor and to preserve the empire has direct consequences for the temporality of the play. Massimo

Cacciari underscores that the temporality of empire itself derives from the slowness of the katechon:

> the temporality proper to the form of empire is the epoch. The will to power of empire is expressed in epoch making. *Epoché* means suspension, stopping, motionless delay. Time no longer moves from moment to moment (*movimentum*) and in empire time takes on its exact form . . . To *katechon*, neuter, and *ho katechon*, masculine, derive from *katechein*, which means: to detain, to contain, to slow down, and that which slows down or he or she who slows down. To be epoch making means to be able to detain or contain all that dissolves the supremacy of the ruling spiritual-political form. We could differentiate between the power that truly stops the energies that aim at dissolving a given order and those that limit themselves to keeping them at bay or containing them. But it is clear that both dimensions intersect.[43]

Empire, Cacciari reminds us, paradoxically needs the "energy of the adversary to last as long as possible" and achieves this "duration" by "slow[ing] down the energies that constitute the body of the adversary, for it knows that their explosion will also spell the end of empire."[44] Thus, for empire to extend its duration, and to shore up its force, it engages with a conservational, slow temporality, one that conditions and extends life *and* the specter of the adversary: in this case, the transgressive bodies of the fanatics.

Cacciari shows that the empire requires the tempo of the *epoché* (the "suspension, stopping, motionless delay"), but this slow monumentality can be hijacked by revolutionary force, which seeks to accelerate where empire would slow down, as Polyeucte eventually dreams. Polyeucte urges his friend, "Ne perdons plus de temps: le sacrifice est prêt: / Allons-y du vrai Dieu soutenir l'intérêt" (Let us waste no more time: the sacrifice is ready / Let us go there to sustain the interests of the true God [2.6.711–12]). The empire has a temporal weak point: it can only sustain its temporality of freezing by "slowing down the energies that constitute the body of the adversary," as Cacciari suggests.[45] Total elimination of the adversary would spell doom for empire, since without an adversary there is no opponent against the katechon's delaying or withstanding can be enacted. Through haste Polyeucte sees his violence and his actions as justified; not only does haste counter the "slowness" of empire, as Cacciari points out, but haste also characterizes the martyr's desire for the glorious end—*déjà*.

By understanding the temporal governance and violence incited by the katechon, we can better understand Polyeucte's haste as a foundational violence— ripe with potential for new community making. "How," asks Ward Blanton regarding Pauline philosophy, "does a new community form burst into existence on the site of an imperial execution, in which someone is abandoned to the strategic imposition of imperial sovereignty? How, in such a case, can something happen besides the routinization of sovereign power?"[46] Paul, like Polyeucte, tells the story of radical break with tradition, but a break that founds and ignites something new.[47] Furthermore, it is significant that Paul was once a persecutor of Christians whose reversal, or conversion, then signals a founding of the Church (a new kind of Christian identity). Similarly, Polyeucte's reversal not only challenges preexisting norms of governance but also lays the groundwork for another type of community, one rooted in (queer) affinity and identity. As Blanton highlights, "One of the tasks presented by . . . philosophico-Paulinist constellations is to uncover the way radical dispossession irrupts in the contestation of existing, world-constituting logics, allowing for the invention of new identifications oriented around the formerly uncountable, zero-level status of the excluded."[48] In this light, marginalized identities, from the denigrated status of "Christian" to the specter of same-sex love, all coalesce to emerge as new, previously unthinkable nodes of identification.

The Temporality of Paranoia

From the very beginning, the play depicts a mode of governance in which the time of life is both intensively managed and scrutinized, but this intensity is also distilled via the vague "telephone chain" of command from Rome to Armenia. The physical gap itself provokes and ignites the spectator's imagination, as Ibbett suggests: "the spectator is asked to imagine himself in relation to particularly pressing political demands, as the governor figures wrestle with problems . . . Is there room for equivocation in complying with a distant order? When must orders from afar be obeyed, and when ignored?"[49] Diegetically, because of this gap of distance, Félix opts to rule via haste. Politically, we must reconsider the deployment of time within the sovereign state when its rule is delayed in distant colonies—which exposes an essential paranoid structure within colonial power. Because of the "state-affirming" tradition of the katechon, if the state posits itself as the forestaller of the end, then paranoia—probing what dangers or threats lie in wait ahead—becomes its characteristic temporal weapon. In the first scene in which we meet Félix, the appointed Roman governor of Armenia, he seems far from sovereign. Significantly, his paranoia, and the investment in knowing and capturing his family's closeted thoughts conditions much of the future-oriented, fearful temporality of his rule.

Contemporary queer theory elucidates the allure of and addictive qualities of paranoia. Eve Kosofsky Sedgwick shows how the reading practice associated with the "hermeneutics of suspicion" produces a cohesive "strong theory" of reading and interpretation. Paranoid reading "places its faith in exposure,"[50] because it trusts that revealing the hidden meanings of a text or of a situation is the key to preventing, ameliorating, or addressing the situation. For Sedgwick, paranoid reading is strongly associated with a specific kind of temporality, a heighted, fearful relationship to the future: "The unidirectionally future-oriented vigilance of paranoia generates, paradoxically, a complex relation to temporality that burrows both backward and forward: because there must be no bad surprises, and because learning of the possibility of a bad surprise would itself constitute a bad surprise, paranoia requires that bad news be always already known."[51] The temporality of paranoia and that of the katechon would appear to go hand in hand, insofar as the katechon itself is deeply uncertain, and is precisely sustained by certain paranoid questions: is the end near? What will hasten or forestall this demise? The state-affirming tradition thus requires a paranoid "burrowing" back and forth to prevent the "bad surprise" of the arrival of the "lawless one."

Félix urges his daughter Pauline, against her wishes, to see Sévère, but Pauline balks. She had previously been betrothed to Sévère, but because he had long been thought dead, only two weeks prior Pauline had acquiesced to marry Polyeucte. The ever-paranoid Félix fears that the returned soldier will use his status as the emperor's favorite to retaliate against Pauline for her marriage to Polyeucte. Félix insists, "Il faut le voir, ma fille / Ou tu trahis ton père et toute ta famille" (You must see him, my daughter / Or you betray your father and all your family [1.4.249–50]). In Félix's case, solidifying political favor from Décie, staying in Sévère's good graces, and maintaining order all depends on his hasty governance choices. Ironically, as Christopher Semk notes, regarding Félix's clumsy timings and Sévère's arrival, "Sévère nearly always appears on the stage too late to be effective. Sévère arrives too late to marry Pauline, who has already married Polyeucte, he arrives too late to save Polyeucte from death, and he arrives too late to convert at the end."[52] There is an out of timeliness associated with any attempt to create (heterosexual) order.

Overall, Félix's anxieties stem from no clear present cause, but rather from a wildly spiraling imagination of future outcomes. Of course, paranoia proliferates when it is both supported by the facts one uncovers and uncorroborated by them: the absence of the expected secret meaning only prompts deeper digging and more insistent stripping away of layers of obfuscation. Félix's decisions often run counter to the evidence that his daughter and his advisors provide; they stem largely from his own paranoid imagination. Even after Polyeucte has "come out" as a Christian and is set to be executed, Sévère pleads with Félix on behalf of Polyeucte as a gesture of compassion. Yet Félix adamantly refuses to accept this possibility: Sévère's discourse is a trap, Félix believes, because Sévère is simply feigning sympathy to prompt Félix's clemency, which Sévère would then use to indict him.[53] "De ce qu'il me demande il m'y ferait un crime / Épargnant son rival, je serais sa victime" (Sévère would make a crime of the same act he begs of me /Sparing Sévère's rival [Polyeucte, I would become his victim [5.1.1463–64]). With the hypothetical tenses of "il m'y ferait" and "je serais," Félix envisions a future in which he would be the victim of the same kind of trap that he ends up devising for Polyeucte; he "knows" this type of deception so intimately, because it is a fantasy of his own paranoid construction.

Amid this crisis of authority in colonial governance, Félix clings obstinately to one project: he has been charged with the conservation of life, as Ibbett reminds us.[54] The temporal "burrowing" of paranoid reading, the back and forth of imagined and forestalled futures and present-day actions, is the regime under which both the forestalling of the katachonic end and a chronobiopolitical management can take place. One of Félix's governance strategies, to forestall an unwanted (bad surprise) end, is to inoculate against future transgressions. He makes sure that Polyeucte witnesses Néarque's demise.

> Du conseil qu'il doit prendre il sera mieux instruit,
> Quand il verra punir celui qui l'a séduit.
> Au spectacle sanglant d'un ami qu'il faut suivre,
> La crainte de mourir et le désir de vivre
> Ressaisissent une âme avec tant de pouvoir,
> Que qui voit le trépas cesse de le vouloir. (3.2.879–84)

> (He will better understand the orders he must follow
> When he will see the punishment of the one who seduced him.
> He'll be made to follow his friend's bloody, spectacular end

The fear of death and the desire to live
Can seize a soul with so much power
That he who witnesses such an execution will cease to desire it.)

Félix hopes that the bloody spectacle of Néarque's death will detour Polyeucte from his intended plan and augment the martyr's desire for life. In this instance, Félix uses execution as a strategy to increase life ("le désir de vivre"), highlighting that death (the spectacle of death) is necessary to increase the investment in life and to heighten the biopolitical governance of life. But his governance via the future-oriented temporality of paranoia falls short, as we shall see.

Sex and Sects: Conversion through Seduction

It is significant that Félix's threat of death targets "the one who seduced him," in other words, using the death of Néarque (the "seducer") to change Polyeucte's position. On one level, this does follow the source text and the pathos-filled moment analyzed above, when Polyeucte cannot bear the thought of being separated from his beloved Néarque. On another level, with the phrase "the one who seduced him," instead of using Néarque's name, Félix pinpoints the crime on Néarque's transgressive act and alludes to the fact that what must be inoculated against is not just the politically disobedient conversion, but also the possibility of future wayward affinities and attachments. Pierre Richelet's *Dictionnaire françois* (1680) scene defines "séduction" as a deceptive form: "Tromperie dans des choses qui regardent la Religion, ou les moeurs" (Deception in affairs regarding religion or mores).[55] Complicating this understanding that seduction is rooted in deceit, the verb "séduire" contains a certain ambivalence about whether the deception is religious or a pleasurable (sexual) one. Antoine Furetière's *Dictionnaire universel* (1690) notes this divide more clearly: "Séduire. Abuser quelqu'un, luy persuader de faire le mal, ou luy mettre dans l'esprit quelque mauvaise doctrine . . . Les plaisirs nous seduisent & nous empeschent de songer à notre salut"[56] (To exploit someone, to persuade him to do evil, or to put in his mind some bad doctrine . . . Pleasures seduce us and impede us from thinking about our salvation). The possibility of seduction, and the uses of deception, only serve to augment a paranoid mentality, especially in the case of Polyeucte. How might one augment the desire for life, and the pleasures of life, while at the same time discerning between deception and reality, seduction or fanaticism? When Stratonice complains that Néarque has seduced Polyeucte, the implication the seduction-conversion took place not through lies and deception, but rather by planting the seeds of interest toward a competing set of (sexual) values ("quelque mauvaise doctrine"). But what does it mean to be converted through seduction?

Conversion itself, of course, carries multiple connotations. To consider another Pauline example, Jonathan Goldberg reflects on the queerness of Caravaggio's *The Conversion of Saint Paul* (1600), with the saint in a moment of religious ecstasy—or conversion—lying prone in what Goldberg reads as a queer position. Saint Paul is on his back with his legs akimbo, splayed open: "Is [conversion] as the etymology of the word suggests, a turn with? Or is it a turning around? Or back? Does it represent a break? An end? A beginning?"[57] In Goldberg's musings, we see that conversion is intimately tied to temporality, whether it inaugurates the new or completes the old. Paul's conversion, like Polyeucte's, signals a radical break with tradition, but a break that founds and ignites something new. Ward Blanton calls this the Paulinist "clearing," asking: "how is one to construe, historically and theoretically, the new, change, or that which is not captured by current regimes?[58] However, where Paul would disavow fleshly genealogy for spiritual affinity, Caravaggio's aesthetic depicts Paul in the throes of ecstasy, a corporeal, embodied image of *jouissance* that for Graham Hammill "resuscitates the flesh that Paul relinquishes."[59] Conversion, queer pleasure, and fleshly remainders entwine. Similarly, Corneille's play shows that the conversion can be a site of nongenealogic affinity and identity, *and* revitalizes the remnant of flesh in Polyeucte's intensified erotic attachment to Néarque. Flesh is significant in terms of its temporality here: it metonymically marks both a temporal "straightness" and a queerly contingent "veering" or seductive straying. The temporally linear version of the flesh is echoed by the affirmations of others who state that Polyeucte "a du nom, et sort du sang des rois" (Polyeucte has a renowned name, and descends from the blood of kings [2.1.420]). Flesh, however, also retains its queer "stuckness" as the carnal remainder of erotic attachment between the men, marking a strange velocity that tends toward martyrdom (the haste to follow one another) instead of a normative velocity of progeniture and the "blood of kings."

In the drama the multiple senses of conversion, from sexual to religious, are condensed in what Goldberg calls the "condition of unnameability [recalling] the well-known formulation about sodomy as the crime not to be named among Christians";[60] or, to use Stratonice's term, the "secret mystérieux" (mysterious secret). Throughout much of the first act Pauline seeks to know "What is this secret?" (1.2.111) and urges Polyeucte to tell her what is happening between him and Néarque: "Mais mon déplaisir ne vous peut émouvoir! / Vous avez des secrets que je ne puis savoir! / Quelle preuve d'amour!" (But my distress does not move you! / You have secrets that I can't know! / And this is proof of love! [1.2.115–17]). While she invokes (heterosexual) love between herself and Polyeucte to remedy his secretive silence, the literal meaning of her jab is also true: the secrets that Pauline cannot partake in are *indeed* a proof of a hidden love, the love between Néarque and Polyeucte. In these opening scenes, the secret at hand, the secret between Néarque and Polyeucte, can be polyvalently read as that of conversion to another sect (Christianity) or else as that of a type of unnameable sexuality.

For Goldberg, the moment of Paul's unexpected and incomprehensible conversion from Jew to Christian, from the persecutor Saul to the believer Paul, unravels the received notions of identity and identification. In Paul's own conversion narrative as recounted in the Bible's book of Acts, Paul underscores how his companions heard the voice of God, but could not see; and Paul himself, upon opening his eyes, is blinded for three days. Conversion and the representation of the unrepresentable are explicitly and particularly aligned in this event. The theatrical representation of that which is unseeable—whether sexual affinity or miraculous conversion—sets the terrain for alternate, other kinds of representational pathways, all uniquely grounded in velocity.

The "excluded" and "unnameable" statuses of the sexual-religious conversion merge in Corneille's play on words around "sexe" and "secte." Several times throughout the play Christianity is labeled a "secte," an insult that is not too far away from its paired paronomastic twin, "sexe." Thus, just as Caravaggio's particular form and aesthetic offer Goldberg and others an occasion to consider the queer fleshliness that cannot be fully relinquished, Corneille's *Polyeucte* preserves this stubborn remainder (and intimate attachment between Polyeucte and Néarque) through the form of rhetoric.

For first-century Roman rhetorician Quintilian, whose work deeply influenced early modern writing and rhetoric, the trope of paronomasia "attracts and excites the attention of the hearer by some resemblance, equality, or opposition of words,"[61] and is commonly called a pun. For Northrop Frye, paronomasia points to something secretive, private, a sort of sticking moment in the rhythm of conversation: "Paranomasia is one of the essential elements of verbal creation, but a pun introduced into a conversation turns its back on the sense of the conversation and sets up a self-contained verbal-sound-sense pattern in its place."[62] For an instant, the doubled sounds snag the smooth flow of discourse. In Corneille's play, the paronomasia of sect and sexe yields a surprise speed, in which one word and its twinned other are heard simultaneously, almost too quickly to be caught, slipped in together in a unison pair. The rushed language instantaneously creates an "inside" and "outside" to the conversation, the presented word, and its back-turned double.

Corneille's description of "leur secte" echoes the ways one might speak of a marginalized (sexual) identity group and resonates strongly, even anachronistically, with modern homophobic language.[63] Comforting Pauline, who fears Christians, Stratonice says at the beginning of the play: "Leur secte est insensée, impie, et sacrilege / Et dans leur sacrifice use de sortilège" (Their sect is crazed, impious, and sacriligious, / And in their sacrifice, use sorcery" [1.3.257–58]). Later, after Polyeucte has converted, Pauline begs her father to save Polyeucte, saying, "Ne l'abandonnez pas aux fureurs de sa secte" (Don't abandon him to the furies of his sect [3.3.909]); she thereby emphasizes the powerful, irrational passion within this denigrated group. In yet another example, the ever-compassionate Sévère, despite the fact that his rival Polyeucte's death could allow him to marry Pauline, tries to defend Christianity to his friend, noting, "La secte des chrétiens n'est ce que l'on pense, / On les hait, la raison je ne la connais point / . . . Par curiosité, j'ai voulu les connaître" (The Christian sect differ from our conception of them, / We hate them, but I have no idea for what reason / . . . Out of curiosity I wanted to know them [4.6.1412–13; 4.6.1415]). Here, he marks his openness to learn more about these otherwise denigrated people. In fact, in comparison to Stratonice's vitriolic speech, Sévère finds the hatred that the "secte" of Christians experiences to be unjustified, a position of sympathy for those in another "secte" (or affinity for another sect and sex) that extends the parallel between anti-Christian and homophobic speech in the drama. In all these—treasonous sacrilege, crazed passion, and curious temptation—we see that the conceptual and cultural difference between sects and its homonym, sex, are not so far apart. Sévère's comment expresses a longing to mingle with Christians, perhaps to expose himself to the possibility that he too may be "seduced" into the faith, as Néarque seduced Polyeucte; in this case, the religious transformation would occur through knowing ("connaître"), which redoubles the sexually euphemistic quality.

The conflation between sex and sect is most apparent in Stratonice's grasping for a term to describe Polyeucte. Unable to pin down precisely the nature of his crime, she resorts to a logic of accretion. She attempts to explain to Pauline why Polyeucte is no longer the spouse he was, but to do so she pulls together a dozen terms:

> C'est l'ennemi commun de l'état et des dieux,
> Un méchant, un infâme, un rebelle, un perfide,
> Un traître, un scélérat, un lâche, un parricide,
> Une peste exécrable à tous les gens de bien,
> Un sacrilège impie: en un mot, un chrétien. (3.2.780–84)
>
> (He is the common enemy of the State and the gods,
> A villain, an infamous one, a rebel, a perfidious man
> A traitor, a scoundrel, a coward, a parricide,
> A disgusting plague on all the good people,
> An impious blasphemer: in one word, a Christian.)

Ultimately, these insults are not able to fully answer the question of why he is no longer worthy of being her spouse; it is unclear why Stratonice needs to resort to so many insults to prove her point. Pauline herself even says, weakly, in his defense: "Ce mot [chrétien] aurait suffi sans ce torrent d'injures" (This word [Christian] would have sufficed without this torrent of insults [3.2.785]). Stratonice's phrase "en un mot," set up by the colon, promises some sort of logical justification anchoring the avalanche of invectives ("to sum up"). The word is doubly insufficient, not only because it tops off such a hyperbolic stream of insults so weakly but also because, in Stratonice's eyes, Polyeucte has not "merely" converted. He has shattered the former bonds between himself and the state, his family, and more.

As Stratonice renarrates to Pauline the event of Polyeucte's conversion, she still cannot fully name the "thing" that troubles her so deeply. She recounts how Polyeucte retorts to Félix, who tries to stop the pair from further desecration of the temple:

> "Quoi! lui dit Polyeucte en élevant sa voix,
> Adorez-vous des dieux ou de pierre ou de bois?"
> Ici dispensez-moi du récit des blasphèmes
> Qu'ils ont vomi tous deux contre Jupiter même.
> L'adultère et l'inceste en étaient les plus doux. (3.2.835–39)
>
> ("What!" said Polyeucte, raising his voice
> "You adore these gods of stone and wood?"

Here, please spare me the narrative of the blasphemy
That both vomited against Jupiter himself.
Adultery and incest were the sweetest of these blasphemies.)

In her recounting, she highlights that she does not wish to repeat Polyeucte and Néarque's injurious words. The closest she can get to recounting what they said is to hint that, in their "vomited" blasphemous speech, they targeted Jupiter for sexually transgressive actions. She loosely associates their own accusations with her own viewpoint of Christians as sexually and morally deviant.

The pun, then, becomes a node where the velocity or swiftness of mistaking one word for another allows for an unexpected intimacy on the level of signification. Frye suggests, we recall, that paranomasia "turns its back on the sense of the conversation," but this image of back-turning, rather than a simple refusal, generates something private, intimate and contained.[64] The doubled meaning of "sex" and "sects" and the production of excess meaning through sonic sameness, is not simply a metaphor; it is *itself* a pathway of presenting, affirming, and attuning attachments between Néarque and Polyeucte. Laurie Shannon, analyzing classically derived figures of "insistently same-sex friendship with complex relationships to eroticism" in the English Renaissance underscores that "they cast the friend as 'another self' and merged a pair of friends as 'one soul cast in two bodies.'"[65] The pun itself embodied this twinned status: two meanings in the same sound, one soul in two bodies. In this light, the conversion, as well as the desire to convert, highlights the intersections between "sexe" and "secte"; Néarque and Polyeucte's love is not merely a "une vieille amitié" (an old friendship), but a deeply felt, physical and sensuous attachment to one another, affirmed and performed through the doubled quickness of the punned term.

Corneille's version of the story presents the men's bonds through the subtle, repeated ways that Néarque and Polyeucte seek sameness and togetherness rather than separation and difference. After Félix has Néarque executed, he asks, "Et notre Polyeucte a vu trancher sa vie?" (And our Polyeucte saw his friend's life cut short? [3.4.957]). He hopes that witnessing the horrific spectacle of his friend's death will prompt Polyeucte to retract. Albin responds, "Il l'a vu, mais hélas! Avec un oeil d'envie. / Il brûle de le suivre au lieu de reculer" (He saw it, alas, with an envious eye. / He burns to follow Néarque instead of retreating. [3.4.958–59]). Polyeucte's response to seeing his friend executed echoes the corporeality in the historical fragment that Boswell emphasizes.

The deadly cut of martyrdom is not one that Polyeucte resents or fears; rather, his main preoccupation is the very act of separation, not being allowed to follow ("suivre") his dearest Néarque, just as we saw in the source text, where Nearchos fears losing the "unity of our soul."[66]

As Shannon underscores, in *Sovereign Amity*, "likeness in both sex and status *is* (the only) political equality in period terms; on the basis of this likeness, writers stress the making of a consensual social bond or body that is not inherently subordinating."[67] In other words, if "secte" is used as a pejorative term, and wielded to justify execution and denigration, the fact that Néarque and Polyeucte insist on their likeness underscores a "poetically powerful imagining of parity within a social form that is consensual."[68] The autonomous "sovereignty" of their friendship, to take a cue from Shannon, thwarts the chronobio-political governance of life as managed by Félix, since they remain immune to both threats of execution (and thus immune to execution itself, as a political weapon). Therefore, this type of queerly intimate sovereignty, wrought from sameness, becomes troubling on both an affective and political scale.

Racing to Baptism

Because of the emphasis on sameness, whether in the redoubled word of sex ("sects"), or in the fear of separation that propels Polyeucte's affective attachments, much of the language of Néarque "seducing" Polyeucte hinges on the expression of what I have called passionate attunement, as they seek to calibrate their emotions and their intensities of feeling for each other. At the very beginning of the play, Néarque initially assumes that Polyeucte's willingness to defer his baptism is a sign of his wavering faith. Polyeucte asks if the haste is even necessary, wondering if he must continue to repudiate his wife: "L'occasion, Néarque, est-elle si pressante / Qu'il faille être insensible aux soupirs d'une amante?" (Is the occasion, Néarque, so pressing / That it is necessary to be insensitive to the sighs of one's lover [Pauline]? [1.1.21–22]). Néarque's urgent haste is unseemly, Polyeucte initially thinks. He later adds, regarding the baptism, "Bien que je le préfère aux grandeurs d'un empire / Comme le bien supreme et le seul où j'aspire / Je crois, pour satisfaire un juste et saint amour / Pouvoir un peu remettre, et différer d'un jour" (Even though I prefer baptism to the glories of an empire / as the highest good and the only one to which I aspire / I believe, to satisfy such a just and sacred love / To be able to push it back a little bit, and defer it by a day [1.1.49–52]). Importantly, Polyeucte does not cite his fear of retribution or political scandal in the wake of his conversion. Rather, he cites affective markers—the lull of amorous sighs or of feminine charms—as the impetus for delaying his conversion: "Vous ne savez pas ce que c'est qu'une femme: / Vous ignorez quels droits elle a sur toute l'âme, / Quand après un long temps qu'elle a su nous charmer, / Les flambeaux de l'hymen viennent de s'allumer." (You do not know what a wife is like / You don't know what rights she has over your whole soul / When, after having charmed us for a long time, / The flames of marriage have just been ignited [1.1.9–12]). To think back to the katechon, in this instance the delaying force (forestalling the wished-for end of conversion) is linked to Polyeucte's heterosexual love. In Néarque's eyes, Polyeucte's delay is also the measure of his sense of the incompatibility between his love for his wife, his love for Néarque, and his love for God. *Temporality* itself (his delay) becomes imbricated with sexuality and a means of signaling his anxiety about the multiple irreconcilable desires that tug on him. Néarque interprets this delay as a signal that Polyeucte initially wishes to cling to the comforts of his heterosexual life and his respected place in governance. Néarque oddly insists on expediting the rite before the heightened ardor of conversion cools:

> Il est toujours tout juste et tout bon, mais sa grâce
> Ne descend pas toujours avec même efficace
> Après certains moments que perdent nos longueurs,
> Elle quitte ces traits qui pénètrent les cœurs,
> Le nôtre s'endurcit, la repousse, l'égare,
> Le bras qui la versait en devient plus avare
> Et cette sainte ardeur qui doit porter au bien
> Tombe plus rarement ou n'opère plus rien
> Celle qui vous pressait de courir au baptême,
> Languissante déjà, cesse d'être la même
> Et pour quelques soupirs qu'on vous a fait ouïr
> Sa flamme se dissipe, et va s'évanouir. (1.1.29–40)
>
> (He is always ever good and righteous, but his grace
> Is not always bestowed with the same efficacy
> After we've lost key moments through our tarrying
> She (grace) that penetrated men's hearts, now turns her back.
> Our heart, grown hardened, pushes her away and strays,
> The arm that once poured it out becomes more parsimonious

And this holy zeal which should lead us to good
Comes more and more rarely, or fails to move at all
That which pressed you to run towards the baptism,
Languishing now, is no longer the same
And for a few sighs that you were made to hear
This flame diminishes and will vanish.)

Néarque uses corporeal imagery—of arrows penetrating hearts, of open arms—to present the pleasures that he offers in rather sensual, physical, terms. One kind of flesh (same-sex attachment, intimacy) is thus proffered in exchange for another: Polyeucte's relinquishing of his marriage love. In Néarque's language of promptitude counteracts the possibility of delay, a *katechonic* delay that would allow Polyeucte to cede to his wife's fears. Therefore, Néarque's precipitousness also takes on a type of queer velocity: a haste that is wrought from the intensity of their affection for one another, which also aligns with their desire to speed along toward their demise, in contradistinction to the "state-affirming" delay of Pauline and her father.

Polyeucte answers Néarque's accusations of weak Christian faith by insisting on the sameness of their passionate experiences. He says, "Vous me connaissez mal: *la même ardeur* me brûle / Et le désir accroît quand l'effet se recule" (You misunderstand me: *the very same ardor* burns within me / And desire only increases when the effect disappears [1.1.41–42], emphasis mine). Polyeucte affirms that he too is rushing to convert: "Oui, j'y cours, cher Néarque / Je brûle d'en porter la glorieuse marque" (Yes, I run there, dear Néarque / I burn to bear the glorious mark [1.1.93–94]). While religious fervor and sexual ecstasy have long borrowed rhetoric from one another, the particularity of the language is noteworthy here—which is composed not only of eroticized eagerness but also of speed. The haste serves as the sign of his desire; with "j'y cours" and the repetition of "brûle," Polyeucte signals an affirming speed that signals his willingness to leave the delaying force of marriage for another kind of attachment—one to Christianity and to Néarque.

To cinch his argument in favor of conversion, Néarque begins to put forth an even speedier rhetoric:

Nous pouvons tout aimer: il [Dieu] le souffre, il l'ordonne
Mais à vous dire tout, ce seigneur des seigneurs
Veut le premier amour et les premiers honneurs.
Comme rien n'est égal à sa grandeur suprême

Il faut ne rien aimer qu'après lui, qu'en lui-même,
Négliger, pour lui plaire, et femme, et biens et rang.
Exposer pour sa gloire et verser tout son sang.
Mais que vous êtes loin de cette ardeur parfaite
Qui vous est nécessaire, et que je vous souhaite. (1.1.70–79)

(We can love everything: He tolerates it, he orders it
But to tell you the truth, this lord of lords
Wants to be first in love and in honors
Since nothing is equal to his supreme glory
After him, you can love nothing else, other than himself.
You must neglect, to please him, wife, goods, and rank.
Reveal yourself for his glory and pour out your blood.
But how far you are from this perfect ardor
That is so necessary for you, and that I wish you.)

Although "que je vous souhaite" grammatically indicates "that I wish for you" (the conversion and God's love), in Néarque's phrasing it is also possible to read it as an exclamation, "how I desire you!" In the ambiguity of expression within "je vous souhaite," similar to the multiplicity afforded by the pun, Néarque can travel from generalities of loving all ("Nous pouvons tout aimer") to an urgent entreaty with which Néarque presses Polyeucte to accept a specific kind of "ardeur parfaite" (perfect ardor). Desire animates the intensity with which Néarque exhorts Polyeucte to accept Christianity. The "perfect ardor" that Néarque wishes for his friend is both affectively intense and vague.

At work in this speech is the rhetorical figure of metalepsis, indicating a sliding chain of similitudes. It is a trope less popular than its cousins, metonym and metaphor, and its status in early modern rhetoric was a confused one: many people did not know whether to laud or loathe this term for his destabilizing possibilities. For example, the phrase "angel wings on the mountain's back," to signify a snow-covered mountain, requires a slippage of metonym to metonym: the snow is white and soft as like angel feathers, the mountain is covered with snow, the mountain's side looks like a hunched back. In the phrase "angel wings on the mountain's back," however, "snow" as the prime animating figure, drops out. In his rhetorical treatise, Quintilian calls metalepsis "an intermediate step . . . signifying nothing in itself, but affording a passage to something. It is a trope that we give the impression of being acquainted with rather than one that we actually ever need." Later, he says that "we need not waste any more time over it."[69] We should note Quintilian's particular emphasis on rushing over (and effectively effacing) that trope which is, itself, self-effacing: a trope with a temporal implication, whose blatant minimization reveals an implicit forcefulness.

Metalepsis ties together through enchained likenesses: the metonym of a metonym is a strange kinship indeed. Although metaphor is a rather conventional trope trading in similitude, in its cousin, metalepsis, meaning is stretched beyond its clearly linkable significance. If metaphor, according to Brian Cummings, "transfers a name to something unlike but not so unlike itself," metalepsis is the trope that "stretches metaphor a little further than we want to go, perhaps even to the breaking point."[70] Metalepsis generates queer ties, enabling A and C to adjoin together, two terms that "ought not" normally be naturally twinned, but are able to be linked topically, grammatically through ties that rush connections in meaning.[71] Metalepsis is the generating figure that knits together, but must also render invisible the common linking agent: "the peculiar power of metalepsis in Renaissance theory is precisely that it leaves certain steps in the exchange invisible,"[72] notes Cummings. This trope "makes space for imagination, for language as fiction or fantasy. In this figure we do not know how we have got to where we are, as if we have been transported by an unseen mechanism."[73] This sudden propelling forth happens invisibly: we are aware of the thrust of movement, but we don't necessarily "see" the intermediary linkages themselves.

In fact, many scholars have picked up on how Néarque's primary insistence in the first scene of the play dissolves the heteronormative ties that bind Polyeucte to his wife: he urges his friend to ignore his wife's tears and pleas. This zealousness is often explained by religious enthusiasm or the excesses of fanaticism. Left out of his speech, and thereby perhaps overlooked by scholarship, is an attention to an invisible linking mechanism. For Néarque to urge Polyeucte to accept this "ardeur parfaite . . . que je vous souhaite" (the perfect ardor . . . that I wish you"), the intimate, "bodily" affection between the two men, and their fear of being separated from one another, becomes a major impetus. Néarque loves Polyeucte and thereby urges his conversion; Polyeucte loves Néarque and wishes to convert, like his friend. Metalepsis hastens the action along yet remains itself unseen. It deliberately leaves out the crucial linking term—the stubborn, fleshly love that Polyeucte and Néarque hold for each other. The spectator must infer or provide the missing pieces, joining far-stretched concepts together to articulate the connection that can only be seen by the traces it leaves behind. Possibly, implicit in Quintilian's denigration of the trope is an uneasiness about metalepsis's subversive potential.

Attuned Speeds

In the play Polyeucte and Néarque seek not only to speed up their actions (conversion, announcement, martyrdom) but also to hasten the sought-after end. They also attune their tempos to one another; this attunement reveals another way that queer velocity might "directionally" diverge from norms of sexuality and intimacy without outright undoing them. A musical paradigm for this visible secrecy, or the open secret, might be the *overtone* or *harmonic* in music. When two instruments play notes in perfect harmony, an unexpected, higher extra pitch is generated. Importantly, the harmonic tone is not actually "played" by the musicians but produced as a supplementary product of the perfect matching of two notes. The supplementary sonic pleasure can only be grasped through perfected articulation. Instead of being sounded marginally or edged out, such desire is apparent, in plain sight, but only caught by the trained ear to the unexpected, lingering overtones.

Early modern scholars of music theory, physics, and mathematics suspected the presence of overtones, but could not fully account for or explain them. The puzzle was this: when a note was played, say on a vibrating string on a violin, if one listened closely, one could hear a few faint, specific, higher resonances at the same time. Another way of discerning these ghostly higher tones (or "upper partials") was to play a stringed instrument and to watch or touch certain higher-pitched strings while the lower note (called the "fundamental") was being played.

This phenomenon was observed by René Descartes in his "Abregé de la musique," a treatise on music theory, pleasure, and taste. He notes that, "I have seen through experience in the strings of the lute or whatever other instrument that it be, that if you touch one, the force of the sound will vibrate all of the other strings which are tuned higher by a fifth or a major third . . . yet the force of this harmonization can only come, without a doubt, from their perfection or imperfection.[74] For Descartes, the sympathetic vibration of neighboring strings by certain intervals was enough to assert that there was a "natural" basis for certain notes to be harmoniously brought together. Such productive resonances, only effectuated through perfect attunement, provided poetic inspiration for seventeenth-century dramatists to write on the resemblance between music and love. Even if the mechanics of such a phenomenon were beyond their grasp, this trope appears, for example, in Pedro Calderón de la Barca's *El médico de su honra* (1637):

> Dicen que dos instrumentos
> Conformemente templados,
> Por los ecos dilatados
> Comunican los acentos:
> Tocan el uno, y los vientos
> Hiere el otro, sin que allí
> Nadie le toque; y en mí
> Esta experiencia se viera;
> Pues si el golpe allá te hiriera,
> Muriera yo desde aquí.[75]
>
> (They say that two stringed instruments,
> When perfectly in tune,
> Transmit the tones by echoing each other:
> Play the one, and the other, though untouched,
> Is moved by the whisper of the wind.
> And so it is with me:
> If a blow struck you there, I would die here.)

Attunement performs a bond of perfected similitude ("Conformemente templados") that also affirms a bond of love. Yet, like the overtone itself, such a love is "hiding in plain sight"—the connection is apparent but not overtly stated.

The physical and mathematical reason for this mutual vibration would not be discovered until the mid-eighteenth century.[76] These ghostly higher tones, simply put, were byproducts of the string vibrating many different ways *at once*. The string has a main speed, or frequency of vibration, called the "fundamental." At the same time, the string vibrates more quickly, in perfect integer multiples of this fundamental frequency, and the faster vibrations cause the string to be "split" or subdivided into perfect halves, thirds, and so on, divided at places called "nodes." These smaller subsections, because "shortened," produce the faint higher pitches of the overtones.

The overtone depends upon perfectly calibrated speeds of vibration, and similarly, unison and repetition, in Polyeucte and Néarque's language, enact kind of overtone through their calibrated queer velocities. Like paranomasia, this unison can be thought of as a redoubled, swift sameness. In the pivotal scene of act 2, when the two men finally decide to present themselves as Christians (to come out and "montrer qui nous sommes"), while they do not actually speak in unison, they do the next closest thing: repeat and recite each other's words *to the letter*, producing, in effect, a redoubled, intensive sameness and attunement that could allow for an overtone. Polyeucte says, as Néarque hesitates:

> Il faut (je me souviens encore de vos paroles)
> Négliger, pour lui plaire, et femme, et biens, et rang,
> Exposer pour sa gloire et verser tout son sang.
> Hélas! Qu'avez-vous fait de cette amour parfaite
> Que vous me souhaitiez, et que je vous souhaite?
> S'il vous en reste encore, n'êtes-vous point jaloux
> Qu'à grand'peine chrétien, j'en montre plus que vous? (2.6.686–92)
>
> (One must [I still remember your words]
> Neglect, to please him, wife, goods, and rank
> Reveal yourself for his glory and pour forth your blood.
> Alas, what have you done with this perfected love
> That you wished me, and that I wish you
> If there is any left in you, are you not ashamed
> That barely Christian, I show it more than you?)

In his insistence that he is quoting Néarque exactly, Polyeucte reveals that he is alarmed at the disaccord wrought by the "j'en montre plus que vous"—by his demonstrating an intensity that is out of sync with and more than Néarque's. He seeks to rectify this through a performance of "unisson"; his unifying repetition reasserts the "amour parfait," which points to both Christian love and the love between the two men. Polyeucte's inserted parenthetical remark underscores that what he says (or is about to say) are actually Néarque's words, preserved and memorized, and recited to draw his friend in to perfect attunement. The goal is for the two to vibrate with the pleasure of the harmonic sameness. Here, the overtone serves as a figure of supplemental queer affection, hiding in plain sight.

While attunement is the means of highlighting sympathetic resonances between the men's bodies, Corneille also uses the figure of discord to evoke the inviability of an intimate relationship. Pauline expresses her anxiety over feeling terribly disjointed from her husband. Stratonice comforts her, describing marriage as follows:

On n'a tous deux qu'un cœur qui sent mêmes traverses,
Mais ce cœur a pourtant ses fonctions diverses,
Et la loi de l'hymen qui vous tient assemblés
N'ordonne pas qu'il tremble alors que vous tremblez,
Ce qui fait vos frayeurs ne peut le mettre en peine:
Il est Arménien, et vous êtes Romaine
Et vous pouvez savoir que nos deux nations
N'ont pas sur ce sujet mêmes impressions. (1.3.145–52)

(You both have a heart that feels the same hardships
But this heart, however, has various functions
And the hymeneal law that ties you together
Does not command that he tremble when you tremble.
That which makes you afraid cannot affect him:
He is Armenian, and you are Roman
And you should know that our two nations
Do not have the same opinions about this subject.)

This sentiment, of course, is in contradistinction to the attuned, sympathetic vibrations seen before in the Calderón quotation and in Néarque and Polyeucte's language. Stratonice insists on the naturalness of difference between people who love each other. While the two men employ the rhetoric of "sameness" to emphasize their passion (for God, but perhaps also for each other), Stratonice's description of Pauline's relationship emphasizes differences—differences that range from the microlevel of the body to the macrolevel of culture and nationality. Trembling, whether from fear or erotic pleasure, is an action that occurs almost outside of personal agency, motivated primarily by affect, and Stratonice's dismissal that they need not both tremble also shows that their velocities need not be attuned.

Overall, the instantaneity of Polyeucte's conversion shatters the ways that identity was founded before—aligned with blood, genealogy, lineage—and we might also add marriage to this list. Pauline speaks of her marriage to Polyeucte in purely functional terms, comparing her previous love for Sévère with her duty-filled marriage to Polyeucte: "Et moi, comme à son lit je me vis destinée, / Je donnai par devoir à son affection / Tout ce que l'autre avait par inclination" (And I, as I found myself fated for his [Polyeucte's] bed/ I responded with duty to his affection, / But the other [Sévère] had my love from my own inclinations [1.3.214–16]). This marriage is an orchestrated commitment—constructed, false, unnatural—and it stands as a foil to the effortless attunement and sameness exhibited by Polyeucte and Néarque. While *Polyeucte* foregrounds the crisis of the "colonial governor" representing imperial interests from afar, Félix's methods of governance through paranoia falls short. Instead, the intensity of the tempos performed by Polyeucte and Néarque, as well as their confirming "sameness"—both in their speeches and in terms of the proliferating sameness of memetic spread—reveal how speed allows the articulation of certain unnameable desires. As analyzed before, these desires are not only law destroying but also foundational of a new kind of community, or a new kind of love. Desire is a magnetizing force between self and other, between this time and the (desired or foreclosed) future.

In *Polyeucte* the conservative tempo of empire and the state-affirming katechonic force it purports to purvey are destabilized. Félix's governance, as the extension of empire's authority, is shaken when his values and his mandate—the biopolitical maintenance of life through genealogical reproduction—are threatened by the revolutionary transformations represented by Christianity. In Corneille's paronomastic doubling of sex and secte, we see how the shattering, unrepresentable experience of conversion inaugurates a new lawlessness: these new Christians are characterized by unruly attachments, attachments that are reproductive according to a completely different logic from the previous governance paradigms. Where Félix's world is characterized simultaneously by a commitment to the predictable, plodding trajectories of marriages and bloodlines and a paranoid anxiety that such an approach will fail, Polyeucte and Néarque celebrate a love based on passionate attunement. In this way, the "end" of martyrdom that Polyeucte and Néarque hasten toward is not an end at all, but rather a shattering, radical inauguration of the new: an alternative to the chronobiopolitical imagination whose limits are made all too clear in Félix's paranoia and vacillation.

4

Circling the Hymen

The Temporality of Dilation in *Bérénice*

Excess and Minimalism

While Andromaque forestalls marriage to Pyrrhus in the name of preserving her catachrestic attachment to Hector, in Jean Racine's *Bérénice* (1670) delay is orchestrated to produce a different result: to preserve another kind of attachment, a fluid and polyamorous one. This simple act of delaying bidding adieu stands as the primary—and, some might say, the sole—action of the tragedy. Racine's dramas are characterized by a strict adherence to the minimalism privileged by classical aesthetics, and this tragedy is no exception. *Bérénice* is marked by simplicity in the extreme: nearly nothing "active" happens. There are no murders or suicides; indeed, there is no bloodshed at all in this drama. Abbé Villars, in his critique of the play, says "there is hardly a plot/action here" and dismissively calls it nothing more than extended elegiacal fluff: "From the beginning to the end, nothing but a gallant web of madrigals and elegies."[1] The play's action is admittedly quite simple. Titus, who has recently been named the emperor of Rome, must bid farewell to his beloved mistress of five years, Bérénice. Roman law forbids a royal queen to share the imperial throne, implicitly excluding foreigners from marrying into power. Thus, Bérénice, as the foreign queen of Palestine, cannot be allowed to marry Titus. At the same time, Titus's best friend Antiochus takes this opportunity to declare his long-smoldering love for Bérénice. Bérénice, despite her requited love for Titus, must accept Titus's farewells and decline Antiochus's amorous declarations. Tears, hand-wringing, and suicide threats ensue, in a painfully extended breakup. But, at the end of the play, the three must part ways and renounce their love forever.

Literary tradition has it—perhaps apocryphally—that the subject was selected by Henrietta of England for a competition between Racine and Corneille, as Mitchell Greenberg notes, "the reigning literary heavyweights would each pen a play on the same material."[2] In contrast to Corneille's version, which features four characters who try to manipulate and coax each other into loving and committing to one another, leading to the ultimate climax of Bérénice's banishment, Racine's version can seem concentrated and pithy at the level of form, as well as in its limitation of subject matter. As Racine says in the preface, "For a long time, I have wanted to see if I could fashion a tragedy with the same simplicity of action that appealed so strongly to the ancients."[3] Racine's version only features three main characters, and, more importantly in terms of the temporality of the action, the king, Titus, comes onstage *already aware* of the necessity of the split and committed, at least in theory, to sending Bérénice away. One does not wait with bated breath to see if Bérénice might stay; we know from the beginning that she must go. Racine's contemporary critics such as Abbé Villars argued that the only "action" of the piece is Titus's mustering the courage to separate. As Villars says, "Since this whole play, if one is paying attention, is actually nothing more than the stuff of one scene, in which Titus tries to leave Bérénice"[4]; Villars implicitly decries the paucity of material with the derogatory snub of "one scene."

Racine's inspiration for the piece derives from a single line of Suetonius's histories: *Titus reginam Berenicen, cui etiam nuptias pollicitus ferebatur, statim ab Urbe dimisit invitus invitam*. Racine translates this as "Titus, qui aimait passionnément Bérénice, et qui même, à ce qu'on croyait, lui avait promis de l'épouser, la renvoya de Rome, malgré lui, et malgré elle, dès les premiers jours de son Empire"[5] (Titus, loved Bérénice passionately, and who even, it is believed, had promised to marry her, sent her away from Rome, against his own will, and against hers, in the first days of his being Emperor). Even in his preface, Racine seems concerned with responding to his critics by justifying the richness of this single line of material, asserting that Bérénice and Titus's story, much like sad farewells of Dido and Aeneas, offers more than enough poetic and dramatic matter to craft a tragedy: "And who could doubt that that which could provide matter for a whole song of a heroic poem, where the action lasts for several days and the narration is sizeable ["occupe beaucoup de place"], could not suffice for the subject of a tragedy?"[6] But perhaps Racine's overinsistence on the sufficiency of his material's temporal duration reveals and reflects anxieties over the critical scrutiny of time onstage. The same play is read as either scanty material—"hardly any action,"[7] as Abbé Villars terms it—or else an excessive action that could otherwise last "several days" and whose narration "occupies a fair amount of space." How can such a tragedy be both nothing ("rien") and excess?

Despite the supposed simplicity of the tale, the classic story of lovers being separated, *invitus invitam* (malgré lui, malgré elle [despite him, despite her]), resonated deeply with audiences. Villars himself reports that once he abandons "my damsels, the rules [of the theatre] at the door" he is immediately drawn into the spectacle: "I found it powerfully sad, and I wept like a simpleton."[8] And indeed it is the public's unbidden emotion in their responsive overflowing of tears that Racine holds up as evidence of his work's success: "But nor do I believe that the public can be dissatisfied with me for having given them a tragedy which has been honored by so many tears, and whose thirtieth performance was as well attended as its first."[9] Repeated enjoyment, in Racine's evaluation, becomes a marker of the play's success. *Bérénice*'s (nearly) nonaction of bidding adieu, as well as the condensed neoclassical restraint in terms of style and form, yields an excessive spilling of tears and emotion. Paucity and excess paradoxically intertwine.

Some spectators and critics in Racine's time complained that if the substantive action of this play consists of saying goodbye and mourning the loss of the beloved, why would it need to be repeated so many times? Georges Forestier cites Racine's dictum "Toute l'invention consiste à faire quelque chose de rien" (All invention is making something out of nothing). In response to this aphorism, Forestier remarks: "A surprising and yet involuntary reminder of the proximity of the principles of dramatic composition to rhetorical composition, as if *Bérénice* had been developed according to the model of the 'chreia,' a rhetorical exercise that precisely consists of making something out of nothing!"[10] Although Forestier means to lightly mock the way that *Bérénice* could be read as a schoolboy's practice of writing goodbye a hundred different ways, I would like to reconsider this flourishing of repetition not as a mere rhetorical exercise. Far from being merely repetitive or superfluous, *copia* and *chreia* were essential techniques used in training Renaissance schoolboys in the arts of rhetoric. Taken from Erasmus's *De copia* (1512), the Renaissance textbook prompted students to write the same phrase—for example, "your letter pleased me greatly," dozens of different ways, taking on different styles, figures of speech, and varied articulations. Thus, at heart, copia exercises were practices of rhetorical expansion and amplification of a seemingly simple term (or retooling a famous anecdote, in the case of the chreia). Lynn Enterline's *Shakespeare's Schoolroom* sheds light on how such mundane repetitive practices constituted a powerfully affective classroom scene of shame, emotion, mastery, imitation, and more.[11] While Enterline's research focuses on the English classroom, there is a compelling case to extend her particular angle of analysis to France, particularly because Racine had exposure to an exceptional amount of classical pedagogy and training in Latin and Greek and, in particular, the copia style, thanks to his schooling at Port Royal. Therefore, Racine was likely cognizant of the emotional and affective potential that lay in "mere" repetition.

In *Bérénice* the supposed paucity of action and excess of rhetorical chreia intertwine to generate a queer erotics. Far from being aesthetic faults of the drama, what critics have dismissed as nonaction or as repetition results from reading and understanding the play through a normative temporal lens: expectations of diegetic progress are derived from fixed notions of what tragic drama or historical sovereignty "should" look like. Notably, the rhetorical repetition returning and expanding repeatedly on the same (sad, sorrowful, longing) affective sentiment is redoubled by the strangely circular temporality within the play. Titus says of Bérénice: "Depuis cinq ans entiers chaque jour je la vois, / Et crois toujours la voir pour la première fois" (For five whole years I've seen her every day, / And felt each time I saw her was the first [2.2.545–46]),[12] putting forth a queer temporality of nonprogress and rich repetition. The pleasurable, surprising renewal begins again each day, a circular time that stands in contrast to the sovereign temporality of progress, decision making, and change. Such a time—an imagined velocity that curves repeatedly toward its beginning—stymies the time of Titus's sovereign decision making when he must finally bid her farewell.

This chapter traces the ways that nonprogressive temporality competes against the linearity of sovereign progress characterized by futurity and the exclusion of "fruit illégitime" (illegitimate fruit) or Bérénice's royal blood. Titus's advisor, Paulin, says:

> Elle a mille vertus. Mais, Seigneur, elle est reine.
> Rome, par une loi, qui ne se peut changer,
> N'admet avec son sang aucun sang étranger,
> Et ne reconnaît point les fruits illégitimes,
> Qui naissent d'un hymen contraire à ses maximes. (2.2.376–80)

(She [Bérénice] has great virtues. But, sir, she's a queen.
Rome, by a law that may never be changed,
Admits no foreign blood to join its own,
And will not recognize the offspring born
From any marriage counter to its code.)

Paulin reminds Titus of his obligation to Roman law. But in his description we see that it is a law not only concerned with precedent, maxims, and traditions (of the past) but also intimately controlling of the future: preventing unwanted (unrecognized) mixed-blood children of Titus and Bérénice, and thereby detouring the bloodline of future heirs to veer toward the foreign (Judea, the East) rather than remaining resolutely Roman. Titus's pleasurable repetition, returning again and again to Bérénice, is in opposition to the progress and marriage expected of him.

In addition to the rhetorical (and gendered) dilation of the repetitive chreia, the other excess in the play that critics have flagged is the character of Antiochus. The introduction of Antiochus into the play has been critiqued as merely a means to expand the simple action of saying goodbye into a full five-act play. Villars complains that "[Antiochus's] goodbyes ["adieux"] to Bérénice were invented by the author to gain some time, to cheat and to stretch it out to fill up an Act."[13] Forestier points out that Antiochus could be seem as a "purely functional" superfluous character, fleshing out what would have otherwise been a ridiculously short tragedy. Racine, however, seems to insist on Antiochus's necessity in the drama: Antiochus is the character who speaks both the opening and closing lines of the play, and he still lingers long after he has bared his feelings to his dearest friends.[14] In my reading, I home in on the most obvious and perhaps the queerest explanation of Antiochus's centrality. He serves as necessary third figure in the play, not simply to open and close the drama, but rather to sustain it in a strangely suspended temporality. He acts as a prism or even an erotic conduit through which Titus's and Bérénice's love can be measured, articulated, and witnessed—and held in perpetual deferral.

To expand on this hypothesis of the necessary third, I should underscore that the play is usually analyzed in terms of pairs, of the pathos of the *invitus invitam* (despite him, despite her)—the sorrowful parting of the heterosexual couple. Critics have been blindered by Racine's depiction of Bérénice as specifically Oriental, exoticized and otherized—a racial and gender identity that, in scholarship, serves as both the justificatory principle for her banishment, as well as the original source of her seductive prowess. Such an overdetermined description of Bérénice acts as a "red herring"—such an obvious "Other," presented in excessive Orientalist splendor—thereby distracting us from paying attention to subtler, less obvious sexualities or gender positions, other queer velocities at play. Such binaristic readings erase the queer possibilities of the trio: Antiochus's loving admiration of Titus, the ways that Titus desires and depends on Antiochus's voice and witnessing eyes, and the manner in which Antiochus's love for Bérénice is frequently presented in mirrored comparison to Titus's love. In fact, the primacy of understanding the play through the figure of the couple, or the duo, excludes something more ambiguously polyamorous, fluid, and triadic. The eroticism undergirding the dynamics of this triad relies on a temporality that is "dilated"—undecided, repetitive, yet full of possibilities. This temporality is only possible when the (sovereign) decision fails to take effect.

To explain what a "circular velocity" entails, it is necessary to take a small digression into the realm of physics. We know, according to Newton, that an object in motion will continue in its trajectory (direction and speed) absent any other impeding force. How then does one explain why an object might move circularly, such as the moon orbiting the Earth? The motion can be explained by the Earth's gravitational pull *inward*, a constant tugging toward the center, called a centripetal force. Such forces must be balanced: if the Earth's force were too great, the moon would simply be drawn toward the Earth and collide with it. The moon's own velocity must be strong enough to be in balanced tension with the Earth's gravity: fast enough to sustain the motion around the Earth without succumbing to the centripetal pull but not so fast such that it would escape the orbital trajectory. If one imagines swinging a tennis ball attached to a string around one's head like a lasso, one would have to continually pull inward (the centripetal force) to sustain the movement. Cut the string, though, and the tennis ball would fly off (at an angle perpendicular to the centripetal force). While in its orbit, this shape, this velocity is round, repetitive. It is wrought from the tension between opening up—pulling away—and drawing together. Circular velocity needs a certain amount of dilation (distance) from the center to be sustained.

To bring this model back to the play, the circular movement must be held in moderated, balanced tension. It otherwise threatens to collapse or to spiral out of control. I suggest that the centripetal force that keeps drawing Antiochus, Titus, and Bérénice together is a type of polyamorous attachment that pulls them together and allows the circular motion to be perpetually sustained—until the string is "cut," or when the hypothetical, deferred marriage is finally called off.

Dilation, Delay, Desire

The rhetoric of dilation, both in Renaissance literature and Derridean thought, can help us understand the ways that temporality and sexuality are intertwined, and this paradigmatic figure allows us to reconsider certain paradoxes of the play. Derrida insists on *différance* in French as operating as both a word and as a concept. Instead of providing a definition, he traces the movement of différance by way of semantic analysis, to bring to light the plurality of meanings that différance enacts.

> The Greek *diapherein* does not comport one of the two motifs of the Latin *differre*, to wit, the action of putting off until later, of taking into account, of taking account of time and of the forces of an operation that implies an economical calculation, a detour, a delay, a relay, a reserve, a representation—concepts that I would summarize here in a word I have never used but that could be inscribed in this chain: temporization.[15]

We are familiar with différance's role in structuralist meaning, how the sign signifies as it indicates its difference from what it is not (what is not there but what is not it). Différance also works temporally, since it defers meaning's presence. But Derrida also highlights the necessity of mediation (temporizing); instead of the intensity of immediacy, the added element of time (deferral) moderates and neutralizes meaning's arrival. Even as Derrida drums up the word "temporization" to describe the arrival of meaning, he also *performs* temporization. "I would summarize here in a word" enacts a forward pointing that heightens the anticipation of the word's arrival, but instead of actually receiving the word, the reader is whiplashed from the near future to the past ("a word I have never used"). From this backward glance we then move to the conditional future ("that could be inscribed"). In this linguistic performance of temporization, Derrida's writing simultaneously incites and dampens desire; the reader might increasingly desire the word's revelation while also growing impatient with the wordplay, toggling back and forth between anticipation and loss, boredom and desire. Derrida continues:

> *Différer* in this sense is to temporize, to take recourse, consciously or unconsciously, in the temporal and temporizing mediation of a detour that suspends the accomplishment or fulfillment of "desire" or "will," and equally effects this suspension in a mode that annuls or tempers its own effect . . . this temporization is also a temporalization and spacing, the becoming-time of space and the becoming-space of time, the "originary constitution" of time and space.[16]

Meaning is thus always *mediated*. Returning to our query regarding the "superfluity" of the additional character of Antiochus, we might keep in mind that "to temper" also has the connotation of adding something to moderate, dilute, or even neutralize the extremes.

Derrida enacts and describes a balanced tension (between the possible yet to come and that which is possibly foreclosed): will he reveal the word (that he has never used, that he could use) or will the word's pronouncement fall short of our anticipation? A similar rhetorical moderation mixed with affects of desire and anticipation appears in the tragedy, specifically in the figure of Antiochus. The addition of Antiochus as a neutral third, to moderate or mediate, is indeed the operative key that enables the whole dilatory operation of circular velocity. While Racine inaugurates his play with Titus's tragic acceptance of his duty to banish his beloved—a simple story of a tragic twosome—once Racine "tempers" the play by adding Antiochus to the simplicity of the duo, we cannot fully anticipate how Titus's love for Antiochus or Antiochus's love for Bérénice will alter the anticipated politically normative action. One aspect that Derrida highlights here is the "becoming-time of space and the becoming-space of time." While the previous chapters have considered the affordances of queer velocity (in fostering new kinds of temporal sensations and intensities), here I make an argument for a spatialized, dilatory aspect of queer velocity as well.

Such spatialization is elucidated by Parker in her "Deferral, Dilation, Différance," and in her seminal study *Literary Fat Ladies* she adds a gendered (third) supplement to the spatial and temporal "spacing" inherent in différance. She argues that the relationships between delay, gender, and rhetorical excess coincide in the Renaissance figure of dilation:

> Derrida's punning "différance" is silent on this third term from that single Latin root, that of *dilatio* or dilation, which in the Renaissance usage in its verbal form meant not only to expand,

> disperse, or spread abroad, but also to put off, postpone, prolong, or protract—meanings that still linger in the modern English "dilatory." But it is, as we shall see, this particular term for the combination of temporal deferral and spatial extension which crucially defines the self-reflexive strategies of a wide range of Renaissance texts, in which "dilation" as delay functions as a kind of semantic crossroads, a complex in which constructs rhetorical and narrative, philosophical and theological, judicial and erotic overlap as figures for the space and time of the text itself.[17]

Parker's work highlights the spatial and sexual dimension of the Latin *differe*, which she relates to but distinguishes from Derrida's différance. Parker reads the Renaissance concern with dilation and delay as "finally caught within the horizon of a telos or ending, however tentatively or self-consciously construed," whereas she reads Derrida's différance as being potentially and productively unlimited.[18] The Renaissance context in which Parker reads dilation requires some sort of eschatological horizon, or an end, against which or in sight of which writings struggle, desire, and turn away.

Parker associates the figure of dilation with the "literary fat lady." While not necessarily physically large, this figuratively fat lady highlights the role that phobias, objectifications, and anxieties over feminine excess plays in Renaissance texts. Parker remarks on the gendered and geographical associations of excessive speech:

> This tradition of rhetorical *dilatio*—with references to the "swelling" style or its relation to the verbal "interlarding" produced through an excessive application of the principle of "increase" provides its own link between fat bodies and "discoursing at large" . . . Ascham's *Schoolmaster* treats of the use of "epitome" in reducing the inflated bulk of an oration through the example of the need to put an "overfat" and "fleshy" style on a diet.[19]

This literary fat lady might be represented in a variety of largenesses: as excessive female speech, the manipulative temporality of feminine coquettish delay, or even the unfillable space of unsatiated feminine desire. The supposed "pithiness" of Ascham's epitome, or example, stands as a "point" that would bring a meandering, repetitive discourse to a close. While literal fatness is not present in the text, there is, analogously, an anxiety about corporeality, progeniture, and generational increase.

Racine's play strictly follows the classical ideals of the bienséances and the règles classiques discussed in chapter 1. In his tragedies blood and death are so fully and completely banished from the stage that one could say that the tragedy turns not around embodiment but around a glaring absence of embodiment. Mitchell Greenberg, also taking up Racine's aphorism "Toute l'invention consiste à faire quelque chose de rien" (All invention is making something out of nothing) suggests that the site of this "rien" indicates an unrepresentable, even obscene excess:

> By eliminating death as a necessity for his tragedy, Racine shifts the locus of tragic intensity from a culpable body, a body that is the site of sin, and places it in a noncernable "other space." The trace scenario shifts from the palpable, the tactile, the manipulable, from the thing, the body itself, and becomes rather a purely undefinable, ungraspable, absence: a no/thing, a *rien*. It is precisely this "no/thing" that Racine tells us, in his preface, that *Bérénice* represents.[20]

But, instead of thinking of *rien* (nothingness) as an allegorical placeholder for the body's banishment on the French neoclassical stage, on which the chreia or repetitive fluff could be embroidered, we need to consider the rhetorical strategies by which this *rien* is produced. The "feminine fatness" theorized by Parker is thus not necessarily corporeally present, but rather rhetorically, temporally, and abstractly evoked in its very absence: as a type of abyss or ample emptiness.

Against the comparatively streamlined speech of a sovereign declaration, *Bérénice* is characterized by inflated, excessive speech, present in hyperbole as well as in repetition. At the play's end, Bérénice threatens suicide faced with Titus's abandonment. Antiochus also entertains the thought of ending his life, and Titus yearns to abandon the throne in favor of loving Bérénice. In the final act Titus gives a speech that reveals his indecision. While he had previously confirmed to others that he would send Bérénice away, here he tries to take back his declaration:

> Oui, Madame. Et je dois moins encore vous dire
> Que je suis prêt pour vous d'abandonner l'empire,
> De vous suivre, et d'aller trop content de mes fers
> Soupirer avec vous au bout de l'univers.
> Vous-même rougiriez de ma lâche conduite
> Vous verriez à regret marcher à votre suite

Un indigne empereur sans empire, sans cour
Vil spectacle aux humains des faiblesses d'amour. (5.6.1399–406)

(And, madam, even less should I declare
That I'm prepared to give the Empire up
And follow you, contented in my chains,
To sigh my life away at the world's end.
You'd blush yourself at such a craven course.
You'd rue the sight, among your followers,
Of a base emperor, without court or power,
Vile spectacle of the slavery of love.)

In this instance Titus paints himself as weak and felled by emotion, but he also uses this "fat" style of overrepetition, fixating at length on the fact that he is ready to abdicate his position simply to trail after Bérénice forever. The citation above is only a seven-line sample of a sixty-line monologue in which he expresses much the same sentiment. This excess, overall, proves too much for Bérénice:

Arrêtez. Arrêtez. Princes trop généreux
En quelle extrémité me jetez-vous tous deux!
Soit que je vous regarde, ou que je l'envisage,
Partout du désespoir je rencontre l'image.
Je ne vois que des pleurs. Et je n'entends parler
Que de trouble, d'horreurs, de sang prêt à couler. (5.7.1469–74)

(Stop, all too generous princes, stop.
In what a plight you cast me, both of you!
Whether I look at you, or else at him,
The image of despair is all I see.
I see only weeping. And I hear no word
That's not of pain and blood that must be shed.)

Bérénice's final speech, punctured by the brusque "Arrêtez," is given in a comparatively shorter, cleaner style than that of Titus's romantic ramblings.

Parker reminds us that Ascham prescribes a lean and spare epitome to cut the "fat" of overly repetitive style. Indeed, epitome can be thought of as the most exemplary example, a condensation in miniature of everything that the ideal could encompass. Notably, the very word "example" itself brings the drama, almost abruptly, to a close:

Je l'aime, je le fuis. Titus m'aime, il me quitte.
Portez loin de mes yeux vos soupirs, et vos fers.
Adieu, servons tous trois d'exemple à l'univers
De l'amour la plus tendre, et la plus malheureuse,
Dont il puisse garder l'histoire douloureuse. (5.7.1500–504)

(I love and flee him; he loves and leaves me.
Take far from my eyes your sighing and your swords.
Farewell, we three shall serve as an example to the world
Of the most tender and unhappy love
That it could bear the doleful history of.)

Example here counteracts the circular nature of dilation (its repetitions and hyperboles) by compressing it to a pithy point, a condensed kernel that is imitated by future generations to come. Temporally, there is a proleptic futurity associated with example. Plotted as such on a linear, pedagogically progressive trajectory, it marks a definitive exit from the dilatory, circular temporality of love, delay, and sorrow that the three had indulged in earlier.

Racine justified his take on Bérénice via an analogy to the tale of Dido and Aeneas but this very tale, founded on the myth of Aeneas's detour, also points to a discord between temporal economies: a system of sovereign progress pitted against that of seductive dalliance. Paulin, Titus's advisor, draws on a similar history of female temptresses to illustrate his point that Titus can no longer put off his repudiation of Bérénice:

Jules, qui le premier la soumit à ses armes,
Qui fit taire les lois dans le bruit des alarmes,
Brûla pour Cléopatre, et sans se déclarer,
Seule dans l'Orient la laissa soupirer
Antoine qui l'aima jusqu'à l'idolâtrie
Oublia dans son sein sa gloire et sa patrie
Sans oser toutefois se nommer son époux
Rome l'alla chercher jusques à ses genoux
Et ne désarma point sa fureur vengeresse
Qu'elle n'eût accablé l'amant et la maîtresse. (2.2.387–97)

(Julius, who first curbed their power by force,
And drowned out law with noise of his alarms,
Burned for Cleopatra, but said nothing,
And let her languish in the East alone.

Antony, who loved her to idolatry
Forgetting home and duty in her arms,
Still never dared to name himself her spouse.
Rome sought him out and brought him to his knees
And did not slacken her revengeful rage
Until she [Rome] had secured both lovers' deaths.)

Paulin here points to the dangers of such romantic delay, since it numbs and neuters the force of sovereignty, whether through the silencing of laws or the forgetting of obligations. Paulin and others are preoccupied with managing delay, or what Parker calls the "narrative topos of overcoming a female enchantress or obstacle on route to completion and ending,"[21] revealing that such slowness represents not just a simple detour but also a political threat. And yet, even in Paulin's warnings, we can see that while the specter of "female enchantresses" are meant to serve a cautionary tale, the experience of delay and silence is transformed from political peril to sexualized enjoyment.[22]

Finally, let us pause over the tragedy's most prominent figure of dilatory temporality: frozenness and ballooning silence. When the play's first line, "Arrêtons un moment," is spoken by Antiochus, we are launched into a paradoxical temporality, where the beginning is that of stasis, or rather the beginning of an extended, staged paralysis. We can compare Antiochus's frozen paralysis with other moments that forestall the instant of departure. Despite having already made his decision, Titus cannot find the language or even the force to abide by the rules of sovereign conduct expected of him:

Résolu d'accomplir ce cruel sacrifice
J'y voulus préparer la triste Bérénice.
Mais par où commencer?
Vingt fois depuis huit jours,
J'ai voulu devant elle en ouvrir le discours,
Et dès le premier mot ma langue embarrassée
Dans ma bouche vingt fois a demeuré glacée. (2.2.471–76)

(Resolved to make this cruel sacrifice,
I knew I must prepare sad Berenice.
But how to start? This week, a score of times,
I've planned to start talking about it before her
And at the first word my encumbered tongue
A score of times has frozen in my mouth.)

In this sense "opening" the dialogue ("ouvrir le discours"), another form of dilation, is impeded by Titus's "langue embarrassée." Roland Barthes remarks, "and we know to what degree the voice is sexualized in the Racinian theatre, and singularly in Bérénice, the tragedy of aphasia."[23] The sexualized double entendre of the tongue's impotence is underscored by the organ's inability to "open" discourse because of its frozen immobility.

The erotics of struggling to speak allows us, however, another angle onto the temporality of aphasia. Barthes's characterization of this speechlessness as tragedy orients the stalled velocity toward a particular end: success is in speech, and inarticulacy is tragic. And yet, paradoxically, all three seek to sustain the aphasia, for the nonspeech itself affords a range of sensations and feelings *not* directed to the "end" of speech. The aphasia itself can be experienced as erotic, and this temporality of not speaking, or waiting for speech, can itself be its own queer "end." Therefore, similar to Andromaque's deployment of silence, silence itself is not merely a refusal to engage with the terms laid out. Once we bracket the expected "ends" of how a sovereign or wife should act, we can see other kinds of directional ends and intentions emerge—such as how this silence *also* sustains and nourishes their three-way relationship.

Silence is essential to this trio for many unexpected reasons; it is not necessarily always experienced as explicitly tragic. Antiochus's own proximity to his beloved Bérénice is predicated on five years of commanded silence:

> Votre bouche à la mienne ordonna de se taire
> Je disputai longtemps, je fis parler mes yeux.
> Mes pleurs et mes soupirs vous suivaient en tous lieux.
> Enfin votre rigueur emporta la balance,
> Vous sûtes m'imposer l'exil, ou le silence[.] (1.4.200–204)
>
> (Your mouth commanded silence from my own.
> I made my eyes my voice and fought you long
> My tears pursued you everywhere you went
> You steeled yourself at last: you knew
> Silence or banishment must be my lot[.])

Whereas Titus attempts to open discourse by dilating his frozen-shut mouth, Antiochus gives an account of mouths being silenced by pressed-together lips (with all the erotic implications of the proximity of "votre bouche à la mienne" [your mouth to mine]). In response to this bodily closure, Antiochus struggles against the excess leakages of tears, sighs, and gazes that he cannot contain. And yet, more than experiencing silence as a limitation or aphasia, Antiochus seems to perform his desiring body, and staging his suffering under the imposed silence in a quasi-eroticized masochism. His eyes, tears, and sighs are all part of this mise-en-scène. For five years, he has dared not defy his mistress's command, instead suppressing his desires and sustaining an obedience to her word. As Deleuze suggests in *Coldness and Cruelty*, "waiting and suspense are the essential characteristics of the masochistic experience,"[24] and thus perhaps it is not the pain (of her cruel rejection, or of losing her to Titus) that is at stake, but rather the dilated, anticipatory time *prior* that Antiochus desires. Although Bérénice has already left for Rome, Antiochus's deliciously suspended state of desire, unspeakable and unfulfillable, means that he can only retrace again and again the path of their history together: "Je demeurai longtemps errant dans Césarée, / Lieux charmants, où mon coeur vous avait adorée. / Je vous demandais à vos tristes États, / Je cherchais en pleurant les traces de vos pas" (What long months I wore out in Caesarea, / Among the dear scenes of my love for you. / Again I sought you in your sad domains, / I searched in tears the places where you'd trod [1.4.235–39]). The postponement of erotic fulfilment only heightens his desire to see and speak, and to be either reciprocated or rejected. At the same time, the lengthy wait time only seems to amplify not only his longing but also his seeking of further temporal suspension and incompletion: "Exemple infortuné d'une longue constance / Après cinq ans d'amour, et d'espoir superflus / Je pars, fidèle encore quand je n'espère plus" (I, hapless figure of long constancy / After five years of futile love and hope / Must part, still faithful though I hope no more [1.2.44–46]).

Silence, for Antiochus and Titus, is both an obstacle and a desire: they draw on silence in a way that eroticizes the delay itself. Both seek to "open" (mouths, discourse), but it is not actual speech that they seek, but rather the anticipatory temporality of *waiting* to puncture the silence that they cultivate and develop. When Titus describes the delay that such silence engenders—"Ma bouche, et mes regards muets depuis huit jours / L'auront pu préparer à ce triste discours" (My silent lips, and looks, these eight days past, / Will have prepared her for these sorry words [3.1.737–38])—he refers to his silence by describing his tongue, mouth, and eyes, giving a sensuous, sexualized corporeality to his experience of this imposed delay. Similarly, in the scene in which Antiochus is meant to reveal to Bérénice the cause of Titus's silence, her desperate demands to be satisfied aurally have palpable sexual undercurrents: "Et vos refus cruels, loin d'épargner ma peine / Excitent ma douleur, ma colère, ma haine" (And your cruel refusals, far from sparing me, / Excite my grief, my anger, and my hate [3.3.875–76]). Antiochus's silence, delaying the moment of truth, does not neutralize or numb, but rather arouses her emotions. Finally, when Antiochus agrees to divulge Titus's news, he says: "Madame, après cela je ne puis plus me taire / Hé bien, vous le voulez, il faut vous satisfaire / . . . Je connais votre cœur. Vous devez vous attendre / Que je vais le frapper par l'endroit le plus tendre" (Madam, after this I must speak at last. / You wish it, and you must be satisfied. / . . . I know your heart. You must expect from me / Blows that will strike where it is tenderest [3.3.887–88; 3.3.891–92]). The innuendo of "satisfying" Bérénice's desire to know, and the revelation of knowledge—the end of the delay—are framed in terms of striking a tender spot, the sexual overtones of which cannot be ignored.

In response to Villars's critique that "nothing" happens, once we understand the temporal dynamics that sustain and amplify this appearance of nothingness, we see characters resort to repetitive, emotionally overflowing speech, akin to the copia. Silence and other figures of frozenness and delay point to the dilation of narrative time, and the strategies to detour or deviate from the plot's telos. I contend that this "nothingness" appears not as the plain lack of action, but rather as the accumulation of activities and affects stemming from delay: anxieties about delay or discoursing over delay's imagined future effects. This type of pleasure deriving from stalling reveals the sexual and political implications of dilatory time. Just as in physics the circular velocity requires a balanced tension to perpetually self-renew, dilation in *Bérénice* is necessarily balanced against restraining figures that I identify: the aforementioned "point"—as in Ascham's imagined end point of the long dilatory delays or the pithy kernel puncturing the fattened rhetoric.

Enter the Hymen, Between

Parker reminds us of another figure of dilation: a "wall" or partition that paradoxically subdivides the text (multiplying it into "members") while also producing (and controlling) increase.[25] The puncturing "point" and dividing wall, the temporality of romantic completion and that of erotic delay, and their relationship to the dilatory female body all converge in the figure of the *hymen*. The hymen, in Renaissance discourse as well as in early modern French, indicated both "marriage" and the "invisible yet fetishized part of the female body."[26] As Margaret Ferguson notes in "Hymeneal Instruction," a deep ambiguity surrounding the hymen itself existed in the Renaissance worldview: "the absence of either medical or theological certainty or even the existence of the hymen as a material phenomenon" provoked a proliferation of instructional literature speculating on "different possible meanings of the hymen, as a word, as a concept, and as an element in the rituals and legitimation of a much debated social institution."[27] The membranous quality of the hymen, in its veiled undecidability (visible and yet obscuring), illuminates my reading of ambiguous eroticism and competing temporal economies in *Bérénice*.

The hymen is simultaneously both abstracted and singularized in the drama. At varying points, it becomes yoked to a temporality either of completion or of reinauguration. The hymen, as rupture—as the literal referent of the broken-off engagement or the foreclosed future marriage, stands as the prosthetic affirmation of Titus's glory and place as sovereign; thus the rupturing hymen underscores his ability to sacrifice his desiring, mortal body to the law of the State. The hymen, as marital unity, in an opposite sense, would crown of years of preceding love as the apotheosis of a long relation between Titus and Bérénice. For Antiochus, the hymen could close the suspended time of waiting, a definitive end to years of yearning for Bérénice and watching Titus from afar. To add to the confusion, the uses of the hymen are also inconsistent, ambivalent, and ambiguous: where in one act the broken hymen signaled Titus's decisiveness and sovereign strength, later in the play, after Titus has already told Bérénice she must leave, he is so stricken by the sight of her tears that he promises her, "Par un heureux hymen je tarisse vos larmes" (I mean to dry your tears with a happy hymen [5.6.1392]). He holds out the hymen as the possibility of a fresh start, circling back to the prelapsarian moment when the ambiguous, dilatory eroticism could be sustained.

The hymen, Derrida suggests, is a figure that inscribes différance within itself. Derrida writes that the hymen confuses the temporality of desire with the temporality of desire's accomplishment. It confounds the will have been (the future anterior of marital union) with the yet to be (the still untouched virginity), since in fulfilment (*accomplissement*) of the marriage hymen, the membrane hymen ceases to exist:

the existence of hymen confuses before and after, prior and posterior. For this reason, Derrida links the hymen with the *pli* (the fold).[28] This folded time might be thought of as a queer velocity, since the hymen posits an end that is both deferred and desired, and temporality becomes circular, spiraling, and curling back on itself.

Derrida reminds us of the double sense of the word *hymen* in French: the nuptial union and the virginal membrane that is torn. It is in fact *entre* (between) both in the sense of being the marriage between two spouses and the tissue between the two vaginal walls, as well as being aurally "between" two meanings. In the sound of the word one can also hear the word *antre*, which in French indicates a "an empty, hollow, concave space in the form of a vault,"[29] resonating with Parker's "bignesse" of the dilatory space.[30]

Fittingly, the play takes place in a very hymeneal space: a "cabinet" or an antechamber between the queen's bedroom and Titus's:

> Souvent ce cabinet superbe et solitaire
> Des secrets de Titus est le dépositaire
> C'est ici quelquefois qu'il se cache à sa cour,
> Lorsqu'il vient à la reine expliquer son amour.
> De son appartement cette porte est prochaine
> Et cette autre conduit dans celui de la reine. (1.1.3–8)
>
> (This proud and private chamber often guards
> The secrets of the Emperor himself.
> Here Titus can seek refuge from his court,
> And come to confess his love for Berenice.
> His own apartment lies beyond that door,
> While this door here gives access to the queen's.)

The *antre* of the space of this chamber (the sole setting of the entire play) literalizes and redoubles the "entre" ambiguity of the hymen. Such a room, an empty space like Derrida's *antre*, is a neutral, apolitical space separated from the activities of the court. This "cabinet" is the passage between ("entre") Titus's and Bérénice's rooms while remaining distinct from (and prior to) the bedroom. Such a tense division is highlighted in a scene where Bérénice, confronted with Titus's rejection, threatens suicide, but her crisis occurs at the same time that the Senate demands to speak to Titus. The birfurcation of Titus's duties pulling him between his lover's desires and the Senate's demands is evidenced in the line's split *hémistiches* (six-syllable halves):

PAULIN: Venez, Seigneur, passons dans la chambre prochaine.
Allons voir le Sénat
ANTIOCHUS: Ah! Courez chez la reine. (4.8.1247–48)

(PAULIN: Come, sir, let's pass into the other room.
Let's see the Senate
ANTIOCHUS: Ah! Hasten to the queen.)

This *entre* and *antre* of the cabinet carves out a zone that is neither public nor private, but still divided between the two.

As such, the hymen stands as the marker of the convergence of two distinct bodies. We might think of the ways in which marriage (hymen) signals the merging of spouses, or in terms of the other, physical hymen, it denotes the unified, intact membrane. But the hymen also stands for difference, in the mark of hymenal rupture in the sexual act, or the corporeal hymen's dividing "wall" between the inside (*antre*) and outside. In other words, one could think of the hymen as materializing and temporalizing différance itself. Derrida writes that the hymen itself plays on the *entre*," verbalizing the noun, to highlight not only the sexual act of "entering" but also the imperative of *entre* (as in to bid someone to enter a room). The hymen effectively performs a multiplicity of *entre*, remaining undecided and "between" dialectically opposed meanings:

> The hymen, the consummation of differends, the continuity and confusion of the coitus, merges with what it seems to be derived from the hymen as a protective screen, the jewel box of virginity, vaginal partition, the fine, invisible veil which, in front of the hysteria (*l'hystère*), stands *between* (*entre*) the inside and the outside of the woman, consequently between desire and desire's fulfillment. It is neither desire nor pleasure, but between the two. Neither future nor present, but between the two.[31]

The hymen figures in multiple instances throughout the play, and while it is used most specifically, and literally, to mean "marriage," the characters still refer to a plurality of significations that the word holds.

Derrida often employs *voile* (veil) as another euphemism or punning play on the membranous hymen (a corporeal, virginal veil), or the synecdoche of the hymen as marriage (a wedding veil). In the play the word "voile" is referred to indirectly through the name Bérénice. Saint Veronica (the latinized version of Bérénice) is associated with the miracle of her veil, which purportedly became imprinted with the image of Jesus's face after he wiped his sweat with her offered cloth; such imprinting and duplication might be thought of as yet another fold. The *voile* becomes a literalized metaphor for the hymen. After Antiochus reveals to Bérénice that Titus intends to call off the marriage (hymen), the verb employed is "séparer": "qu'à jamais l'un de l'autre il faut vous séparer" (That you and he must separate forever [3.3.894]), says Antiochus reluctantly. Bérénice's exclaims in disbelief, "Nous séparer? Qui? Moi? Titus de Bérénice!" (Separate? Who? [Me?] Titus from Berenice? [3.3.895]), which enacts this separation textually, beginning with the unity of the "nous" and then literally splitting the couple into individual names at the end of the alexandrine line.

Veils appear again as a figuration of the marriage or hymen later in the play. After Bérénice, in disbelief, sends her friend Phénice to summon Titus to her, Phénice tries to calm Bérénice and prepare her for Titus's visit: "Remettez-vous, Madame, et rentrez en vous-même. / Laissez-moi relever ces voiles détachés" (Calm yourself, Madam, and regain your poise. / Let me arrange these sundered veils for you [4.2.969–70]). Bérénice refuses to fix her torn veils, saying, "Laisse, laisse, Phénice, il verra son ouvrage" (Let it alone, he'll see his handiwork [4.3.972]), implying that Titus must be made to reckon with the multiple kinds of ruptures that he has wrought. The detached veils literalize Bérénice's emotional disarray and symbolically evokes both the broken-off nuptials and the separation of a detached bodily hymen (or deflowering). The future, anticipated marriage will not have been held, but Bérénice is always already detached from and attached to Titus. We are again presented with an in between, even paradoxical temporality of not yet and too late.

In the ambiguity of the word *hymen* in French, the hymen poses both a temporal and spatial confusion. Its betweenness is not innocent; in fact, it is the evidence of (non)violence, of pending rupture (since the physical hymen is torn in the marital union of hymen). Derrida writes:

> It's the hymen that desire dreams of piercing, of bursting, in an act of violence that is (at the same time or somewhere between) love and murder. If one or the other were to take place, there would be no hymen. But neither would there simply be a hymen in (case events go) no place. With all the undecidability of its meaning, the hymen only takes place when it doesn't take place, when nothing really happens, when there is an all-consuming

> consummation without violence, or violence without a hit, or a hit without a mark, a mark without a mark (a margin), etc., when the veil is, without being torn.[32]

For Derrida the dissolution of the hymen is the fulfillment of the hymen. It seems that *Bérénice* offers the tragic version of the same—the bloodless rupture, or the "consummation without violence, or violence without a hit." Bérénice herself must depart, in a soft non-rupture, before the actual rupture/link of the hymen as marriage can take place.

The hymen stands as both *pli* and *accomplissement* (fold and fulfilment, respectively). In the dilatory, cyclical temporality of the play, the hymen reappears again and again, like a refrain. Each repetition or fold adds new importance to the multiple meanings of the word itself—that it could be both rupture and jouissance, fair compensation, and token of sovereign glory. In all the hymen's meanings, from mundane to sublime, what is staged is not the majestic sovereign decision of Bérénice's repudiation, but rather the gentle pathos of foreclosed pleasures, or the sorrows of undecidable, sustained time.

The Impossible Threesome and Veil of Friendship

The presence of frozen eroticized delay, the dilatory temporality of the paradoxical rupture or fulfilment of the hymen highlight what I have been calling circular velocities in *Bérénice*—the kinds of velocities that "go" nowhere yet require great force, energy, and attention to maintain in balanced tension. But what kinds of sexual dynamics are specifically enabled by this? The "voile" (veil) in this play, as a metaphor and synecdoche for the hymen, is sometimes employed to indicate the hymen (in all its sexual connotations). In this section I explore the opposite connotation of the veil: asexuality, or neutrality. Antiochus refers to a "voile d'amitié" (veil of friendship) indicating the neutral (and neutered) cover of friendship that he uses to cloak his true affections and remain close to both Bérénice and Titus. In his opening monologue, he says, "Je me suis tu cinq ans. Et jusques à ce jour / D'un voile d'amitié j'ai couvert mon amour" (Five years I have been silent—and till now / The veil of friendship has disguised my love [1.1.25–26]). I propose that this act of neutering or veiling makes the dynamics of substitution, sublimation, and circulation (the circular velocities) between the three possible in the first place.

Since Titus's father's death and his subsequent ascension to the imperial throne, Titus has been in mourning for eight days, but he still refuses to make a pronouncement about his marriage to Bérénice. Given Titus's ambiguous silence during his period of grief, we enter the story from Antiochus's perspective. Antiochus wants to see Bérénice, intending to confess his love to her, and then leave immediately afterward, saying, "Sur son hymen j'attends qu'elle s'explique" (I'm waiting to hear how she explains this marriage [1.3.127]). His friend and confidant Arsace is surprised by Antiochus's desire to flee. Arsace says:

> Je suis surpris sans doute, et c'est avec justice.
> Quoi depuis si longtemps la Reine Bérénice
> Vous arrache, Seigneur, du sein de vos États,
> Depuis trois ans dans Rome elle arrête vos pas,
> Et lorsque cette reine assurant sa conquête
> Vous attend pour témoin de cette illustre fête,
> Quand l'amoureux Titus devenant son époux,
> Lui prépare un éclat qui rejaillit sur vous . . . (1.3.79–86)[33]

> (I am astonished, sir, and with good cause.
> What? When Queen Berenice so long ago
> Removed you from the bosom of your lands;
> When she has stilled your steps three years in Rome;
> And when this queen, now, triumphing in love,
> Waits for you as witness to this noble rite,
> When adoring Titus, becoming her groom,
> Gives her a shine [burst of glory] that splashes back on you . . .

Arsace points to the dilatory time that Antiochus has spent, lingering in Rome away from his own kingdom. At the same time, this ballooning, "dilated" temporality allows the dynamic between the three characters to flourish in an odd way; Bérénice and Titus can't simply be together, and Antiochus, as the superfluous third, can't simply depart. She asks Antiochus to be present as the "témoin" (witness) to her union, as a reflection of her attachment to Antiochus, and Antiochus's presence at the marriage erupts in an "éclat qui rejaillit sur vous" (shine [burst of glory] that splashes back on you), replete with erotic connotations.[34] To apply a contemporary model to this triadic dynamic discussed in this chapter, we might consider the three characters—Bérénice, Titus, and Antiochus—to be entwined in a polyamorous trio. As alluded to earlier, circular velocity is only made possible through a balanced tension between the moving object's trajectory and the centripetal force. The "gravity" that draws the three central characters of *Bérénice* in a circular orbit together is their triangulated threesome.

One might ask why Antiochus, the king of Comagène, would ignore his own kingdom for so long. Antiochus's long-enduring love for Bérénice seems to be one component of his own extended stay. But another bond may be his loving admiration for and jealous rivalry with Titus, which are all magnetic affects that draw him to remain in Rome. Antiochus recounts how he was initially the main contender for Bérénice's hand, yet Bérénice ultimately chose Titus over him:

> Madame, il vous souvient que mon coeur en ces lieux
> Reçut le premier trait qui partit de vos yeux
> J'aimai, j'obtins l'aveu d'Agrippa votre frère.
> Il vous parla pour moi. Peut-être sans colère
> Alliez-vous de mon coeur recevoir le tribut. (1.4.189–93)
>
> (Madam, you will recall in those lands too
> My heart received the dart of your first glance.
> I loved—your brother gave me his consent.
> He spoke to you for me. And without anger perhaps
> You would have borne the tribute of my heart.)

Antiochus participates in traditional homosocial "traffic in women,"[35] as Gayle Rubin puts it, by asking Bérénice's brother for her hand, rendering love and marriage secondary to soldering ties between the patriarchal forces (fathers, brothers, male suitors) who circulate the women between their households. Mapping such a romantic alliance, such as asking permission, requiring a familial go-between, or receiving the bride, posits a certain kind of normative temporality to that desire, one that would progress by certain steps and finally come to fruition with Bérénice's receipt of Antiochus's tribute.

Titus's arrival marks a swerve from the planned betrothal between Antiochus and Bérénice and sets into motion a different type of affective temporality. Antiochus reminisces:

> Titus, pour mon malheur, vint, vous vit, et vous plut.
> Il parut devant vous dans tout l'éclat d'un homme
> Qui porte entre ses mains la vengeance de Rome.
> La Judée en pâlit. Le triste Antiochus
> Se compta le premier au nombre des vaincus. (1.4.194–98)

(But Titus, to my grief, came, saw, and pleased you.
He stood before you with the force of a man
Who held all Roman vengeance in his hands.
Judea grew pale. The wan Antiochus
Of all the vanquished knew himself the first.)

What is interesting here, however, is that Antiochus is neither resentful nor bitter. Titus is presented in terms of glorious, virile masculinity, underscored by the vibrating "v" in the first line. In the phrase "dans tout l'éclat d'un homme," "l'éclat" here replicates the near-sexual "éclat" in the gushing "burst of glory" that Antiochus referenced in the earlier scene. The spectacle of virility transforms, in the following line, into the dilatory openness of "u" and "ou" vowels ("parut," "vous," "tout"). Struck by the magnificence of this vision, "La Judée en pâlit" (Judea grew pale) taking the synecdochal country, also coincidentally gendered feminine, to condense both the country's colonized submission with Bérénice's romantic ravishment. Thus far this narrative seems to adhere to the stereotype of an exoticized feminine Other falling prey to the virile spectacle of the masculine dominating country. Yet, what is most intriguing about this tale is that Antiochus inserts himself into the story of seduction, counting himself among the vanquished. "Le triste Antiochus" (the wan Antiochus) shares the alexandrine line with "La Judée en pâlit" (Judaea grew pale), the two halves completing the unified line, and he puts himself "au nombre des vaincus" (of all the vanquished) merging with strange equivalences: the scene of seduction, vanquishment, and domination.

As Antiochus narrates his experience watching Titus seduce Bérénice, his memories emphasize his mixed emotions of jealousy and admiration, and the triangulation of his desire as he observes Titus. And it is indeed his affection for Titus that tempers what would have been jealous anger: "Inutiles périls! Quelle était mon erreur! / La valeur de Titus surpassait ma fureur. / Il faut qu'à sa vertu mon estime réponde" (What useless dangers! And how wrong I was! / Titus's valor far surpassed my own. / My esteem had to match his virtue [1.4.217–19]), implying that the spectacle of Titus's strength and virility could be responded to not with jealousy but rather with esteem or love. A dynamic of simple rivalry is transformed into a queer triangulation through this tempering. The excesses of Titus's glory and Antiochus's sadness are moderated by Antiochus's affection for Titus.

ANTIOCHUS: Chéri de l'Univers, enfin aimé de vous
Il semblait à lui seul appeler tous les coups
Tandis que sans espoir, haï, lassé de vivre
Son malheureux Rival ne semblait que le suivre
. . . .
Il dompta les Mutins, reste pâle et sanglant
Des flammes, de la faim, des fureurs intestines
Et laissa leurs Remparts cachés sous leurs ruines. (1.4.221–24, 1.4.230–32)

ANTIOCHUS: (Loved by the world, loved above all by you,
He seemed to draw all blows upon himself,
While hopeless, hated, weary of his life
His wretched rival could but follow him.
. . . .
Titus quelled those final rebels, bleeding, pale
From famine, flame, and internecine strife,
And left their ramparts crushed beneath their ruins.)

While Antiochus intends, in this scene, to convey his love to Bérénice, his whole speech is primarily about Titus and Titus's exploits. Antiochus places himself in the position of "suivre," which has the doubled connotation of coming in second place, trailing behind, but also closely following and observing. And this mixed vision of jealous admiration is highlighted in the narrative, where he takes on Bérénice's perspective and vision, imagining how bold, brave, and virile Titus must have appeared in her eyes as he quelled the Judean uprising.

Antiochus's vision of a conquering, virile Titus not only aligns his vision and admiration with that of Bérénice but also underscores his necessary position as neutral, or the "halfway between"—the "entre," in other words—that enables such triangulation. His jealous anger was tempered, but Antiochus *himself* becomes the figure of tempering, muting, and neutralizing that allows this dynamic triadic to persist for five years. To do so, a necessary neutrality is enacted, even performed, as a symbolic castration wherein Antiochus is ordered by Bérénice to silence his love: "Votre bouche à la mienne ordonna de se taire" (Your mouth commanded silence from my own [1.4.200]). Antiochus's position as a necessary third, then, underscores his capacity as *neutre* (which, we recall, in French means both neutral and neutered), deprived of voice and speech, both of which were sacrificed toward the (futile) goal of eventually winning Bérénice's love.

Bérénice needs to silence Antiochus to neutralize his love to friendship ("amitié"), thus enabling the dilation of triadic dynamics. Similarly, Titus also requires Antiochus to be a neutral (neutered) conduit of expression, both giving and receiving love, farewells, explanations, and more: "Et je veux seulement emprunter votre voix" (I only want you to lend me your voice [3.1.694]). Titus emphasizes that Antiochus's own voice and sentiments must be suppressed or neutered in order for Titus to use him as a conduit. This silencing both tempers (moderates) and temporalizes Antiochus's desire. Through silence, Antiochus can continue to remain under cover of the "voile d'amitié" (veil of friendship), a veil that allows an ambiguously indefinite circulation of emotion, replacement, and substitution: "Je me suis tu cinq ans. Et jusques à ce jour / D'un voile d'amitié j'ai couvert mon amour" (Five years I have silenced myself—and till now / The veil of friendship has disguised my love [1.1.25]). If we associate such imposed silence with the veil of friendship that Antiochus uses to remain in Rome, and keeping in mind that "veil" is another term Derrida uses to discuss the hymen, it is in silence's opposite—speech—that forces the rupture of the veil/hymen.[36] As Antiochus describes his desolation after Bérénice's departure from Caesarea (having left for Rome), we must not forget that it is not only Bérénice but also Titus who has left. Antiochus speaks of an empty loneliness, but it is sufficiently ambiguous whether he is mourning Bérénice's absence or the absence of both her and Titus, the rival whom he used to follow ("suivre"):

> Rome vous vit, Madame, arriver avec lui
> Dans l'Orient désert quel devint mon ennui
> Je demeurai longtemps errant dans Césarée
> Lieux charmants, où mon cœur vous avait adorée.
> Je vous redemandais à vos tristes États,
> Je cherchais en pleurant les traces de vos pas
> Mais enfin succombant à ma mélancolie,
> Mon désespoir tourna mes pas vers l'Italie.
> Le Sort m'y réservait le dernier de ses coups.
> Titus en m'embrassant m'amena devant vous.
> Un voile d'amitié vous trompa l'un et l'autre;
> Et mon amour devient le confident du vôtre. (1.4.233–44)
>
> (Rome, Madam, saw you enter in with him.
> Abandoned in the East, how deep my woe!
> What long months I wore out in Caesarea,
> Among the dear scenes of my love for you.

Again I sought you in your sad domains,
I searched in tears the places where you'd trod.
At last my sadness grew too great for me,
And in despair I turned my steps to Rome.
There fate reserved its final blow for me.
Titus, embracing me, led me to you.
A veil of friendship fooled both you and him;
My love became the confidant of yours.)

In this narrative, the "vous" is on the surface addressed to Bérénice, but there are strange doublings in which the "vous" might refer to them both. Antiochus refers to the "vous" in the plural: "vous trompa l'un et l'autre" and "mon amour devient le confident du vôtre" (A veil of friendship fooled both you and him; / My love became the confidant of yours). It is sufficiently ambiguous to suggest that he is seeking them both in the first two lines: "où mon Coeur vous avait adorée . . . je cherchais en pleurant les traces de vos pas" (Among the dear scenes of my love for you . . . Sobbing, I searched the places where you'd trod). What is interesting is that after so much waiting, seeking, and following, upon Antiochus's arrival in Italy, the first recounted action is Titus's embrace. And the three are able to be united together and to express their affection for one another because of this veil of friendship.

After Antiochus's confession, Bérénice's refusal of his love also takes on a strange rhetoric; instead of outright rejecting him, she begins to intertwine her feelings for him with her feelings for Titus:

À regret je reçois vos adieux.
Le ciel sait, qu'au milieu des honneurs qu'il m'envoie,
Je n'attendais que vous pour témoin de ma joie.
Avec tout l'Univers j'honorais vos vertus,
Titus vous chérissait, vous admiriez Titus.
Cent fois je me suis fait une douceur extrême
D'entretenir Titus dans un autre lui-même. (1.4.266–72)

(I hear your farewells with regret.
Amid the honors heaven has bestowed
I waited but for you to share my joy.
With all the world, I praised your qualities
Much loved by Titus, you admired him too.
It has been my delight, a hundred times,
To feel a second Titus spoke in you.)

As her speech continues, she braids together their three affections for each other ("honorais," "chérissait," "admiriez") culminating in a strange substitution: "Titus dans un autre lui-même" (a second Titus). After Antiochus's departure, Bérénice admits, "cette prompt retraite / me laisse, je l'avoue, une douleur secrète" (His sudden flight / Gives me, I must admit, some secret pain [1.5.287–88]), effectively mirroring Antiochus's earlier aside, "Je vois que vous cœur m'applaudit en secret / Je vois que l'on m'écoute avec moins de regret" (I see your heart applauds me secretly, / I see you hear my words with less regret [1.4.225–26]). While Bérénice does not elucidate why her own sorrow (or previous heart's applause) must be "secret" or hidden, it may gesture toward a deeper melancholia regarding the ungrievable, foreclosed types of sexualities and relationships that cannot be fully articulated. Perhaps Bérénice is alluding to a more obscure source of sadness, since that which has been lost, the ambiguously erotic tripartite dynamic, is itself difficult to name.

Bérénice fantasizes about Antiochus as a second Titus, but, before Antiochus can leave, Titus actually *asks* Antiochus to stand in for him, as Titus's double. Titus begins by asserting the strength of their three-way bond: "Elle ne voit dans Rome et n'écoute que vous. / Vous ne faites qu'un cœur et qu'une âme avec nous" (You are the only friend she has in Rome. / You are of one heart and one soul with us [3.1.697–98]). Because of this unification of heart and soul, Titus believes it is feasible to have Antiochus serve as his double. As Barthes observed, in *Bérénice* the act of speaking and the intimacy of serving as a *porte-parole* (spokesperson) become imbricated within an eroticized economy. Titus geographically replicates Antiochus's role as a vital passage or conduit between himself and Bérénice. He promises Antiochus land as a prize for his conduit action of carrying Titus's words to Bérénice. This recompense is, significantly, between ("*entre*") Antiochus's kingdom and Bérénice's:

Pour rendre vos États plus voisins l'un de l'autre
L'Euphrate bornera son Empire et le vôtre
Je sais que le Sénat tout plein de votre nom,
D'une commune voix confirmera ce don.
Je joins la Cilicie à votre Comagène. (3.1.764–67)

(To make your lands more neighbor to each other,
Euphrates shall be your two empires' bourn.
I know the Senate, ringing with your name,
Will ratify this gift with one accord.
I join Cilicia to your Comagene.)

In this description of land, geography becomes intimacy. With the river's common caress and jointly touching territory, land united together becomes a figural stand-in for the marriage ceremony. Thus, the gift of territory that is between "entre" materializes and literalizes the role of "entre" that Antiochus must serve, a betweenness that is *only* possible under the veil, or cover, of neutral friendship. This neutrality is precisely what allows Antiochus to be "hollowed out" and to take on the role of Titus's voice, Titus's adjunct, or another Titus ("un autre lui-même"). This evacuation can be thought of as representing another form of "antre"—the cavernous hollow. Antiochus, however, is not merely a convenient scapegoat for the duties that Titus shirks; there is a real dynamic and interdependency intertwining them. As Arsace observes of the trio: "Trois Sceptres, que son bras ne peut seul soutenir / Vos deux États voisins, qui cherchent à s'unir. / L'intérêt, la raison, l'amitié, tout vous lie" (Three scepters, that she cannot wield alone, / Your two states neighbors, longing to be one. / Interest, reason, friendship, bind her to you [3.2.825–27]).

Both Titus and Bérénice rely on Antiochus's presence to witness, speak, and substitute. Titus, before going into make his final declaration of love to Bérénice, requires Antiochus's presence: "Venez, Prince, venez, je vous ai fait chercher. / Soyez ici témoin de toute ma faiblesse. / Voyez si c'est aimer avec peu de tendresse. / Jugez nous" (Come, Prince, come, I sent to look for you; / Bear witness to my every weakness here. / See if I love with too scant tenderness. / Judge me [5.7.1426–29]). This witnessing is also demanded by Bérénice, when she is disappointed by the fact that Antiochus is leaving: "Je n'attendais que vous pour témoin de ma joie" (I waited but for you to [witness and] share my joy [1.4.268]). Titus, when asking Antiochus to speak on his behalf, begs him, "Soyez le seul témoin de ses pleurs, et des miens" (You be sole witness to her tears and mine [3.1.744]), a position of witnessing that, we recall, Bérénice hoped to place him in as well. *Témoin* ("witness"), Derrida reminds us, derives from *testis*, which gives us both "testimony" but also, in its root, indicates both *le tiers* ("the third") as well as testes.[37] Witnessing, or watching, or being made to watch becomes eroticized here. Antiochus is simultaneously neutered (reduced to a mere witness) and eroticized, but his vision becomes erotically charged precisely *because* he is neutered.

Scholarship on the play has largely ignored this polyamorous, triadic connection. Critics simplify the dynamic by minimizing Antiochus entirely or else by feminizing him, thus reducing *Bérénice* as a simple story about a dyad—the repudiation of the feminine Orient (symbolized by Bérénice and Antiochus) in favor of the masculine Occident (Titus), as Michèle Longino notes, an analysis that veers alarmingly close to reinforcing, not subverting, Orientalist stereotypes. Longino argues that Antiochus is "hardly a man by Western standards. Not only his hopeless love for Bérénice, but his compromised status as a man, make of him doubly a woman, and as such a strong signifier of the East for the West."[38] The Titus-Bérénice pair is consistently the primary analytic for simplicity's sake. Greenberg's analyses of the play drop Antiochus from the equation. He reads the repudiation as allegorical of the problematic of the king's two bodies and sees the rejection of the feminine (allegorized in the figure of Bérénice) as the victory of the king's body politic over the (desiring, lustful) body mortal.[39] This allegory hinges on a male-female binary by underscoring the "maternal" aspect of Bérénice and Titus's relationship, as well as the feminine Orient to which Bérénice is linked. Forgetting Antiochus or collapsing him on to the side of femininity is necessary for such a narrative binaristic duality to be enacted. These readings ignore the ways that Antiochus is, in fact, actively depended on not only by Titus but also by Bérénice as well as Antiochus's own desire for both of them. In terms of the play's action, Antiochus relays messages for and speaks on the behalf of one and the other. Far from having a merely mechanized function in the play, Antiochus, as tempering third, or neutral-neutered middle, or even as a necessary (sexualized) witness, prevents Titus from making a clean cut or announcing a definitive decision. In other words, as long as the gravitational pull of polyamorous love keeps everything in orbit and in balanced tension, nothing will spiral out of control.

The Hymen's Deixis

Much of the diegetic action of neutralizing, covering, or diminishing intensities in *Bérénice* neatly echo what Leo Spitzer has called Racine's classical *piano*, in which emotion reaches the apotheosis of its expression not through exaggeration or stress but, paradoxically, through that which is blurred, softened, or dulled. Spitzer suggests that the power and strength of Racine's poetry derives from his use of "distinguished restraint, of self-enclosure" akin to the dampening or "piano" pedal of the pianoforte, or the musical indication "*piano*" in Italian, meaning "softly quiet." For example, Titus's crisis is not necessarily dramatized according to a spectacularly glorious action or decision, but rather it is presented in the most minimal, even most dampened piano terms. The amount of energy and force it takes to restrain and soften a passionate cry *is* the measure of its pathos. The whisper becomes more powerful than the scream. Spitzer draws on the subtlest of words, such as the use of the indefinite article, the third-person reference, the demonstrative "ce" to suggest that "unsaid emotion takes its revenge by energizing its verbal expression, by exercising a counterpression on the words that repress it. So we have a *piano* strung with tension."[40]

It has been derided that in this "bloodless" tragedy, Titus's only action, or decision, is a very subtle one: to decide on the deictic present. Deictics, in rhetoric, are indexical, "pointing" words, such as "this" or "here" or "now." In Titus's case, he grapples with deploying the temporal deictic, the "now" that would cleanly cleave Bérénice from Titus, marking the definitive point of departure and separation. Titus attempts to declare such a deixis, using anaphora to evoke a ritualist rhythm: "Maintenant que je puis couronner tant d'attraits, / Maintenant que je l'aime encor plus que jamais" (Now it's mine to crown such loveliness, / Now that I adore her more than ever [2.2.441–42]). However, ultimately he is undone by indecision and the line, like his resolve, crumbles: "Je vais, Paulin . . . O Ciel! Puis-je le déclarer?" (I [shall], Paulin . . . Heavens! Can I say it? [2.2.445]). While ellipses (*points de suspension*) typically indicate interruption, here Titus seems to indicate a self-interruption, a schism between his resolute self and his loving self.[41]

His failure to announce the "now" highlights the tragedy of the sovereign. To return again to the figure of temporal dilation I offered in the beginning of this chapter, the "now"—a decisive, fixed time—cuts short the dilatory, circular temporality that was so necessary to the flourishing of their polyamorous love. If Bérénice, Antiochus, and even Titus himself are anxious about the deictic present, it is because this deixis, especially in relation to the sovereign declaration of "en ce moment" (at this moment) or "aujourd'hui" (today) is doubly allegorical and significant. First, it marks the transition from dilatory, circular time to a more linear time that is marked, represented, and measured. Second, Titus's decision making was supposed to instantiate the Roman law (of the performed repudiation, of Bérénice's exclusion). Instead of conjuring the "now" and sticking to that moment, his anxiously repeated "now" stages the sovereign's (in)ability to commit to an ontological "now" or a "real" present.

The hymen, in its unreadable status of "entre," in its undecidability, most troubles the nature of the present or the givenness of the deictic "now." As Derrida notes, the temporality of the hymen is one that scrambles notions of a governable, graspable time:

> The intermission or interim of the hymen does not establish time: neither time as the existence of concept (Hegel) nor lost time nor time regained, and still less the moment or eternity. No present in truth presents itself, be that as it may a dissimulation. What the hymen thwarts, under the space of the present (temporal or eternal) is the assurance of mastery.[42]

The hymen reappears throughout the play in its manifold figural incarnations, whether in the necessary impossibility of marriage or separation, or in the neutral status of "*entre*" (and "*antre*") that its undecidability performs. But as Derrida underscores, the hymen's paradoxical status inherently troubles the notion of mastery.

In the tragedy, as the moment of deciding on the hymen's fulfilment or rupture draws nearer, the characters discuss temporality differently. In the previous idyllic, triadic eroticism, time was discussed in the vague multiplicity of "cent fois" (a hundred times), a temporal (non) measure invoked when the characters wished to allude to their undecided, dilated dynamic.

> J'ai même souhaité la place de mon père,
> Moi, Paulin, qui cent fois, si le sort moins sévère
> Eût voulu de sa vie étendre les liens,
> Aurais donné mes jours pour prolonger les siens. (2.2.431–44)
>
> (I even coveted my father's place,
> I, who a hundred times, if gentler fate
> Had wished to stretch the limit of his days,
> Would have given some of my days to lengthen his.)

In Titus's fantasy, time takes on a fuzzy round number (e.g., "cent fois"), but the temporality of his language also itself posits a hypothetical, alternative past in which destiny would have wanted to extend his father's life, or he would have given his life for his father's. Already, early in the play, we see that "cent fois" signals a fantasizing outside of time or figures an alternative temporality. Leo Spitzer suggests that "the use of exaggerated round numbers looks at first glance like an expression of affectivity, but when one has got used to the constantly recurring thousands, hundreds and scores, the figures have more the effect of a dull formula, corresponding to the Latin *sescenti* ('six hundreds' = 'a large number')."[43] As such, the repeated "cent fois" has the "dampening" effect so prized by Spitzer. "The thousands and hundreds are obviously exaggerated numbers, but in as much as they are round numbers they serve to spread a mood of calm and lucid orderliness."[44] Bérénice says, for example:

> Il craint peut-être, il craint d'épouser une reine
> Hélas ! s'il était vrai . . . Mais non, il a cent fois
> Rassuré mon amour contre leurs dures lois.
> Cent fois . . . Ah ! qu'il m'explique un silence si rude. (2.5.630–43)
>
> (He fears perhaps, he fears to wed a queen
> Alas! If so . . . But no, a hundred times
> He's strengthened me against their cruel laws.
> A hundred times . . . Ah! I wish he could explain so harsh a silence.)

Similar to Titus's earlier self-interruption, the ellipses here show that Bérénice interrupts her own trains of thought, cycling through polarities of feeling. Her anxiety is interrupted by her self-soothing, her sense of reassurance is interrupted by resurgent fears ("Ah!"). With the rounded numbers, Bérénice gives the impression of orderliness, but an order that is belied by her nervous repetitions. The "softness" of a simplified, round number dampens the sharp poignancy of her realization that she must leave. She also is accumulating, in an innumerably large number, a whole host of memories of his previous declarations of love. The tragic pathos, then, stems from the ways that such large and imprecise numbers, the repeated frequency of the declaration of Titus's love, falls short in the face of just one, singular deictic "now" when Titus must send her away.

"Cet hymen est rompu," says Arsace, underscoring both the legalistic sense of the marriage (hymen) being broken off, as well as the sexualized sense of the physical membrane (hymen) being broken or split. As the decision regarding the hymen comes to the fore, the characters turn from the vaguely dilatory, undecided time of "cent fois" (a hundred times) to a fragmented sense of "moments." After Bérénice has been informed by Antiochus that Titus will break off the hymen/marriage, she sends her friend Phénice to see if Titus will come to clarify the situation himself. As she waits, Bérénice gives a monologue that is mostly about her experience of time itself: "Phénice ne vient point? Moments trop rigoureux, / Que vous paraissez lents à mes rapides voeux! / Je m'agite, je cours, languissante, abattue, / La force m'abandonne, et le repos me tue" (Phenice not here yet? Ah! excruciating moments, / How slow you seem to my tumultuous thoughts! / I run, I tremble, languishing, cast down; / My strength deserts me, but to rest is death [4.1.953–56]). In this period of waiting and unknowing, before the decision has been confirmed by Titus himself, Bérénice remarks on the jarring effect that these competing temporalities have on her. The infinitely dilated, pleasurably repeated time must finally come to a moment of decision, and the struggle between these incompatible temporal economies ends up feeling too intense ("trop rigoreux").

Puncturing this undecidable temporality, the temporal "now" gives the illusion of control or rather, maps the desire for mastery over dilatory time. Roland Racevskis has touched on Racine's treatment of temporality in *Bérénice*:

> In its singular and plural forms combined, the word "moment(s)" occurs 40 times in *Bérénice* . . . the prevalence in this play of the term "moments(s)" constitutes evidence that Racine sought to develop the representation of intimate, individual experiences of time into its smallest manifestations as a way of ornamenting and internally fragmenting the minimalistic action of the story chosen for this play. What results from the multiple references to the moments of characters' lives is a diversity of subjective temporalities.[45]

Bérénice's monologue does present such a minimalized time, as well as the jarring discord she experiences as she waits. Although the Freeman-Batson concordance (1968) has aided scholars in theorizing the density and frequency of particular keywords in Racine, Racevskis neglects to distinguish between "moment" and the collocation "en ce moment" ("now") and he primarily analyzes the former.[46] I therefore build on Racevskis's assertions about temporality in *Bérénice* to suggest that we need to consider not only the importance of the microscopic temporal fragment of the "moment" but also the priority that Racine affords to the "now." The puncturing status of the "now" forces a decision on the ambiguously eroticized triad, or the undecidable hymen. "Now" becomes the "point" that destabilizes the dilation of time in the play, much like Ascham's pithy epitome that cuts through the "fat" of dilatory speech.

Drawing on a different deictic phrase, Antiochus says, "Aujourd'hui qu'il peut tout, que votre hymen s'avance" (Today, he can do anything, his marriage advances [1.2.43]), in his monologue of imagined speech to Bérénice, linking Titus's all-powerful sovereign capacities ("il peut tout") with the impending marriage. But taking on this mantle of sovereignty is explicitly linked to a different kind of linear temporality, one that, as we have seen, resists the dilatational increase of pregnancy that would result from a "hymen odieux" (detestable marriage [2.2.402]). Later, Titus confesses to Antiochus, "Mes transports aujourd'hui s'attendaient d'éclater. / Cependant aujourd'hui, Prince il faut la quitter" (Today my joys should have known no bounds. / And yet today, Prince, I must part from her [3.1.713–14]), and in the folded doubling of "aujourd'hui," Racine highlights the pathos of the most joyously anticipated day turning into the most sorrowfully dreaded one. If we are to take the notion of repetition (*la chrie*) seriously, in the repeated invocations of "en ce moment," "ce jour," or "aujourd'hui" (at this moment, this day, or today), there is not only an anxiety expressed over the marriage or the separation (the hymen) but also a focus on the conjuring power of the deictic "now" itself and its very undecidability. This "aujourd'hui" (today), as deixis, marks a temporal threshold between the continuity of previous emperors' pasts and an acceptable sovereign future for Titus.

When Bérénice confronts Titus after hearing that he plans to send her away, she acknowledges that he is following Roman law and tradition. But her main argument targets his choice of the "now": "Ignoriez-vous vos Lois / Quand je vous l'avouai [my love] pour la première fois? / À quel excès d'amour m'avez-vous amenée [?]" (Did you not know your laws, / When I declared my love for the first time? / To what excess of love have you not led me [?] [4.5.1065–67]), and "Tout l'Empire a vingt fois conspiré contre nous. / Il était temps encor. Que ne me quittiez-vous?" (The Empire threatened us before, twenty times. / There was still time. Why not desert me then? [4.5.1073–74]). Bérénice employs the "dampened" softness of round numbers (twenty times) as a counterpoint to the height of pain she experiences. She effectively criticizes him for not having accepted earlier that they could never be together and resents his indulgence in the amatory delay. At the same time, she insists that the logic of the separation taking place *that day*—that particular, puncturing "now"—does not make sense, underscoring the arbitrary nature of his decision: "Hé bien, Seigneur, hé bien, qu'en peut-il arriver? / Voyez-vous les Romains prêts à se soulever?" (Well, then, my lord, and what could come of it? / Do you see Rome ready to rise up? [4.5.1137–38]). In other words, she insists that there is no "state of emergency," actual or pending, and thus her repudiation does not adhere to any kind of logic, except for one that invests in a certain kind of Roman-only future. Such a separation could have taken place earlier or could have been deferred for years. They could still, for example, live in the dilatory temporality of the deferred, future "hymen." In a rather contemporary gesture, Bérénice even argues against the institution of marriage, hoping that they could remain together, unmarried: "Ah Seigneur! S'il est vrai, pourquoi nous séparer? / Je ne vous parle point d'un heureux hyménée" (Ah sir! if that is true, why separate us? / I speak no more of happy marriage vows [4.5.1126–27)]. There is not any logical or real reason that either the separation or the marriage has to happen today, right now, if at all.

Titus himself remarks on the absurdity of the necessary violence of the deictic present. He highlights the violence of the hymen's rupture with the verb "percer" (to pierce):

> Je viens percer un cœur que j'adore, qui m'aime
> Et pourquoi le percer? Qui l'ordonne? Moi-même.
> Car enfin Rome a-t-elle expliqué ses souhaits?
> L'entendons-nous crier autour de ce Palais?
> Vois-je l'État penchant au bord du précipice?
> Ne le puis-je sauver que par ce sacrifice?
> Tout se tait, et moi seul trop prompt à me troubler,
> J'avance des malheurs que je puis reculer. (4.4.999–1006)
>
> (I pierce a loving heart that I adore.
> Why pierce it? Who ordains it? I myself.
> Indeed has Rome yet made its wishes known?
> Do we hear shouting round the palace walls?
> And do I see the state perched on the brink?
> Must I make this sacrifice to save it?
> All's quiet—I alone, to wound myself
> Advance misfortunes that I might dispel.)

As he seeks to find the animating logic behind his sorrow, he ends up tumbling into a mise en abyme. Who is the villain orchestrating this cruel separation, and who or what is forcing him to make this decision? He indicates an ultimate *piano*—the softest quiet—"Tout se tait" ("All's quiet") as he points to himself, alone.

The play plots a trajectory from a nebulous temporality of "cent fois," or a dampened, circular repetition, to a temporality that is broken down, measured, and fragmented. Before, the dilatory temporality, and the triadic threesome it sustained, was structured by the remote, if distant, possibility of an end point: the hymen. However, once the hymen is (or is not) broken, then the dilation of time and infinite repetition feels overwhelming and threatening, as Bérénice mentions in her "Moments trop rigoureux" monologue. In this moment of indecision, the clash of the two temporalities—the circularity of polyamorous substitution and the linearity of sovereign progress—means that even common temporal markers seem absurd and ridiculous to Bérénice:

> Dans un mois, dans un an, comment souffrirons-nous,
> Seigneur, que tant de Mers me séparent de vous?
> Que le jour recommence et que le jour finisse
> Sans que Titus puisse voir Bérénice?
> Sans que de tout le jour je puisse voir Titus? (4.5.1113–1117)
>
> (In a month, in a year, my lord, how shall we bear [endure]
> Our sundering across so many seas?
> Or that the day begin again and end
> With never Titus seeing Berenice,
> With never all day long my seeing you?)

Enjambment itself becomes a marker of textual dilation, with the line's logic spilling over its twelve-syllable container, replicating textually the fact of Bérénice being pushed out of Rome. Bérénice, however, employs this dilation to her advantage, marking a dual position in affect. As we first hear "souffrirons" it may lead us to believe that Bérénice is hysterically building to a final complaint of her suffering: "And how (much) shall we suffer." With the "que" in the next line, however, she draws herself together, quietly, like the queen she is, and the phrase becomes modified to mean "and how shall we bear [endure]." The tragedy consists of this very restraint: as sovereigns, they must endure. Bérénice conjures images of extended time and distance ("so many seas"), but with the ambiguous hinge "que" and the cold formality of "Seigneur," she creates infinitely greater *emotional* distance than can be alluded to in markers of time and space. It is because her sensation of temporality itself is shifting, moving from an ambiguous circularity (one in which "Titus sees Bérénice and Bérénice sees Titus") to a temporality of acceptable sovereign progress in which they live separately. Therefore, Bérénice's questions regarding the deictic present—"why now? Why today?"—actually take on greater rhetorical and even political import.

Pathos of Example

Bérénice ends almost anticlimactically. “Adieu, servons tous trois d’exemple à l’univers / De l’amour la plus tendre, et la plus malheureuse, / Dont il puisse garder l’histoire douloureuse” (Farewell, let all three of us serve as an example to the world / Of the most tender and unhappy love / That it could bear the doleful history of [5.7.1502–4]). All the characters’ suffering, heartbreak, and loss must surely be in the name of some greater purpose, we would imagine. But the entirety of the play comes to an ambiguous close when their sacrifice of one another is merely an example. The inscription of their story is aligned with a proper sovereign history, eschewing the excesses of Antony and Julius, obeying the very same matrimonial law that other emperors Caligula and Nero—even with all their uncontrollable appetites—still respected. Such an example marks a proscription that guides sovereign and civic behavior. And yet this sadly inglorious—even mundane—ending to the drama seems almost fitting with Benjamin’s diagnosis of *trauerspiel*:

> The baroque knows no eschatology, and for that very reason it possesses no mechanism by which all earthly things are gathered in together and exalted before being consigned to their end. The hereafter is emptied of everything which contains the slightest breath of this world, and from it the baroque extracts a profusion of things which customarily escaped the grasp of artistic formulation and, at its high point, brings them violently into the light of day, in order to clear an ultimate heaven, enabling it, as a vacuum, one day to destroy the world with catastrophic violence.[47]

But this catastrophe, as emblematized in Bérénice’s departure, is one that is particularly softened, or to use Spitzer’s term, “dampened.”

Titus needs to repeat (again and again) the necessity of deciding on Bérénice’s fate and sending her away: “Si le Peuple demain ne voit partir la Reine, / Demain elle entendra ce Peuple furieux/ Me venir demander son depart à ses yeux” (If Bérénice does not leave Rome tomorrow, / Tomorrow she will hear the furious people come / In rage to bid me send her from their sight [3.1.732–33]), repeating “demain” twice in the hopes of sounding resolute, but Titus’s supposedly sovereign declaration ends up timidly retreating behind his excuse of “ce Peuple furieux” (furious people). And later, he points out that if he allowed Bérénice to stay, he would be breaking the very laws that he himself is responsible for upholding: "Maintiendrai-je des Lois que je ne puis garder?" (Could I enforce the laws I cannot keep? [4.5.1146]). At the same time, he is unable to decide whether to break the law for personal gain, make an exception for himself, or stick to one declaration. Bérénice points out that he is making this sacrifice to uphold laws—but laws that he himself is capable of changing: "Quoi, pour d'injustes Lois que vous pouvez changer / En d'éternels chagrins vous-même vous plonger? / Rome a ses droits, Seigneur. N'avez-vous pas les vôtres?" (Why plunge yourself into unending pain / For cruel laws that you yourself could change? / Rome has its rights, my lord. Have you not yours? [4.5.1149–51]). In all these discourses, the responsibility of the decision itself is displaced onto the "people" or the "law," and the example itself of governance and decisiveness seems rather muted.

In the fractional moment between the sovereign's logical decision (for the good of the state, to keep chaos at bay) and not deciding, there is a movement from the realm of the impossibly illogical to the absolutely necessary. Yet this movement always presupposes a flicker of indecision, a moment before the decision being made. Derrida suggests that the sovereign's relationship to decision making inevitably debases him, much like Benjamin's creaturely fallen sovereign:

> Because every decision (by its essence every decision is exceptional and sovereign) must escape the order of the possible, of what is already possible, of what is already possible and programmable for the supposed subject of the decision, because every decision worthy of the name must be this exceptional scandal of a passive decision or decision of the other, the difference between the deciding decision and the undecided decision itself becomes undecidable, and then the supposed decision, the exceptionally sovereign decision looks, like two peas in a pod, just like an indecision, an unwilling, a nonliberty, a nonintention, an unconsciousness and an irrationality, etc. and then the supposed sovereign subject begins, by an invincible attraction, to look like the beast that he is supposed to subject to himself (and we already know, having often—last time too—verified it, that in place of the beast one can put, in the same hierarchy, the slave, the woman, the child).[48]

Titus's indecision reduces him to a shadow of his former self, the one who was, Bérénice reminds us, heralded by "Ces flambeaux, ce bûcher, cette nuit enflammée, / Ces aigles, ces faisceaux, ce people, cette armée, / Cette foule de rois, ces consuls, ce Sénat / Qui tous de mon amant empruntaient leur éclat" (That pyre, those torches, the whole night on fire, / Those eagles, those banners, the troops, the throng, / That crowd of kings, the consuls and the Senate, / Who all lent their acclaim to him I love [1.5.303–6]). This flicker of a "nonintention" or a "nonliberty" reduces him, as Derrida suggests, from the exalted status of sovereign to a diminished status, more akin to a beast or animal that can only be motivated by pure instinct or affect.

Titus's sovereignty is reproduced through passed-down diachronic traditions—through the valuation of certain kinds of (Roman) lives, as well as xenophobic exclusion—all in the interest of promoting and prolonging a Roman-only heritage. And yet sovereignty is figured here as a "machine" that is both prostatist and prosthetic, which Derrida merges together in a portmanteau hybrid of "prothétatique." The temporality of this prosthetic pro-State is one that is both ephemeral and eternal: as a machine, it is of course eternal, but as a prosthetic in the service of life (preserving the quality of life, of precarious lives) it trades in ephemerality—the fear of life's fleetingness—to extend and subtend itself. The duration of a proper sovereignty, aligned with the trajectory of history that Paulin has laid out in act 2, is one that depends on the duality of the necessity of (infinite) sovereign continuity, as well as the specter of life's fragility (that the sovereign alone can control and protect). Thus, the *prothétatique* nature of the sovereign resides, itself, in a monstrous temporality that wavers between, and in this wavering covers over, the threat of death and a biopolitically controlled life and future.

The baroque without eschatology—since it has, according to Benjamin, "no mechanism by which it gathers all earthly things in together and exalts them before consigning them to their end"[49]—places the German *trauerspiel* in an ephemeral-eternal temporality akin to Derrida's *prothétatique*. Whereas the eschatological mechanism could formerly be counted on as a meaning-making cap to the tragic present, the numbing, nearly animal quality of the *prothétatique* state indicates an incessant sovereignty that will—and must—continue. Since sovereignty prolongs its reign of power through the prosthetic and machinic, there is no glorious end point. Given this sense of a (non)end, *Bérénice*'s own ending dramatizes the ways that propulsion through history occurs rhetorically, passed down not through grand sacrifice or sovereign declarations but, rather, passively through "example": "Adieu, servons tous trois d'exemple à l'univers / De l'amour la plus tendre, et la plus malheureuse, / Dont il puisse garder l'histoire douloureuse" (Farewell, let all three of us serve as an example to the world / Of the most tender and unhappy love / That it could bear the doleful history of [5.7.1502–4]), says Bérénice. The play stages the shift from a dilatory ambiguity, of pending exclusion and possible hymen, to the clearly pedagogic and ascertainable clearing of the exemplum, one that is properly inscribed in a history to be imitated, by the universe to come, like so much copia that takes up one phrase or one example and amplifies and embroiders it endlessly.

If Parker suggests that Renaissance dilation differs from Derridian *différance* since dilation is "finally caught within the horizon of a telos or ending,"[50] this is an ending that is dampened, in a Spitzerian *piano*: to serve as an "example" is neither glorious nor clearly beneficial nor directly necessary. And yet it is in the smallness of such telos that renders the wrenching difficulties of the drama all the more poignant. The excesses of waiting, laboring over speech, confessing love—all of it is reduced to a mere point, or example, exerting what Spitzer would analyze as an equal-and-opposite counterpressure against the spiraling amplification of emotion. The measure of that sorrow is then *in the very force* it takes to condense and minimize it to nothing more than a brief mark in the book of history, a small example to be noted. If Racine attempted to "faire quelque chose de rien," (make something out of nothing), the rhetorical effect of Bérénice's "exemple" is to "faire rien de quelque chose" (make nothing out of something).

Perhaps what makes the tragedy draw out such an excess of tears ("weep like a simpleton," as Villars remarks)[51] is its touching on the types of desires, intimacies, and relationships that can only be mourned as what Bérénice called "douleur secrète" (secret sorrow). Titus's "langue embarrassée" (encumbered tongue) seems to denote both his inability to speak and language's own inability to be adequate to any type of expression that he might need. In this sense, it is a tragedy not only of the loss of the beloved(s) but also of the inability to speak of the dynamics of such a love, whether it be strangely triangulated and polyamorous, full of substitutions, fantasies, and voyeuristic "witnessing." The encumbered tongue may also point to the impossibility of speaking of the loss of the pleasurably renewed, circular temporality in favor of properly progressive sovereign time. It is fitting that Bérénice's announcement of their exemplarity is one that is future oriented, forward thinking, but at the same time it seems to proleptically imagine their emotions and sorrows as being neatly condensed into a few lines of history to come. Just as Paulin devotes an alexandrine or two to Antony and Cleopatra, Bérénice's repudiation will become a small example in a long list. And perhaps poignantly enough, the line in Suetonius's history is precisely nothing but a tiny fragment of this story, the *invitus invitam* (despite him, despite her) to which this entire tale is softened, dampened, and reduced.

Conclusion

Stepping Out of Time

"Queerness's time is a stepping out of the linearity of straight time," writes José Esteban Muñoz. For Muñoz, "Straight time's 'presentness' needs to be phenomenologically questioned, and this is the fundamental value of a queer utopian hermeneutics. Queerness's ecstatic and horizonal temporality is a path and a movement to a greater openness to the world."[1] While Muñoz does not specifically invoke the word "velocity," with the phrases "stepping out" and "path and a movement," he alludes to what I have expressed with the concept of queer velocity: a tempo with a directional component. In *Cruising Utopia* he tracks a striving toward a horizon of possibility, toward new forms of worldmaking and collectivity. One of the polemical stances his book takes is a dissatisfaction both with an Edelmanian queer antirelationality—an antisociality that rejects futurity and its norms outright—and with the settledness of the present.[2] Likewise, in *Queer Velocity* the directional component of velocity manifests as a waywardness that unsettles the phenomenology, assumptions, and values associated with and produced by "straight time."

In these concluding pages I want to think about velocity's relationship to utopianism, building on Muñoz's reflections. The queerness of the velocities I have analyzed shows that the affects and sensations wrought from slowness and speed can forge sites of unruly feeling, nonnormative relationships, or attachments to objects, same-sex friends, or even queer triangles. This book has mapped ways of "stepping out" of temporal norms of neoclassical tragedy, both in fleeting moments and sustained relational formations. Such a striving for this rich openness or glimpsed connections is necessary because, as Muñoz insists, "The present is not enough. It is impoverished and toxic for queers and other people who do not feel the privilege of majoritarian belonging, normative tastes, and 'rational' expectations."[3]

Much of my book's argument has hinged on the wager that neoclassical tragedy affords a particular "frame" of enclosed temporality that makes particularly visible the effects of velocity's waywardness and snags; the rules and *bienséances* governing conduct (or, as Foucault might say, the "conduct of conducts") sediment the "presentness" of straight time and foreclose questions about its phenomenological hegemony. But beyond a hermeneutic of visibility, theater rules contribute to a specific kind of normalizing impulse: there is a tautological relationship between the *vraisemblance* and bienséances and what Muñoz calls the "temporal stranglehold" of the present.[4] Muñoz's evocations of rationality and "majoritarian belonging" are strongly illustrated by the kind of "presentness" produced by seventeenth-century French theater. Theater practitioners, writers, and critics of the seventeenth century were invested in cementing the rules of and practicing a certain type of verisimilitude and conduct; these regulations were necessary to reflect a believable reality. D'Aubignac says authoritatively, "these rules being nothing but an Art allowing beautiful moments to succeed with verisimilitude, it appears fairly evident how necessary they are, for through a common consensus one approves what conforms to them and one rejects that which the rules do not tolerate."[5] With the language of rejection and intolerance, it is clear, as I have argued, that the rules had a moralizing component. But this represented theatrical reality was believable only because it reinforced (by performing, iteratively reproducing) structures of rationality, pragmatism, and normality. Therefore, as I argued in chapter 1, the theater rules were political, but not for the top-down disciplinary reasons that many theater historians have alluded to—for example, the installation of social order under Cardinal Richelieu's projects, the establishment of absolutist dazzlement at Versailles—but rather for the biopolitical management of the present that these rules conditioned and afforded.

Velocity signals a queer utopian impulse. Because queer velocities don't "go" where one anticipates that they should, or could go, they carve out the possibility of "stepping out" of the present, or the trajectory of the present. Muñoz writes:

> The not-quite-conscious is the realm of potentiality that must be called on, and insisted on, if we are ever to look beyond the pragmatic sphere of the here and now, the hollow nature of the present. Thus, I wish to argue that queerness is not quite here; it is, in the language of Italian philosopher Giorgio Agamben, a potentiality.[6]

While writing this book, I have often been asked if velocity is resistance, or if there was an element of resistance to velocity. Here I have attempted to show how this question somewhat misses the mark. Velocity can be more closely aligned to what Deleuze called pouvoir-vital that was an intensification of life, rather than an outright push against the management of life. As I described in the introduction, Deleuze argues that, since life is the ultimate prize at stake in the game of biopolitical discipline, life itself becomes a means of "hijacking" such monitoring: "Life becomes resistance to power when power takes life as its object . . . when power becomes bio-power, resistance becomes the power of life, a vital power that cannot be confined within species, environment or the paths of a particular diagram."[7] Deleuze's reading of biopolitics imagines redeploying the object of prey (life) as the very means of resistance. I take this model and apply it to temporality. When power takes the time of life as its object and objective, resistance becomes a matter of the time of living. We can divert disciplinary vigor into an alternative vitality that stems from velocity. If time is the object, then attention to temporalities—divergent tempos, swerving speeds—becomes critical. Deleuze's pouvoir-vital becomes not a matter of life, but a matter of speed. To give a material analogy for this, seventeenth-century English dramatist John Dryden, well versed in the French neoclassical tradition, picks up on the essential quality of temporality to generate theatrical affect. Stuart Sherman emphasizes that for Dryden theater's temporality could be thought of as "'the compression of the Accidents,' by which the author 'crowds together' in the narrow 'compass' of the play's few hours as many events and quick turns as possible [to] '[produce] more variety and consequently more pleasure to the Audience;'"[8] Dryden therefore pinpointed theatrical pleasure as deriving from a specific temporal experience. Deleuze's strategy of pouvoir-vital might suggest that instead of shattering the temporal vise, one might enjoy, even welcome, the pinch, compression, or pressure.

Therefore, rather than examining the outright expression of resistance or dissent on the macrolevel, I zoomed in on some more molecular components of temporal management, showing how queer velocities are flagged and made present not only through diegetic references but also through rhetoric. Rhetoric, I wagered, had capacity to convey velocity, since trope could be thought of *as* a form of movement, or transport (*translatio*). Figures such as catachresis and paralipsis convey their own, fleeting moments of velocity within the smaller frame of the regular, twelve-syllable alexandrine verse, since they enact microtemporalities between the sign and its meaning.

One of my book's points of departure was how the particularity of the early modern world—from the developing French theater rules to the newness of time pieces—allowed for what I called a new onto-epistemology of temporality. I will use these concluding pages to plant the seed of further inquiry. Haunting the invocation of the norm is the larger context of non-Western temporality. That is, even as I invoke "normativity," I recognize that I am implicitly making the center of the norm Europe (specifically France, or Versailles). My dramatic archive examined in the book, spanning from the mid-to-late seventeenth century, hovers on the cusp of French colonial endeavors, and thus lurking in the aesthetic and biopolitical normalization of temporality that I trace lies the latency for it to be deployed as a specifically otherizing force.

In *Time and the Other*, anthropologist Johannes Fabian points to what he calls the "denial of coevalness," or the presumed temporal "lag" between otherized "unmodernized" societies and the West.[9] For Fabian, by positing the existence of a "natural" or "evolutionary Time," anthropology—dedicated to intellectually justifying colonialism—organized societies along an axis of a "stream of time—some upstream, others downstream."[10] This organizing principle was not neutral, as it produced and projected hegemonic values flattering to the West and further served to cement an imaginary divide between others and us. Fabian goes so far to suggest that these are merely conceptual mythologies: "Civilization, evolution, development, acculturation, modernization . . . are all terms whose conceptual content derives, in ways that can be specified, from evolutionary Time . . . *Primitive* being essentially a temporal concept, is a category, not an object, of Western thought."[11] Therefore, primitivity can be more closely thought of as a hermeneutic or a sieve that winnows between the "now" of modernity and the "not yet" of undeveloped peoples.

Fabian suggests that this lag has not always existed; in medieval thought, temporality was more closely aligned with the idea of salvation, not progress, and "the Others, pagans and infidels (rather than savages and primitives), were viewed as candidates for salvation."[12] Wayward nonbelievers needed only to be drawn (metaphorically, literally, or spiritually) to the "centers" of Christendom: Rome or Jerusalem. In contrast, the Enlightenment naturalization and rationalization of time reconfigures temporal relations as "exclusive and expansive"; in other words, the savage is held in another not-yet time that is always lagging behind modernity. Time as progress becomes deeply linked to the conception that reason enables progress, replacing the instantaneity of faith and salvation. Or, as Fabian puts it, "The pagan was always *already* marked for salvation, the savage is *not yet* ready for civilization."[13] At the very moment of transition between the former and latter models, the Other is redeemable and relegated to the not yet.

This turning point is illustrated by Voltaire's tragedy *Zaïre (1732)*, famously one of the "last" French tragedies written that adhere to the neoclassical unities.[14] It thematically rhymes with many of the plays that this book has examined: like *Andromaque*, the play depicts a captor who has fallen in love with his captive; and like *Polyeucte*, the plot hinges on an illicit conversion that must be undertaken in haste. Similar to *Bérénice*, *Zaïre* has moments of foreclosed mutual love that must be renounced. The play's particular form, thanks to its neoclassical adherence to the unity of time, affords the visibility and amplification of queer velocities (dragging and haste). While François-René de Chateaubriand famously said of *Zaïre*, "Ici tout est tragique: les lieux, l'homme et la Divinité"[15] (Here everything is tragic: the location, man, and divinity), what is also tragic, I would wager, is also time and, more specifically, velocity. *Zaïre* is set against the backdrop of the thirteenth-century Crusades, in which the French Christian soldiers are attempting to wrest control of Jerusalem from the sultan Orosmane. Onstage, however, the violence is more internal than explicit. The eponymous Zaïre is a French Christian who has been raised since infancy in Orosmane's harem. She has fallen reciprocally in love with the sultan and is poised to marry him. The whole tragedy ends in an *Othello*-like turn, however, when the racialized lover (Orosmane) misreads Zaïre's cues of velocity (deferral and haste) and murders her in a fit of jealousy.

At first glance, the Muslim sultan's inability to felicitously manage temporalities relegates him to a state of undeveloped primitivism and hasty, irrational action. But, once we take velocity into account, we can see that one aspect of the tragedy can be mapped on to Fabian's conceptual turning point: over the course of the play, Orosmane changes from redeemable pagan to irredeemable primitive. It is not only a failure of Enlightenment philosophy's ideals but also the collapse of a certain kind of queer utopianism gestured at the beginning of the play.

In the drama's optimistic opening, we are presented with a fantasy of universality, a flattening of difference. Zaïre imagines different forms of relationality and becoming (what she could have been, what she would like to be). In her imaginings, many of these are adamantly not determined by reason, location, hegemony of bloodline, or more.

Unaware of her origins or her true identity, she expresses a certain open-mindedness toward the dogmatism of religion and nation:

> L'instruction fait tout, et la main de nos pères
> Grave en nos faibles cœurs ces premiers caractères
> Que l'exemple et le temps nous viennent retracer,
> Pour moi, des sarrasins esclave en mon berceau,
> La foi de nos chrétiens me fut trop tard connue. (1.1.109–13)
>
> (Instruction does everything, and the hand of our fathers
> Engraves in our weak hearts the first letters
> That example and time come to retrace,
> For me, slave to the Saracens in my crib
> The Christian faith was made known too late to me.)

The particularities of religious identity and belief, in her first major speech of the play, are all minimized and smoothed away by the work of time. Repetition (and the early exposure to religious ideology are key, in her mind; she could just as easily have been exposed to another faith, but the Christian doctrines were simply taught to her too late to be impactful. Therefore, time and timing cement identity, in Zaïre's view, not the persuasiveness of religion or inherited (blood) identity. Zaïre's musings about identity and relationality interrogate conceptions of human potentiality. She also describes a type of determinism by place: "J'eusse été près du Gange esclave des faux dieux, / Chrétienne dans Paris, musulmane en ces lieux" (I could have been close to the Ganges River the slave of false gods / Christian in Paris, Muslim in this place [1.1.107–8]). Finally, is important to remember that Zaïre's world, and the temporality that characterizes it, is the enclosed space of the "sérail" (seraglio, or harem). She says to her friend Fatime,

> Au sérail des soudans dès l'enfance enfermée
> Chaque jour ma raison s'y voit accoutumée.
> Le reste de la terre, anéanti pour moi,
> M'abandonne au soudan qui nous tient sous sa loi. (1.1.21–24)
>
> (Shut away in the sultan's seraglio from childhood,
> Each day my reason becomes more accustomed to it
> The rest of the earth, annihilated for me,
> Abandons me to the sultan who keeps us under his rule.)

Therefore, Zaïre seems to embrace multiple forms of becoming. She presents one form of potentiality through training, another as a type of place-based determinism, and a third as a complete self-yielding of reason through a deep affective and law-bound attachment to the sultan. None of these forms of becoming hinge on race, origin, family, or bloodline, or the normative temporalities that these concepts engender. This is not to say that Zaïre embraces a necessarily queer potentiality or that her reasoning is without cultural prejudices and hierarchies. But, rather, her descriptions show that she is equally open to multiple, even utopic, pathways of development.

Just as captive Andromaque's temporality is conditioned by the single time per day that Pyrrhus allows her to see her son, Zaïre and her fellow captive Fatime seem to spend most of their time waiting for a single, highly anticipated moment. They fantasize about the return of the mysterious Nérestan who has promised to ransom the freedom of Zaïre and other enslaved Christians. Fatime says, "Avez-vous oublié / ce généreux Français, dont la tendre amitié / Nous promit si souvent de rompre notre chaîne? / Combien nous admirions son audace hautaine!" (Have you forgotten the gallant Frenchman who, in tender friendship, promised us so often that he would break our chains? How we admired his haughty audacity [1.1.27–30]). Zaïre does not dwell on this slow time of waiting. She instead uses the past tense to close the book on this tempo, while admitting that she did share in Fatime's admiration and wonder at this brave warrior: "J'admirai trop en lui cet inutile zèle; / Il n'y faut plus penser" (I admired too much this useless zeal in him / It should not be thought of again [1.1.45–46]). Fatime responds with a conditional future tense, insisting on dreaming of a world in which this gallant Frenchman could return: "Mais s'il était fidèle, / S'il revenait enfin dégager ses serments, / Ne voudriez-vous pas?" (but if he were faithful / were he to return to fulfil his promises, wouldn't you want? [1.1.46–48]), but Fatime's "wouldn't you want" question is cut off by Zaïre's insistence that "Il n'est plus temps / tout est changé" (It is no longer time / everything is changed [1.1.48–49]). Thanks to Zaïre's interruption, we never hear the end of Fatime's question: what is she imagining that Zaïre would desire? Freedom? Conversion? The young man himself? Fatime? We are left only to imagine the end of the question, because, as Zaïre insists, there is no more time.

In chapter 1 I suggested that the marshalling of the bienséances in the theater was a way of leveraging rules of shared feeling or shared sentiment. In this way one unexpected affordance of the unity of time was not only to install aesthetic-temporal propriety but also to coordinate a shared sensitivity to temporal rhythms and sexual-sensual expression, perhaps akin to what Beth Freeman has called a "hypersociality." She defines hypersocial as "not just excess sociability but sociability felt and manifested along axes and wavelengths beyond the discursive and the visual—and even beyond the haptic, for the synchronization of bodies does not require their physical touch, but rather a simultaneity of movement in which the several become one."[16] After Zaïre reveals to Fatime her secret—that she intends to marry Orosmane—Fatime begins to count herself among Zaïre's future subjects. But Zaïre refuses this gesture. Much like Bérénice's queer desire to share her happiness with Antiochus on the cusp of her (anticipated) wedding day, Zaïre seeks a shared enjoyment with Fatime: "Sois toujours mon égale, et goûte mon bonheur; / Avec toi partagé, je sens mieux sa douceur" (Be always my equal, and taste my happiness; / shared with you, I can better feel its sweetness [1.1.79–80]). With the sensual words "goûte" (taste) and "sens" (to feel), Zaïre insists on a mutual fabric of sensation that synchronizes them and augments her own sense of belonging (to each other). This scene echoes Bérénice's attachment to Antiochus, when she wishes to share the joy of her impending marriage: "Je n'attendais que vous pour témoin de ma joie" (I waited but for you to share my joy [1.4.268]).

While Zaïre emphasizes the hypersociality of the harem, Orosmane, in his speech to Zaïre declaring his love, insists on forgoing the multiplicity of pleasures of the Orient in favor of a singular, Occidental-style love: "Je sais que notre loi, favorable aux plaisirs, / Ouvre un champ sans limite à nos vastes désirs" (I know that our law, favoring pleasures, opens an unlimited field for our vast desires [1.2.163–64]). He promises Zaïre "de ne choisir que vous pour maîtresse et pour femme / de vivre votre ami, votre amant, votre époux" (to choose only you as mistress and wife, to live as your friend, your lover, your husband [1.2.190–91]). His declaration of monogamy and performance of repudiating the field of "vastes désirs" is reinforced by his employment of time. At the end of act 1, he says, "Je vais donner une heure aux soins de mon empire, / Et le reste du jour sera tout à Zaïre" (I'll commit an hour to taking care of my empire, and the rest of the day will be entirely for Zaïre [1.5.313–14]). Sexual purity, and the performance of monogamy, is replicated by his temporal purity, by dedicating his day almost exclusively to Zaïre.

This first act serves to illustrate Zaïre's belief in something like queer utopic thinking: where rank is abolished in favor of a hypersociality (in Freeman's sense), where the seraglio is no longer a prison but an intimately shared space, where religious difference and national origin mean less than an inexplicable love attachment. It is not necessarily a true utopia, but while mourning the given conditions of their status—as captive and far from family—the main characters still begin to imagine a "stepping out" of the traditionally prescribed roles, sexualities, religions, and tempos conditioned by the state.

The tragedy is catalyzed when Zaïre's queer longing is confronted by the temporal expectations of her familial relations. Nérestan, the dreamy French warrior, does return to offer himself up for ransom and is shocked to discover that Zaïre does not wish to be freed; she will stay with her beloved Orosmane in Jerusalem. Furthermore, the one political prisoner whom Orosmane refuses to release is the deposed Christian king Lusignan, who has languished in a sunless cell for the past twenty years and must there remain due to his potential disruption of Orosmane's absolute authority.

Once Zaïre is able to convince Orosmane to let Lusignan at least see his countrymen, she is brought to tears by the sight of Lusignan, even though she does not know him. She says, offering another example of Freeman's hypersociality: "Mes larmes, malgré moi, me dérobent sa vue; Ainsi que ce vieillard, j'ai langui dans les fers; / Qui ne sait compatir aux maux qu'on a soufferts!" (My tears, despite myself, impede my vision / Much like this man, I have languished in chains / Who cannot empathize with troubles one has undergone oneself? [2.2.514–16]). With "much like" and "empathize with," she insists on an expression of tender, involuntary kinship—here, another hypersocial queerness—wrought from their shared temporal-carceral experience. This unexpected affective response foreshadows the shocking and sudden revelation that follows: Zaïre learns that Lusignan is none other than her father and Nérestan is her brother.

The means of identification are crucial here: the near-blind Lusignan deduces Zaïre's identity through a series of contiguous objects. Zaïre produces a cross found on her person as a baby. Lusignan, by touch, confirms that it is the same cross that he had given to his deceased wife: "Oui, c'est elle" (yes, it is she [2.3.611]), he affirms, but his ambiguous use of "elle" could refer to either Zaïre or the cross. This chain of association affirms that Zaïre is indeed his daughter. In contrast, Nérestan is identified by a scar on his chest; his unmistakable embodiment ties him to his father, while Zaïre is linked to her family through an object that had passed through many hands. Fittingly, Nérestan and Lusignan cry out to each other in terms of family endearment: Lusignan cries out, "Approchez, mes enfants" (come here, my children,) and

Nérestan says, “Moi, votre fils!” (I, your son! [2.3.632–33]). Zaïre, in contrast, can only gasp, “Seigneur!” In this depiction of the reunited family, hypersocial, carceral kinship can feel more “real” and powerful than the sudden imposition of family ties and relations.

Because of the haste of the revelation of Nérestan’s identity—as Zaïre’s brother—the reader or spectator may still have in her mind the sense impression that Fatime and Zaïre gave of the dashing, courageous Frenchman. Fatime’s open question “wouldn’t you want?” lingers seductively. To shift so suddenly from Nérestan as “admirable” (as lover and hero) to Nérestan as brother can cause some overlap and confusion. The “persistence of vision” refers to an optical illusion effect where two sides appear to blend into one image: take for example, a top that has one-half blue sides and one-half red sides. When spun quickly, the red and blue sides appear to merge into a single purple tone. Similarly, the viewer may likewise carry a “persistence of vision” from act 1 to act 2, which suggests that the velocity of the abrupt transition and revelation queers the relation between Zaïre and Néréstan. Is he a potential future lover? Or was he always her brother? What is clear is that Néréstan’s and Lusignan’s revelations begin to uninstall the regulations and rules that structure the possibilities of the seraglio, as well as to import to Jerusalem the nonutopic conventions of family, France, and Christianity.

Zaïre insists that she could never renounce her family ties and her bloodline, reminding them that she is already baptized. But Nérestan relegates her to the primitive zone of the “not yet,” saying, “cette loi n’est pas la vôtre encore; Le jour qui vous éclaire est pour vous à l’aurore; / Vous n’avez point reçu ce gage précieux” (This law is not yet yours / The enlightening day is only at its dawn for you / You have not yet received the precious gage [baptism] [3.4.783–85]). In a second peripeteia, her brother is devastated to realize that she will be marrying the Muslim sultan Orosmane. Nérestan urges her to be rebaptized in Christianity and subsequently risk dying for her faith, as a martyr. He says, using a language of merciless violence: “Il [ce bras] ne souffrira pas qu’à son culte engagé, / Entre un barbare et lui ton cœur soit partagé. / Le baptême éteindra ces feux dont il soupire, Et tu vivras fidèle, ou périras martyre” (My arm will not tolerate that, engaged to its cult / Your heart should be shared between a barbarian and my arm [myself] / Baptism will extinguish these flames that the heart longs for / And you will live in faith or die a martyr [3.4.881–84]). This speedy conversion and urged renunciation of other faiths can be contrasted to Zaïre’s opening speech where she spoke of the slow “engraving” of her heart and her openness to take on another faith, mirrored by Orosmane's willingness to take on the sexual mores of another culture. In this light, baptism and conversion to Christianity appear to be the prosthetic acts necessary to appease her brother's irate fury.

Furthermore, Voltaire was familiar with Corneille's *Polyeucte* and the scene of hasty baptism that the play opens with (as he dismissively calls Polyeucte a "fanatic"); in the preface of the 1738 and 1742 editions, it notes that "it is called *Christian Tragedy* in Paris and often performed instead of *Polyeucte*."[17] Whereas Polyeucte and Néarque's calibrated tempos of revolutionary haste served to suture their relationship, Nérestan and Zaïre seem to be out of sync. He simultaneously demands a hasty baptism and a deferral of the matrimony: "Ne peuvant t'arracher à ce palais honteux, / Je reviendrai bientôt par un heureux baptême / T'arracher aux enfers, et te rendre à toi-même" (Not being able to tear you away from this shameful palace, / I will soon return and, by means of a happy baptism, / Tear you from this hell and return you to yourself [3.5.894–96]); she has to be "arrachée" (torn) from her hellish deception to be reinstated as a proper and true Christian woman, which must happen "bientôt" (soon). This disjunction itself, far from merely accidental, produces a strategic winnowing effect. The commanded distribution of temporalities—deferring and hastening——reinforces the idea that she inhabits a paradoxical temporality, a temporal fold. As a Muslim, she is still a primitive "other" unaware of what is best for her own good, but with "te rendre à toi-même" (return you to yourself) Nérestan insists that this other, modernized identity is always already latent within herself. Zaïre stands at the temporal fold as a redeemable (baptizable) pagan and the sexually transgressive primitive, illustrating Fabian's conceptual turning point.

Meanwhile, Orosmane, unaware of the family ties that have been revealed, suspects that the surreptitious goings-on between Zaïre and Nérestan indicate a romantic betrayal. Again, the persistence of vision and the velocity of Nérestan's return create queer confusion between brother and lover. After observing Nérestan and Zaïre together, Orosmane begins to replay their interaction. He asks his friend, "Corasmin, que veut donc cet esclave infidèle? / Il soupirait. Ses yeux se sont tournés vers elle; / Les as-tu remarqués?" (Corasmin, what does this infidel slave want? He was sighing and his eyes turned to her. / Did you notice them? [1.5.297–99]). Caroline Weber has highlighted that Orosmane has an "anxious, almost prurient wish to know what the infidel wants" but merely reads this probing imagination as evidence of Orosmane's jealousy.[18]

At this point, the mismatching of velocities becomes tragic. Whereas Orosmane initially employed his time to illustrate his promise of monogamy—"Et le reste du jour sera tout à Zaïre" (and the rest of the day will be entirely for Zaïre [1.5.314])—here, he begins to *equate* velocities and sexual desire. At the hour of their intended matrimony, he says, "Paraissez, tout est prêt, et l'ardeur qui m'anime / Ne souffre plus, madame, aucun retardement" (Appear, everything is ready, and the ardor that animates me / Does not tolerate, madame, any delay [3.6.920–21]), and urges Zaïre, "Digne et charmant objet de ma constante foi, / Venez, ne tardez plus" (Worthy and charming object of my constant faith / Come, don't delay [3.6.941–42]). Zaïre hesitates, because she has given her word to her brother not to marry Orosmane, or at least she intends to be baptized first. She asks for a delay, to slow down time: "Souffrez que l'on diffère" (Accept that we defer [3.6.964]), and is unable to complete her request.

To defer, here, becomes differentiation—or as Derrida might put it, "différer c'est différer." By deferring the matrimonial union that would signify the zenith of their sameness (their unity, monogamy, and shared religion), she also insists on and articulates a difference. The presence of this delay tears them apart. Orosmane now resolutely sees them as different. He not only differentiates them as two separate beings within a couple but also attributes this delay to a Western power strategy:

> Mais il est trop honteux de craindre une maîtresse;
> Aux mœurs de l'Occident laissons cette bassesse.
> Ce sexe dangereux, qui veut tout asservir,
> S'il règne dans l'Europe, ici doit obéir. (3.7.1036–38)
>
> (But it is too shameful to fear a mistress,
> To Occidental mores let us leave this vileness
> This dangerous sex, which wants to enslave all
> Though it reigns in Europe, here it must obey.)

Similar to Félix's temporality of paranoia, which I discussed in the chapter 3 on *Polyeucte*, the splitting occasioned by difference triggers in Orosmane a paranoid "temporality that burrows both backward and forward."[19] This burrowing is necessary to prevent the unexpected: "because there must be no bad surprises, and because learning of the possibility of a bad surprise would itself constitute a bad surprise, paranoia requires that bad news be always already known."[20] Zaïre's request for delay itself *performs* delay, halting the wished for velocity moving toward the marriage. This unexpected interruption provokes the uncontrolled blossoming of Orosmane's paranoia. He says:

> Je t'aimerai toujours. Mais d'où vient que ton cœur
> En partageant mes feux, différait mon bonheur?
> Parle, était-ce un caprice? Est-ce crainte d'un maître,
> D'un soudan, qui pour toi veut renoncer à l'être?
> Serait-ce un artifice? épargne-toi ce soin;
> L'art n'est pas fait pour toi, tu n'en as pas besoin:
> Qu'il ne souille jamais le saint noeud qui nous lie! (4.2.1177–83)
>
> (I will love you forever. But why did your heart,
> While sharing my ardor, defer my happiness?
> Speak, was it a caprice? Is it fear of a master,
> Of a sultan, who for your sake wants to renounce being so?
> Could it be artifice? Spare yourself that care,
> Art was not made for you, you do not need it:
> Let it never sully the holy knot that binds us!)

With the future tense "je t'aimerai" he tries to reassure himself of the constancy of a future orientation that is pleasing to him. But the paranoid questions creep in and begin to spiral out of control. He scrutinizes every possibility that could have caused such delay: from Zaïre's capriciousness to fear and to feint. As Orosmane confronts the possibility of Zaïre's unfaithfulness, he is not content to face stoically the possibility of rejection; he must know it, investigate it, and stage it for himself.

When Zaïre rushes to meet her brother Nérestan at night for her secret baptism, Orosmane misinterprets the meeting as a romantic tryst and murders Zaïre in a fit of jealousy, crying out, "Misérable Zaïre, tu ne jouiras pas" (Miserable Zaire, you will not enjoy [orgasm] [5.7.1514]). As Weber has shown, both the Muslim lover and Christian brother "recoil from her incomprehensible desire—the obscene enjoyment she would ostensibly attain through the simultaneous entertainment of mutually exclusive symbolic claims—and so work pitilessly toward its elimination."[21] The fantasy of universality that Zaïre posited at the beginning has shattered. She uses a wedge of time (deferral) to engage in this "simultaneous entertainment," trying to keep both her lover and her family. The implosion of Zaïre's strategies of both deferral and haste—techniques that she draws on to sustain two identities at once—shows the clash between body's rhythms, sexualities, and sensualities are all being evaluated and governed in new kinds of ways, all oriented toward the unicity or purity demanded by chrononormativity. That is, with Orosmane's and Nérestan's repeated invocations of "infidèle" (with the dual invocations of unfaithful or infidel), Zaïre's behavior is sifted into the categories of either monogamy or infidelity, with little or no space for fantasy, hypersociality, or other forms of intimacy. Whether she buys time ("différer") to convert before the marriage, it is through her uses of velocity that she *brings to light* the mutually exclusive nature of the categories. In other words, velocity operates as a hermeneutic to illuminate the structures of mutually exclusive identities. Orosmane's haste—to judge Zaïre and to rush to murder—begins to otherize him. As Orosmane begins to speak, Nérestan spits out, "qu'ordonnes-tu, barbare?" (what are you ordering, barbarian? [5.10.1622]), which might be taken not only as an insult to the murderer of his sister but also as a particularly primitivized, racialized slur.

The impoverishment of the available categories with which to describe desire extends to the legibility of desire. Affinities like Zaïre's and Fatime's are not sustainable in the long term, as the tragedy tells us. The temporal-racial categories of primitive and barbarian are beginning to take hold. The deeply intimate relationships sketched out in the play are portrayed as directly competing against each other: familial, erotic, carceral, religious, or amical. The play's open-minded multiplicity in the first act, with the variety of ways of becoming that Zaïre describes, is ultimately crushed at the end. Therefore, what is remarkable is that the tragic aspect that Chateaubriand pointed to is not caused by villainous machinations (like *Othello*) nor by the barbarian-primitive Sultan's evildoings or incompetence. Rather, Chateaubriand unwittingly puts his finger on the fact that "tout est tragique" (everything is tragic)—because the given world, itself, cannot accommodate a multiplicity of velocities, pathways of potentialities, or different forms of hypersociality.

In a letter to a certain M. Falkener, to whom the play is dedicated, Voltaire complains about some aspects of the translation of *Zaïre* into English.[22] He especially targets the heavy-handedness with which the English tend to make French allusiveness too explicit: "If everything is known right away, one is satiated; there is nothing left to desire, and one arrives suddenly to languor while believing one is racing to sensuousness."[23] In particular, Voltaire is offended by the melodramatic theatrics that the translator included: "to only say what is necessary, and in the necessary manner is, it seems to me, a merit which the

French (if you'll allow me) have better approximated than the writers of other countries."[24] In many ways Voltaire emphasizes what my book has been trying to argue: that French theater, *because* of its particular neoclassical form and its restraint, allows us to see the slownesses and hastenings more clearly than any other archive of theater. What I have argued in this book is that one affordance of the bienséances and the unity of time is the Foucauldian "conduit des conduites" (conduct of conducts). This is an apparatus that is not only aesthetic but also latently political; thus, I have illuminated the biopolitical and queer angle of this unique aesthetic function. The unity of time, as discussed in chapter 1, was integral to the development of the idea of "properness" and thus part of a larger apparatus (*dispositif*) that shaped and coordinated desire and the expression of erotics to a normative rhythm. Such a coordinating of life's rhythms could be understood as the basis for a type of biopolitical seizing of the time of life. It could *also* allow, as I suggested, a type of emancipated spectatorship or an imaginative theatrical engagement.

Theater exhibits a utopian impulse since it plays with the mechanisms of representation and helps us imaginatively push the boundaries of the phenomenological or of the given. In chapter 2 I suggested that an attention to velocities might help us rethink what looks like tarrying or delay on Andromaque's part, in response to her impossible ultimatum either to marry her captor or to relinquish her son. The very imperceptible slowness of her action signaled the possibility of a queerly animate object attachment to Hector's ashes themselves. In chapter 3 the velocity of haste, directionally "detouring" away from the norms of marriage or governance, offered a kind of legibility to the passionate attunement of the queer friendship between Polyeucte and Néarque, as they "came out" as Christians together. And finally, in chapter 4 on *Bérénice*, I wagered that the time of repetition or of "dilation"—sustaining a "not yet" or a capacious potentiality—allowed for the ambiguity of a queer triad to be held together. Altogether, these plays that show how theater, in the words of Alain Badiou,

> Stylizes and amplifies, to the point that it produces the obviousness of, the fact that a confused world is uninhabitable for the subjects who make it up, even and especially when they believe that the confusion is simply life's natural state. The theatre makes appear on stage the alienation of those who do not see that it is the law of the world itself which has lost its way, and not bad luck or personal incapacity.[25]

Let us then consider velocities to be part of the arsenal of theater's stylization and amplification. Velocities offer a way for characters to make their worlds livable—there is a latent optimism in Zaïre's use of various tempos in the play's beginning. The theater, through these multiple velocities, permits other possibilities of being-with each other. But velocities in the theater also push back against the stuckness of an "impoverished" larger world.

Although I stressed before that not all velocities are necessarily queer, the queerness of the velocities I analyzed shows the "uninhabitable" nature of the world for certain kinds of relationships, attachments, and modes of feeling that have no place in an "impoverished" present. While Fabian underscored how temporality served to demarcate the "us" from the primitive Other, what I have illustrated with my reading of *Zaïre* and in this book more broadly is that we might shift the focus from the arc of "evolutionary time" or the hegemony of past, present, and future to the rich possibilities of multiple kinds of tempos, speed, and velocities that exist in every present moment. By staying attuned to these velocities, we can begin to abdicate our affinity for identity-based categories of sexuality and begin to sense and feel our relations (however ephemeral, impossible, or queer) differently.

NOTES

Introduction

1. Christian Biet and Christophe Triau remind us that the theater was lit by candles, a subtle element that changes how we think of the temporal and sensory experience of theatergoing in the seventeenth century. They describe how "the stage would be poorly lit by a meagre row of candles, which were decidedly inferior to the court productions that everyone tried to imitate. The candle lighting forced each act to last only around twenty-five to thirty minutes. The wicks of the candles would then be trimmed so they could keep burning." Christian Biet and Nicolas Triau, *What is the Theater?* trans. Joanne Brueton (New York: Routledge, 2019), 108–9.

2. Isaac de Benserade, *Iphis et Iante: Comédie*, ed. Christian Biet and Lise Leibacher-Ouvard (Paris: Lampsaque, 2000), 94. All translations by Marie Satya McDonough unless noted.

3. Benserade, *Iphis et Iante*, 94.

4. In this study I understand "affects" to indicate a range of emotive intensities, from the subtlest gradient to the most powerful sway, which provoke a charged experience in an embodied subjectivity. The notion of affect as a force that agitates body and feeling draws on Gilles Deleuze's work on Baruch Spinoza. See Gilles Deleuze, *Spinoza: Practical Philosophy* (San Francisco: City Lights, 1988), 48–51. Affect also hearkens to a French seventeenth-century articulation of an adjacent term: *sentiment*. *Sentiments*, as described in the 1694 Académie Française dictionary, not only indicate sensations and emotions, but also refer to "the affections, passions and all the movements of the soul." Therefore, *sentiments*, much like "affects" in the current theoretical milieu, capture a feeling and a capacity of sensation, the impression of movement—being moved or experiencing an emotive force—as well as, curiously, an association with the "natural" that is haunted by the sense of unnaturalness. *Dictionnaire de l'Académie françoise dedié au roy* (Paris: Coignard, 1694).

5. I acknowledge the slight anachronism of the term as a figure; *vélocité* does appear in Furetière's 1690 dictionary, but only to indicate speed. Antoine Furetière, *Dictionnaire universel, contenant généralement tous les mots françois tant vieux que modernes et les termes de toutes les sciences et des arts* (The Hague and Rotterdam: Arnout and Renier Leers, 1690), http://gallica.bnf.fr/ark:/12148/bpt6k50614b. Velocity as a speed with a directional component is more fully fleshed out as a concept in Isaac Newton's *Principia* (1687).

6. Sara Ahmed, *Queer Phenomenology: Orientations, Objects, Others* (Durham, NC: Duke University Press, 2006), xxvii.

7. Ahmed, *Queer Phenomenology*, xxviii.

8. Vincent Duclos, Tomás Criado, and Vinh-Kim Nguyen, "Speed: An Introduction," *Cultural Anthropology* 32 (2017): 1–11.

9. Cymene Howe, "Timely," Theorizing the Contemporary, *Fieldsights*, January 21, 2016, https://culanth.org/fieldsights/timely.

10. Elizabeth Freeman, *Time Binds: Queer Temporalities, Queer Histories* (Durham, NC: Duke University Press, 2010), 7.

11. Pierre Corneille, *Trois discours sur le poème dramatique*, ed. Bénédicte Louvat and Marc Escola (Paris: Flammarion, 2006), 137.

12. Gary Ferguson, *Queer (Re)Readings in the French Renaissance: Homosexuality, Gender, Culture* (Aldershot, UK: Ashgate, 2008); Carla Freccero, *Queer/Early/Modern* (Durham, NC: Duke University Press, 2006); Todd Reeser, *Setting Plato Straight: Translating Ancient Sexuality in the Renaissance* (Chicago: University of Chicago Press, 2015); Joan DeJean, *The Reinvention of Obscenity: Sex, Lies, and Tabloids in Early Modern France* (Chicago: University of Chicago Press, 2002); Lewis Seifert, *Manning the Margins: Masculinity and Writing in Seventeenth-Century France* (Ann Arbor: University of Michigan Press, 2009).

13. Jose Esteban Muñoz, *Cruising Utopia: The Then and There of Queer Futurity* (New York: New York University Press, 2009), 65.

14. Iante says:

> Ce mariage est doux, j'y trouve assez d'appâts
> Et si l'on n'en riait, je ne m'en plaindrais pas:
> Je n'aurais pas regret qu'on nous joignît ensemble,
> Si l'on ne profanait le nœud qui nous assemble. [Benserade, *Iphis et Iante*, 105]
>
> (This marriage is sweet: in it I find plenty of delight
> And if people didn't mock it, I wouldn't complain.
> I would have no regrets that we have been joined together
> If people didn't profane the knot that binds us).

15. Joseph Harris describes the potential illegibility of Iphis's and Iante's love, given the presumed impossibility of lesbian sexual desire in the early modern period. See Harris, "Disruptive Desires: Lesbian Sexuality in Isaac de Benserade's *Iphis et Iante* (1634)," *Seventeenth Century French Studies* 24, no. 1 (2002):153–56.

16. Peter Coviello, *Tomorrow's Parties: Sex and the Untimely in Nineteenth-Century America* (New York: New York University Press, 2013), 7.

17. Benserade, *Iphis et Iante*, 112–13.

18. Johannes Fabian, *Time and the Other: How Anthropology Makes Its Objects* (New York: Columbia University Press, 2014), 31.

19. Michel Foucault, *The History of Sexuality, Vol. 1: An Introduction*, trans. Robert Hurley (New York: Vintage Books, 1978), 179.

20. Eric Santner, *The Royal Remains: The People's Two Bodies and the Endgames of Sovereignty* (Chicago: University of Chicago Press, 2011).

21. See Timothy Murray, *Theatrical Legitimation: Allegories of Genius in Seventeenth-Century England and France* (1987); and Déborah Blocker, *Instituer un 'art': Politiques du théâtre dans la France du premier XVIIe siècle* (Paris: Champion, 2009), to consider the relation between absolutist ideology and the standardization of the theater in early modern France.

22. Michel Foucault uses "*dispositifs*" as a term for any number of structures in (e.g., discourse, architecture, rules, signs) that are intended to capture, monitor, surveil, condition, or otherwise manage the body and its concomitmant desires. Therefore, the *dispositif* is that which limns and brings into the being the body itself as a site of power. See Michel Foucault, *Discipline and Punish: The Birth of the Prison*, trans. Alan Sheridan (New York: Vintage Books, 1995) or Michel Foucault, *The History of Sexuality, Vol. 1: An Introduction*, trans. Robert Hurley (New York: Vintage Books, 1978).

23. Michel Foucault, *Discipline and Punish: The Birth of the Prison*, trans. Alan Sheridan (New York: Vintage Books, 1995), 161.

24. Stuart Sherman, *Telling Time: Clocks, Diaries, and English Diurnal Form, 1660–1785* (Chicago: University of Chicago Press, 1997), 5.

25. Carlo Cipolla, *Clocks and Culture: 1300–1700* (New York: W. W. Norton, 2003), 58.

26. The exact nature of who, between Hooke or Huygens, first developed the spring balance gave rise to a bitter dispute between the two men (who were based in London and Paris, respectively). Huygens's notebook reveals a design for the spring watch dating from 1675, but Hooke claimed that he had invented the idea as early as 1658 but was unable to develop a prototype since funds were lacking. See A.R. Hall, "Robert Hooke and Horology," *Notes and Records of the Royal Society of London*. 16, no. 2 (1951), 167–77.

27. David S. Landes, *Revolution in Time: Clocks and the Making of the Modern World* (Cambridge, MA: Belknap Press, 1983), 128.

28. In addition to Landes and Cipolla, see also Gerhard Dohrn-van Rossum, *History of the Hour: Clocks and Modern Temporal Orders* (Chicago: University of Chicago Press).

29. This tripartite notion of "proper" and its relation to gender and sexuality in English literature was developed by Patricia Parker, *Literary Fat Ladies: Rhetoric, Gender, Property* (London: Methuen, 1987). In France the 1690 Furetière dictionary shows the wide range of definitions associated with *propre*, including "qui appartient à quelqu'un" (proper possession); "ce qui est convenable" (propriety); and "un heritage qui est venu par succession" (the sense of property as place).

30. Gerhard Dohrn-van Rossum alludes to a (somewhat disproven) story that Charles V "installed striking clocks in his residences at Vincennes and St. Pol and built the public clock at the Louvre. Subsequently he issued an ordinance requiring all churches in Paris to regulate their tolling . . . by the clock at the royal palace . . . Jacques Le Goff and Krzysztof Pomian emphasize that the new, rational time 'thus became the time of the state.'" Dohrn-van Rossum, *History of the Hour: Clocks and Modern Temporal Orders*, 217. Although Dohrn van-Rossum weighs eyewitness evidence for and against such a myth, what is most pertinent to my analysis here is the very persistence of the myth and the fantasy-generating origin that it allows.

31. Roland Racevskis, *Time and Ways of Knowing under Louis XIV: Molière, Sévigné, Lafayette* (Lewisburg, PA: Bucknell University Press, 2003), 92–96.

32. Silvio Bedini, "European Timekeepers in China and Japan," in *Encyclopedia of Time*, ed. Samuel L. Macey (London: Routledge, 2013), 189.

33. Ernst H Kantorowicz, *The King's Two Bodies*, reprint edition (Princeton, NJ: Princeton University Press, 1997).

34. "Ce corps Glorieux, qui fonctionne comme une horloge, entraîne une cérémonial mécanisé à l'extrême à la cour . . . Saint-Simon note que'avec une horloge et un almanach, à trois cents lieues de la cour, on savait ce qu'à une heure donnée le roi faisait.' A la gesticulation du roi-machine correspond celle des courtisans qui l'approchent quotidiennement dans l'espoir d'une faveur ou d'un regard bienveillant." Jean-Marie Apostolidès. *Le roi-machine* (Paris: Éditions de Minuit, 1981), 156.

35. As I argue in chapter 1, the word *regulier* in the seventeenth century carried connotations of order, orderliness, and adherence to norms and normality.

36. Racevskis, *Time and Ways*, 19.

37. Foucault, *Sexuality*, 145.

38. Foucault, *Sexuality*, 146.

39. Freeman, *Time Binds*, 4.

40. Foucault, *Sexuality*, 139.

41. Lee Edelman, *No Future: Queer Theory and the Death Drive* (Durham, NC: Duke University Press, 2004), 5.

42. Notable texts include Carolyn Dinshaw, *Getting Medieval: Sexualities and Communities, Pre-and Postmodern* (Durham, NC: Duke University Press, 1999); Carla Freccero, *Queer/Early/Modern* (Durham, NC: Duke University Press, 2006); Freeman, *Time Binds*; J. Jack Halberstam, *In a Queer Time and Place: Transgender Bodies, Subcultural Lives* (New York: New York University Press, 2005); and Heather Love, *Feeling Backward: Loss and the Politics of Queer History* (Cambridge, MA: Harvard University Press, 2007).

43. Edelman, *No Future*, 15.

44. Edelman finds shared structural terrain between queerness and futurism: "thus queerness could never constitute an authentic or substantive identity, but only a structural position determined by the imperative of figuration; for the gap, the noncoincidence, that the order of the signifier installs both informs and inhabits queerness as it inhabits reproductive futurism" (*No Future*, 24). But it is important to remember that these two kinds of gaps or lacks are not identical (even though Edelman views them as structurally resonant); one kind of gap catalyzes our future-oriented energies to accomplish the gap's eventual suturing (Imaginary), while the other is a foreclosed lack (Real) that is aligned with queerness's destabilizing powers: "Where futurism always anticipates, in the image of an Imaginary past, a realization of meaning that will suture identity by closing that gap, queerness undoes the identities through which we experience ourselves as subjects, insisting on the Real of a jouissance that social reality and the futurism on which it relies have already foreclosed" (*No Future*, 24–25).

45. Edelman, *No Future*, 9.

46. Muñoz, *Cruising Utopia*. 1.

47. Coviello, *Tomorrow's Parties*, 7.

48. Tom Boellstorff, "When Marriage Falls: Queer Coincidences in Straight Time," *GLQ: A Journal of Lesbian and Gay Studies* 13, nos. 2–3 (2007): 229.

49. L. O. Aranye Fradenburg and Carla Freccero, eds. *Premodern Sexualities* (New York: Routledge, 1996); Carolyn Dinshaw. *How Soon Is Now?: Medieval Texts, Amateur Readers, and the Queerness of Time* (Durham, NC: Duke University Press, 2012).

50. Madhavi Menon, M. *Unhistorical Shakespeare: Queer Theory in Shakespearean Literature and Film* (Palgrave Macmillan US, 2008).

51. Carla Freccero, "Queer Times," in *After Sex?: On Writing since Queer Theory*, ed. Janet Halley and Andrew Parker (Durham, NC: Duke University Press, 2011), 17.

52. Goldberg builds on Alan Bray to suggest that "sodomy, as the allegation of certain forms of sexual debauch, became visible in the Elizabethan period only when supposed practitioners were charged with violations, usually religious or political, of the social order" to *Sodometries: Renaissance Texts, Modern Sexualities* (New York: Fordham University Press, 2010), 120. Therefore, the term "sodomy" might be more closely aligned with disrupting a good, normative social order instead of specifying the particular act.

53. Ari Friedlander, "Desiring History and Historicizing Desire," *Journal of Early Modern Cultural Studies* 16, no. 2 (2016): 3.

54. Valerie Traub, *Renaissance of Lesbianism in Early Modern England* (Cambridge: Cambridge University Press, 2002), 32.

55. Blocker, *Instituer*, 45.

56. Blocker, *Instituer*, 13

57. Timothy Murray, *Theatrical Legitimations* (Oxford: Oxford University Press, 1987), 111–16.

58. Jacques Scherer, *La dramaturgie classique en France* (Paris: Nizet, 1950), 383.

59. Giovanni Dotoli, *Temps de préfaces: Le débat théâtral en France de Hardy à la Querelle du* Cid (Paris: Klincksieck, 1997), 32.

60. Certainly, this myth of "decorporealization" can be thought of as more idealistic or clichéd than truly practiced. As Sylvaine Guyot has suggested, the cliché of disembodied Racinian theater finds its weak point in the truly rich and affectively corporeal language that draws attention to a stubbornly opaque corporeality (faces, bodies) that resists transcendence to the metaphysical plane. See Sylvaine Guyot, *Racine et le corps tragique* (Paris: Presses Universitaires de France, 2014).

61. Jean Racine, *Théâtre complet*, ed. Alain Viala and Sylvaine Guyot (Paris: Classiques Garnier, 2013), 481.

62. Dana Luciano, *Arranging Grief: Sacred Time and the Body in Nineteenth-Century America* (New York: New York University Press, 2007), 11.

63. Roland Racevskis, *Time and Ways*, 20–21. "Foucault's terms—'meticulous,' 'minute,' 'detailed,' 'micro-physics'—refer to a practice of intense focus on small time quantities in this 'political investment of the body.' A study of the microtemporal dynamics of subjective experience contributes to describing the rhythms of this 'micro-physics of power' in early modern France."

64. Landes, *Revolution in Time*, 89.

65. Sherman, *Telling Time*, 21.

66. Gilles Deleuze, *Foucault* (Minneapolis: University of Minnesota Press, 1988), 92.

67. Jennifer Row, "Queer Time on the Early Modern Stage: France and the Drama of Biopower," *Exemplaria: Medieval, Early Modern, Theory* 29, no. 1 (2017): 59.

68. J. K. Barret, *Untold Futures: Time and Literary Culture in Renaissance England* (Ithaca, NY: Cornell University Press, 2016), 16.

69. Patricia Parker, *Literary Fat Ladies*, 42, 47. Paul Valéry, "Calepin d'un poète" and "Propos sur la poésie," in *Œuvres*, vol. 1, ed. J. Hytier (Paris: Gallimard, 1957), 1449–50; 1372; and Paul Valéry, "Les droits du poète sur la langue," *Œuvres*, vol. 2, ed. J. Hytier (Paris: Gallimard, 1960), 1264.

70. Michel Foucault, "The Subject and Power," in *The Essential Foucault*, ed. Paul Rabinow and Nikolas Rose, trans. F. Duraand-Bogaert (New York: New Press, 2003), 138.

71. Jane Bennett, *Vibrant Matter: A Political Ecology of Things* (Durham, NC: Duke University Press, 2010); and Mel Y. Chen, *Animacies: Biopolitics, Racial Mattering, and Queer Affect* (Durham, NC: Duke University Press Books, 2012).

72. Racine, *Bérénice*, in *Théâtre complet*, ed. Alain Viala and Sylvaine Guyot (Paris: Classiques Garnier, 2017); and *Racine, Berenice and Bajazet*, trans. Alan Hollinghurst (London: Faber and Faber, 2012). Translations of *Bérénice* adapted by Marie Satya McDonough.

73. Johannes Fabian, *Time and the Other: How Anthropology Makes Its Objects* (New York: Columbia University Press, 2014), 31.

74. Robyn Wiegman and Elizabeth A. Wilson, "Introduction: Antinormativity's Queer Conventions," *Differences* 26, no. 1 (2015): 2.

75. Eve Kosofsky Sedgwick. *Touching Feeling: Affect, Pedagogy, Performativity* (Durham, NC: Duke University Press, 2003), 13.

Chapter 1

1. "Il n'y a point eu en notre temps de Question plus agitée, que celle que j'ai à traiter maintenant; Souvent les Poètes en parlent, de leur côté les Comédiens s'en entretiennent en tout rencontre, aussi bien que ceux qui fréquentent le Théâtre; il n'y a point de Ruelles de lit où les femme n'entreprennent d'en faire des leçons." Abbé d'Aubignac, *La pratique du théâtre*, ed. Hélène Baby (Paris: Honoré Champion, 2011), 171. All translations into English by Marie Satya McDonough.

2. D'Aubignac, *La pratique*, 179.

3. Déborah Blocker, *Instituer un 'art': Politiques du théâtre dans la France du premier XVIIe siècle* (Paris: Champion, 2009).

4. D'Aubignac, *La pratique*, 20.

5. Racevskis, *Time and Ways*, 68–69.

6. Scherer, *La dramaturgie*, 120.

7. Charles Sorel, *De la connaissance des bons livres* (Paris: Pralard, 1671), 7. Cited in Scherer, *La dramaturgie*, 122.

8. Michel Foucault, *Discipline and Punish: The Birth of the Prison*, trans. Alan Sheridan (New York: Vintage Books, 1995), 151–52.

9. Christian Biet and Nicolas Triau, *What Is the Theater?*, trans. Joanne Brueton (New York: Routledge, 2019), 388.

10. Scherer, *La dramaturgie*, 383.

11. Biet and Triau, *What Is the Theatre?*, 413–14.

12. Biet and Triau, *What Is the Theatre?*, 413–14.

13. Jean-Marc Civardi, "Quelques critiques adressées au *Cid* de Corneille en 1637–1638 et les réponses apportées," *L'information littéraire* 54, no. 1 (2002): 14.

14. Jean-Yves Vialleton, "Les bienséances: Concept intraduisible ou notion apocryphe?," *Littératures classiques* 96, no. 2 (2018): 65.

15. Vialleton, "Les bienséances," 64.

16. John D. Lyons, *Kingdom of Disorder: The Theory of Tragedy in Classical France* (West Lafayette, IN: Purdue University Press, 1999), 125.

17. Lyons, *Kingdom of Disorder*, 125.

18. Lyons, *Kingdom of Disorder*, 125.

19. Pierre Corneille, *Théâtre complet*, ed. Liliane Picciola (Paris: Classiques Garnier, 2017), 866.

20. Corneille, *Théâtre complet*, 866.

21. Corneille, *Théâtre complet*, 866.

22. Corneille, *Théâtre complet*, 866.

23. Elizabeth Freeman, *Beside You in Time: Sense Methods and Queer Sociabilities in the American Nineteenth Century* (Durham, NC: Duke University Press Books, 2019), 5.

24. Roland Racevskis, *Time and Ways*, 20–21.

25. Freeman, *Beside You*, 12.

26. Vialleton, "Les bienséances," 69.

27. Vialleton, "Les bienséances," 69.

28. René Bray, *La formation de la doctrine classique en France: René Bray* (Paris: Librairie Nizet, 1974), 113.

29. Mitchell Greenberg, *Subjectivity and Subjugation in Seventeenth-Century Drama and Prose: The Family Romance of French Classicism* (Cambridge: Cambridge University Press, 1992), 18.

30. Blocker, *Instituer*, 199.

31. This is not to deny theater's historically vehicular role as a convenient, efficient, and powerful means of conveying political messages to foreign ambassadors. But many of these aforementioned arguments in favor of theater's conveying properties also work by analogy or similitude. Ellen McClure, for example, uses the similar structure of representation and belief to make the case: "A foreign prince dealing with an ambassador should in some sense believe that he is in fact speaking to the king whom the ambassador represents. An audience at a play should, *likewise*, believe that they are genuinely witnessing real actions." Ellen McClure, *Sunspots and the Sun King* (Champaign: University of Illinois Press, 2006), 200 (emphasis mine). See also Ellen Welch, *A Theater of Diplomacy: International Relations and the Performing Arts in Early Modern France* (Philadelphia: University of Pennsylvania Press, 2017).

32. Chloé Hogg, *Absolutist Attachments: Emotion, Media, and Absolutism in Seventeenth-Century France* (Evanston, IL: Northwestern University Press, 2019), 9.

33. Freeman, *Beside You*, 8

34. Michel Foucault, "The Subject and Power," in *The Essential Foucault*, ed. Paul Rabinow and Nikolas Rose, trans. F. Duraand-Bogaert (New York: New Press, 2003), 133.

35. Foucault, "Subject and Power," 138.

36. Foucault, *Discipline*, 154.

37. Foucault, *Discipline*, 201.

38. Foucault, *Discipline*, 201–2.

39. Bray, *La formation de la doctrine*, 113.

40. "la vraisemblance n'est pas le *but* du dramaturge mais plutôt le *moyen* d'obtenir l'adhésion complète du public." John Lyons, "Le Démon de l'inquiétude: La passion dans la théorie de la tragédie," *XVIIe siècle*, 792 (1994): 787–89.

41. Caroline Levine, *Forms: Whole, Rhythm, Hierarchy, Network* (Princeton, NJ: Princeton University Press, 2015), 7.

42. Levine, *Forms*, 7–8.

43. In this section my use of "affords" or "affordances" hearkens to Levine's usage, which draws upon "affordances" of design theory.

44. Biet and Triau, *What Is the Theatre?*, 413–14.

45. Corneille, *Théâtre complet*, 868.

46. Corneille, *Théâtre complet*, 868–69.

47. Judith Butler, "What Is Critique? An Essay on Foucault's Virtue," in *The Judith Butler Reader*, ed. Judith Butler and Sara Salih (Hoboken, NJ: Wiley-Blackwell, 2003), 221.

48. "structurer le champ d'action éventuel des autres." Foucault, "Subject and Power," 138.

49. Jean-Marc Civardi, *La querelle du* Cid *(1637–1638): Édition critique intégrale* (Paris: Champion, 2004), 997.

50. Allison Stedman, *Rococo Fiction in France, 1600–1715: Seditious Frivolity* (Lewisburg, PA: Bucknell University Press, 2012), 38.

51. Corneille, *Théâtre complet*, 866.

52. All plays are hereafter cited parenthetically. Text references are to act, scene, and line of the following edition: Pierre Corneille, *Le Cid*, in *Théâtre complet*, ed. Liliane Picciola (Paris: Classiques Garnier, 2017). All translations of *Le Cid* are by Marie Satya McDonough or else adapted by the author from Pierre Corneille, *Le Cid / Cinna / The Theatrical Illusion*, trans. John Caincross (London: Penguin, 1975).

53. Civardi, *La querelle*, 997.

54. Paul Scott, "'Ma force est trop petite': Authority and Kingship in *Le Cid*," *Forum for Modern Language Studies* 45, no. 3 (July 2009): 300.

55. Christopher Braider, "*Cet hymen différé*: The Figuration of Authority in Corneille's *Le Cid*," *Representations* 54 (1996): 28–56; Jacques Derrida, "Différance," in *Margins of Philosophy*, trans. Alan Bass (Chicago: University of Chicago Press), 19823–27.

56. M. J. Muratore, "The Poetics of Indeterminacy: Corneille's Le Cid," *Romance Quarterly* 60, no. 4 (2013): 244–53.

57. Hélène E. Bilis, *Passing Judgment: The Politics and Poetics of Sovereignty in French Tragedy from Hardy to Racine* (Toronto: University of Toronto Press, 2016), 28.

58. Mitchell Greenberg, *Corneille, Classicism, and the Ruses of Symmetry* (Cambridge: Cambridge University Press, 1986), 52.

59. Greenberg, *Corneille*, 52.

60. Greenberg, *Corneille*, 52.

61. "La bienséance des mœurs d'une fille introduite vertueuse n'y est [pas] gardée par le poète lorsqu'elle se résout à épouser celui qui a tué son père." Civardi, *La querelle*, 947.

62. "Si tost qu'il [Rodrigue] se presente à elle, quoy que teint du sang de son Pere, elle le souffre en son logis & dans sa chambre mesme . . . luy tesmoigne que pour cela elle ne laisse pas de l'aymer . . . C'est trop clairement trahir ses obligations naturelles, en faveur de sa passion; c'est trop ouvertement chercher une couverture à ses désirs." Civardi, *La querelle*, 962.

63. "plus excusable d'attribuer cette faute à Rodrigue qu'à Chimène"; "et son sexe, qui est comme en possession de fermer les yeux à toutes considerations pour se satisfaire en matiere d'amour, eust rendu son action moins estrange & moins insupportable." Civardi, *La querelle*, 963.

64. Foucault, *Sexuality*, 147.

65. Foucault, *Sexuality*, 147.

66. Butler, "Critique," 218.

67. Michel Foucault, *The History of Sexuality, Vol. 2: The Use of Pleasure*, trans. Robert Hurley (New York: Vintage, 1990) 23.

68. Joseph Harris, *Inventing the Spectator: Subjectivity and the Theatrical Experience in Early Modern France* (Oxford: Oxford University Press, 2014).

69. Jean Chapelain, "Lettre sur la règle des vingt-quatre heures," in *Opuscules critiques*, ed. Alfred C. Hunter and Anne Duprat (Geneva: Librairie Droz, 2007), 224.

70. Chapelain, "Lettre sur la règle des vingt-quatre heures," 225.

71. Pierre Bourdieu, *Distinction: A Social Critique of the Judgment of Taste* (Cambridge, MA: Harvard University Press, 1984).

72. Civardi, *La querelle*, 185.

73. Joseph Harris, *Inventing the Spectator: Subjectivity and the Theatrical Experience in Early Modern France* (Oxford: Oxford University Press, 2014), 38.

74. Harris, *Inventing the Spectator*, 39.

75. D'Aubignac, *La pratique*, 171.

76. Harris, *Inventing the Spectator*, 39

77. Harris, *Inventing the Spectator*, 48.

78. Rancière, Jacques. *The Emancipated Spectator*, trans. Gregory Elliott (Brooklyn: Verso, 2011), 2.

79. Rancière, *The Emancipated Spectator*, 2.

80. Déborah Blocker, *Instituer un 'art': Politiques du théâtre dans la France du premier XVIIe siècle* (Paris: Champion, 2009), 45.

81. Jürgen Habermas, *The Structural Transformation of the Public Sphere: An Inquiry into a Category of Bourgeois Society*, Studies in Contemporary German Social Thought (Cambridge, MA: MIT Press, 1989).

82. Hélène Merlin-Kajman, *Public et littérature en France au XVII*e *siècle* (Paris: Les Belles Lettres, 1994), 27.

83. Marine Roussillon glosses that for Chapelain these quarrels were "'Agreeable disagreements.' Agreeable: that which elicits pleasure, but also which makes agree, which produces agreement/harmony, consent. The legitimate quarrel is a disagreement which produces commonality, a dissensus which

opens onto consensus. The Sentiments of the Académie thus seek to define the conditions of legitimacy of literary conflict, both at the level of ethics—by promoting civility and humility—and at the level of aesthetics, by emphasizing the search for a shared pleasure." Roussillon, "'Agréables différends': L'esthétique galante de la querelle dans deux dialogues de Jean Chapelain et Jean-François Sarasin," *Littératures classiques* 81, no. 2 (2013), 51.

84. Foucault, *Discipline*, 27.

Chapter 2

1. *Andromaque*, by Jean Racine, dir. Muriel Mayette-Holtz, Comédie-Française, Paris, France, October 16, 2010, to February 4, 2011.

2. Roland Barthes, *On Racine*, trans. Richard Howard (Berkeley: University of California Press, 1992), 75.

3. . Anne Ubersfeld, introduction to Jean Racine, *Andromaque*, ed. Anne Ubersfeld (Paris: Éditions sociales, 1961), 51. See also William A. Mould, "The 'Innocent Strategème' of Racine's Andromaque," *French Review* 48, no. 3 (1975): 557–65; and Harriet Stone, "The Tragic Implications of Andromaque's Sacrifice," *Romanic Review* 75, no. 4 (1984): 424–31.

4. Sherman, *Telling Time*, 21.

5. Basil Dufallo and Peggy McCracken, *Dead Lovers: Erotic Bonds and the Study of Premodern Europe* (Ann Arbor: University of Michigan Press, 2006), 2. Emphasis mine.

6. Tiphaine Karsenti, "From Historical Invention to Literary Myth: Ambivalences and Contradictions in the Early Modern Reception of the Franco-Trojan Genealogy," in *Early Modern Medievalisms*, ed. Alicia Montoya, Sophia van Romburgh, and Wim van Anrooji (Leiden: Brill, 2010), 93.

7. Karsenti, "From Historical Invention to Literary Myth," 100. Colette Beaune also underscores that the Trojan genealogy bolstered up a notion of French *cultural* superiority as well: "Not content with assuring the ancientness and prestige of the nation as they had always done, [the Trojans] were now the guarantors of its ethnic purity and of a national solidarity based on blood. They justified the kingdom's rank among the European nations and before the Church and the Empire . . . Finally these warriors, having belatedly become civilizing heroes (insofar as France, endowed with political prestige, began to concern itself with its cultural identity quite late), founders of cities, decreers of laws and of words, would assure, at the dawn of the nation, the originality of its culture." Beaune, *Naissance de la nation France* (Paris: Gallimard, 1985), 54.

8. Including Pierre de Ronsard's *La Franciade* (1572) and Robert Garnier's *La Troade* (1579), known to Racine.

9. Racine, *Théâtre complet*, 216.

10. Freeman, *Time Binds*, 3.

11. Certainly, there are other forms of queer desire present in the play, but thus far none of these attachments have been analyzed as operations in tempos or velocities. Queer overtones have been highlighted in Andromaque's motherhood by other scholars, since she borders on treating her son merely as a quasi-incestuous replacement for Hector; see Greenberg, *Racine*, 80. We know, for example, that Pyrrhus describes Andromaque kissing her son:

> C'est Hector, disait-elle en l'embrassant toujours.
> Voilà ses yeux, sa bouche, et déjà son audace,
> C'est lui-même; c'est toi, cher époux que j'embrasse (*Andromaque*, 2.5.652–55)
> (It's Hector, she said, kissing him constantly.
> Here are his eyes, his mouth, and his precocious audacity
> It's him, it's you, dear husband, whom I am kissing)

In this sense, her love for Astyanax seems less like a progress-oriented preservation of the future and more like a redoubled, folded temporality in which the son stands in for the father.

12. Walter Benjamin, "Theses on the Philosophy of History," in *Illuminations: Essays and Reflections*, ed. Hannah Arendt, trans. Henry Zohn (New York: Houghton Mifflin Harcourt, 1968), 260.

13. Judith Butler, *Antigone's Claim Kinship between Life and Death* (New York: Columbia University Press, 2000), 76.

14. Carla Freccero, *Queer/Early/Modern*, 59. See also Christiane Klapisch-Zuber, "La 'Mère Cruelle': Maternité, veuvage et dot dans La Florence des XIVe–XVe siècles," *Annales. Histoire, Sciences Sociales* 38, no. 5 (1983): 1097–109, http://www.jstor.org/stable/27581802.

15. Harriet Stone, *The Classical Model: Literature and Knowledge in Seventeenth-Century France* (Ithaca, NY: Cornell University Press, 1996), 63.

16. Georges Forestier, *Jean Racine* (Paris: Gallimard, 2006), 303–4.

17. Christian Biet, "La veuve et l'idéal du mari absolu: Célimène et Alceste," *Cahiers du dix-septième*, 7, no. 1 (1997): 217.

18. For William Mould, Andromaque's love is less maudlin—less aligned with a contemporary ideal of motherhood—and more in tune with the seventeenth-century maternal ethic: "The aristocracy, deprived in the interim 1637–1667 of any real function, may well have begun to lose the practice of feudal virtue, but certainly retained at least a nostalgia for the *générosité* of preceding generations. The heroic and generous ideal of maternity held by Andromaque would have been readily apparent to Racine's audience" (Mould, 558) and thus for Mould what he defines as a "generous maternity" means that Andromaque's gesture "lifts up" Astyanax into a realm in which "life and death are of little importance" (564). In a similar "heroic" vein, for Anne Ubersfeld, "Andromaque is not caught between two duties, maternal duty and the duty of marital fidelity; she is caught between two *feelings*, maternal *feeling* and another equally powerful feeling, which might be called *national feeling*: she does not refuse to remarry, she refuses to marry the torturer of her people. This would mean killing her people twice over, and when she calls on Hector's memory, it is not only the beloved husband that she invokes, it is the incarnation of Troy . . . She almost never names Hector alone . . . but rather Hector and *Troy*" (Ubersfeld, *Andromaque*, 51). Yet, while both Mould and Ubersfeld argue that Andromaque is refusing social norms of motherhood in the name of higher stakes, they are all trying to reclaim her delay in the name of another type of triumphant temporality: national sentiment or heroic glory. I do not wish to diminish these possibilities, but I also would like to assert that it is only by letting go of a redemptive futurity that we can bring to light other vibrant possibilities of attachments, including queerer ones.

19. "Or à ce moment un sacrifice solennel et des libations funèbres [...] étaient offerts par Andromaque aux cendres d'Hector." Racine, *Théâtre complet*, 213.

20. Samuel Sanchez y Sanchez, "The Flesh and Bones of Politics in Early Modern Spain," in *Dead Lovers: Erotic Bonds and the Study of Premodern Europe*, ed. Basil Dufallo and Peggy McCracken (Ann Arbor: University of Michigan Press, 2006), 119.

21. Jane Bennett, *Vibrant Matter: A Political Ecology of Things* (Durham, NC: Duke University Press, 2010), vii.

22. Amber Jamilla Musser, "Objects of Desire: Toward an Ethics of Sameness." *Theory and Event* 16, no. 2 (2013), muse.jhu.edu/article/509903.

23. Amber Musser, "Objects of Desire."

24. Mel Y. Chen, *Animacies: Biopolitics, Racial Mattering, and Queer Affect* (Durham, NC: Duke University Press Books, 2012), 11.

25. Chen, *Animacies*, 11, 30.

26. Chen, *Animacies*, 2.

27. Patricia Parker, *Shakespeare from the Margins: Language, Culture, Context* (Chicago: University of Chicago Press, 1996), 22.

28. Parker, *Shakespeare from the Margins*, 21.

29. Parker, *Shakespeare from the Margins*, 21.

30. Bennett, *Vibrant Matter*, 18.

31. Stephen Greenblatt, *The Swerve: How the Renaissance Began* (London: Bodley Head, 2011), 5.

32. Bennett, *Vibrant Matter*, 17–18.

33. Ellen McClure, "Sovereign Love and Atomism in Racine's Berenice," *Philosophy and Literature* 27, no. 2 (December 2003): 307–8.

34. Luciano, *Arranging Grief*, 9.

35. "un transport d'égoïsme qui fait reculer Pyrrhus lui-même." Claude Saint-Girons, "Racine et l'amour maternel," *Dix-septième siècle* 7, no. 8 (1950): 231.

36. Cathy Caruth, *Unclaimed Experience: Trauma, Narrative, and History* (Baltimore: Johns Hopkins University Press, 1996), 7.

37. Mitchell Greenberg, *Racine: From Ancient Myth to Tragic Modernity* (Minneapolis: University of Minnesota Press, 2010), 59.

38. Stéphane Natan, "Les questions d'Andromaque: Entre révolte et revelation," *Seventeenth-Century French Studies* 36, no. 2 (November 2014): 136.

39. For more on the exaggerated language of "guerre" (war) in literary debates of the seventeenth century, see Alain Viala, "Un temps de querelles," *Littératures classiques* 81, no. 2 (2013) 5–22.

40. Robert W. Hartle, "Racine's Hidden Metaphors," *Modern Language Notes* 76, no. 2 (1961): 135.

41. Ellen McClure, *Sunspots and the Sun King* (Champaign: University of Illinois Press, 2006); and Timothy Hampton, *Fictions of Embassy: Literature and Diplomacy in Early Modern Europe* (Ithaca, NY: Cornell University Press, 2009).

42. Timothy Hampton, *Fictions of Embassy*, 186.

43. Louise K. Horowitz, "The Second Time Around," *L'Esprit Créateur* 38, no. 2 (1998): 25.

44. Racine, *Théâtre complet*, 207.

45. Quintilian, *Institutes of Oratory*, ed. Lee Honeycutt, trans. John Selby Watson, Kindle edition, 2015.

46. Patricia Parker, "Metaphor and Catachresis," in *Ends of Rhetoric: History, Theory, Practice*, ed. John Bender and David E. Wellbery, 60–73 (Stanford, CA: Stanford University Press, 1990), 72.

47. Gerard Poselt, "The Tropological Economy of Catachresis," in *Metaphors of Economy*, ed. Nicole Bracker and Stefan Herbrechter (Amsterdam: Rodopi, 2005), 86.

48. D'Aubignac, *La pratique*, 260.

49. According to Racevskis, "[they] can only invoke the greatness of their parents, while struggling with the historically petty, amorous concerns of their own sparse present on the threshold to an unknown future. Latecomers, in a parasitically referential relationship to the accomplishments of those who preceded them, the characters in *Andromaque* stand on a void, the constantly vanishing temporality of their own lives, the slippage of their becoming." Racevskis, *Tragic*, 157.

50. Roland Racevskis, *Tragic Passages: Jean Racine's Art of the Threshold* (Lewisburg, PA: Bucknell University Press, 2008), 157.

51. Carolyn Dinshaw, "Temporalities," in *Oxford Twenty-First Century Approaches to Literature: Middle English* (Oxford: Oxford University Press, 2009), 108.

52. Dinshaw, "Temporalities," 108.

53. Christian Biet, "La veuve et l'idéal du mari absolu: Célimène et Alceste," *Cahiers du dix-septième* 7, no. 1 (1997): 217.

54. Leo Bersani, *A Future for Astyanax: Character and Desire in Literature* (Boston: Little Brown, 1976), 50. Emphasis mine.

55. Edelman, *No Future*, 4.

56. Lee Edelman, "Ever After: History, Negativity, and the Social," *South Atlantic Quarterly* 106, no. 3 (2007): 470.

57. Christian Biet, "La veuve et l'idéal du mari absolu: Célimène et Alceste," *Cahiers du dix-septième* 7, no. 1 (1997): 217.

58. See Horowitz, "The Second Time Around" (24) for an extended discussion of the trope of renewal and return. Horowitz emphasizes the proliferation of "re" verbs in the text, as well as the symbolic importance of the name "Phoenix"—as the mythological figure rising out of the ash, surviving past death.

59. In an earlier version of the play, Racine has Andromaque reappear briefly to give a speech ("Deux fois veuve et deux fois l'esclave de la Grèce"; "Twice widowed and twice the slave of Greece") in which she confronts Hermione for her murderous plot and mourns Pyrrhus. Raymond Picard, in the Pléaide edition of the text, notes: "This long variant consists mostly of a speech by Andromaque which interrupted the rhythm of the action . . . Racine, wanting to maintain the inflexible strictness of the drama, removed it." *Œuvres completes*, vol. 1, *Théâtre poésie*, ed. Raymond Picard (Paris: Gallimard, 1976), 1089. For another take on the duality implicit in this speech and the poetics of nonclosure, see Richard Goodkin, "*A Choice of Andromache's*," *Yale French Studies*, no. 67 (1984): 225–47, doi:10.2307/2929917.

Chapter 3

1. *Polyeucte*, by Pierre Corneille, directed by Brigitte Jaques-Wajeman, Théâtre de la Ville-Paris, Paris, January 10–21, 2017.

2. Regarding the critical responses to Jaques-Wajeman, see Shathil Nawaf Taqa, "Polyeucte de Corneille face à la crise du sens," *PHILITT: Philosophie, littérature, et cinéma* (March 22, 2017), https://philitt.fr/2017/03/22/polyeucte-de-corneille-face-a-la-crise-du-sens/; or Barbara Selmeci Castioni, "Déjouer le saint: Le devenir de l'image du saint dans le théâtre religieux en France au XVIIe siècle, à l'interstice du théâtralisable et du théâtralisé," *LHT: Littérature Histoire Théorie* 19 (October 2017), http://www.fabula.org/lht/19/selmecicastioni.html. Castioni writes: "The fact that Polyeucte is represented as a terrorist asks us, though, to be particularly cautious, in a time when the blurring of religious belief and religious extremism poisons our understanding of current events. Polyeucte does not inflict physical violence—or allow it to be inflicted—on anyone other than himself. The blood that is shed is his own, and the hand that sheds it is that of the other. In seventeenth-century theatre, the martyr is not a terrorist: nothing is more foreign to him than the idea of an attack on another's life, whether opponent or coreligionist, man, woman, or child, who might not share his zeal." All translations by Marie Satya McDonough

3. Ross Lerner, *Unknowing Fanaticism: Reformation Literatures of Self-Annihilation*, 1st ed. (New York: Fordham University Press, 2019), 3.

4. Pierre Corneille, *Théâtre complet*, vol. 2, ed. Maurice Rat (Paris: Classiques Garnier, 2014).

5. Serge Doubrovsky, *Corneille et la dialectique du héros* (Paris: Gallimard, 1982), 241.

6. Lerner, *Unknowing Fanaticism*, 4. For "organs," see Edmund Spenser, *The Faerie Queene*, ed. A. C. Hamilton, with Hiroshi Yamashita, Toshiyuki Suzuki, and Shohachi Fukuda, 2nd ed. (London: Longman, 2007) (2.1.32–33).

7. Doubrovsky, *Corneille*, 241.

8. Katherine Ibbett, "Classicism and the Creaturely: Pierre Corneille's 'Polyeucte,'" *Yale French Studies*, no. 124 (2013): 112.

9. Lerner, *Unknowing Fanaticism*, 5.

10. John Boswell, *Christianity, Social Tolerance, and Homosexuality: Gay People in Western Europe from the Beginning of the Christian Era to the Fourteenth Century* (Chicago: University of Chicago Press, 1980), 141.

11. Boswell, *Christianity, Social Tolerance, and Homosexuality*, 141.

12. Boswell, *Christianity, Social Tolerance, and Homosexuality*, 143.

13. Lerner, *Unknowing Fanaticism*, 4. See also John Calvin, *Institutio Christianae Religionis* (Paris, 1559), 1.13.7

14. *Dictionnaire de l'Académie françoise dedié au roy* (Paris: Coignard,1694); also *Trésor de la langue française informatisé*, http://atilf.atilf.fr/.

15. Eric Santner, *The Royal Remains: The People's Two Bodies and the Endgames of Sovereignty* (Chicago: University of Chicago Press, 2011)

16. Carl Schmitt, *Political Theology: Four Chapters on the Concept of Sovereignty*, trans. George Schwab (Chicago: University of Chicago Press, 2006), 6.

17. Schmitt, *Political Theology*, 36.

18. Katherine Ibbett, *The Style of the State in French Theater, 1630–1660: Neoclassicism and Government* (Aldershot: Ashgate, 2009), 66.
19. Foucault, *Sexuality*, 138.
20. Ibbett, *Style of the State*, 59.
21. Foucault, *Discipline*, 208.
22. Santner, *Remains*, 5.
23. While Sylvaine Guyot's work examines the remainder of fleshliness in Racinian theater, not Corneille's, it is relevant here to think of the rhetoricity of embodiment and corporeality in a famously "disembodied" theater tradition.
24. Pierre Corneille, *Théâtre complet*, vol. 2, ed. Maurice Rat (Paris: Classiques Garnier, 2014), 9. All translations by Marie Satya McDonough
25. Scherer, *La dramaturgie*, 116.
26. André Georges, "L'appel de Polyeucte et de Néarque au martyre," *Revue d'Histoire littéraire de la France* 96, no. 2 (March 1996): 193.
27. Julia Reinhard Lupton. "Ablative Absolutes: From Paul to Shakespeare," in *Paul and the Philosophers*, ed. Ward Blanton and Hent de Vries (New York: Fordham University Press, 2013), 282.
28. Ibbett, "Classicism and the Creaturely," 110.
29. Three sites—early modern France, the Roman Empire, and ancient Armenia (known as one of the first Christian nations)—are thus triangulated along these lines of religion and politics, with France reflecting and blending anxieties of both; France as a nascent empire echoed the problems of Roman imperial governance from afar, while France as a Christian nation, albeit with a troubled, riven identity, shared characteristics with Armenia.
30. Ward Blanton, introduction to Ward Blanton and Hent de Vries, eds., *Paul and the Philosophers* (New York: Fordham University Press, 2013), 27.
31. Marc de Wilde, "Politics between Times: Theologico-Political Interpretations of the Restraining Force (*katechon*) in Paul's Second Letter to Thessalonians," in *Paul and the Philosophers*, ed. Ward Blanton and Hent de Vries (New York: Fordham University Press, 2013), 105.
32. De Wilde, "Politics," 106.
33. De Wilde, "Politics," 106.
34. Ironically, then, in this model Polyeucte's conversion to Christianity makes him the structural analogue of the Antichrist/Man of Sin that the state (Roman Empire, with its pagan religion) must hold in abeyance. Thus, while the equivalences between the problems of the katechonic temporality and the play are sound, the placeholder of the Man of Sin/Antichrist is reversed.
35. Marc de Wilde, "Meeting Opposites: The Political Theologies of Walter Benjamin and Carl Schmitt," *Philosophy and Rhetoric* 44, no. 4 (2011): 377.
36. De Wilde, "Meeting Opposites," 376.
37. De Wilde, "Politics," 125–26.
38. De Wilde, "Politics," 107.
39. De Wilde, "Meeting Opposites," 366.
40. Walter Benjamin, *Toward the Critique of Violence: A Critical Edition*, ed. Peter D. Fenves and Julia Ng (Stanford, CA: Stanford University Press, 2021), 57
41. De Wilde, "Meeting Opposites," 369.
42. De Wilde, "Meeting Opposites," 373.

43. Massimo Cacciari, *Europe and Empire: On the Political Forms of Globalization*, ed. Alessandro Carrera, trans. Massimo Verdicchio, 1st ed. (New York: Fordham University Press, 2016), 145, 146.
44. Cacciari, *Europe and Empire*, 150, 151.
45. Cacciari, *Europe and Empire*, 151.
46. Blanton and De Vries, *Paul and the Philosophers*, 20.
47. Ward Blanton calls this the Paulinist "clearing," asking: "how is one to construe, historically and theoretically, the new, change, or that which is not captured by current regime? Blanton, introduction to *Paul and the Philosophers*, 30.
48. Blanton, introduction, 25.
49. Ibbett, *Style of the States*, 63.
50. Sedgwick, *Touching*, 138.
51. Sedgwick, *Touching*, 130.
52. Christopher Semk, *Playing the Martyr: Theater and Theology in Early Modern France* (Lewisburg, PA: Bucknell University Press, 2017), 109–10.
53. This false sympathy bait and switch is precisely how Félix will later attempt to trick Polyeucte (act 5, scene 2).
54. Ibbett, *Style of the State*, 75.
55. Pierre Richelet, *Dictionnaire françois* (Widerhold: Geneva, 1680).
56. Antoine Furetière, *Dictionnaire universel, contenant généralement tous les mots françois tant vieux que modernes et les termes de toutes les sciences et des arts* (The Hague and Rotterdam: Arnout and Renier Leers, 1690), http://gallica.bnf.fr/ark:/12148/bpt6k50614b.
57. Jonathan Goldberg, *The Seeds of Things: Theorizing Sexuality and Materiality in Renaissance Representations*. 1st ed. (New York: Fordham University Press, 2009), 8.
58. For Blanton, "In this respect, the nondialectical 'event' of Alain Badiou, the 'time that remains' of Giorgio Agamben, and the radical apocalyptic passivity of Jacob Taubes are all analytic devices to think in, with, and against Paul an alternative way of construing such lines of flight than mere clearing and reconstruction or negation and overcoming." Blanton, introduction, 30.
59. Graham Hammill, *Sexuality and Form: Caravaggio, Marlowe and Bacon* (Chicago: University of Chicago Press, 2000) 79.
60. Greenberg, *Seeds of Things*, 11.
61. Quintilian, *Institutes*, 9.3.66.
62. Northrop Frye, *Anatomy of Criticism: Four Essays* (Princeton, NJ: Princeton University Press, 2001), 276.
63. Another example of the association between "sectes" and so-called sexual deviance is the typical Christian discourse on the Muslim world in early modernity: members of the "secte" of Islam are "sodomites." See Toby Wikström's forthcoming book *Staging and Erasing the Global in Early Modern France* analyzes such overlapping denigrations.
64. Northrop Frye, *Anatomy of Criticism: Four Essays* (Princeton, NJ: Princeton University Press, 2001), 276.
65. Laurie Shannon, *Sovereign Amity: Figures of Friendship in Shakespearean Contexts* (Chicago: University of Chicago Press, 2001), 3.

66. Boswell, *Christianity, Social Tolerance, and Homosexuality*, 143.

67. Shannon, *Sovereign Amity*, 3.

68. Shannon, *Sovereign Amity*, 7.

69. Quintilian, *Institutes*, 37.

70. Brian Cummings, "Metalepsis: The Boundaries of Metaphor," in *Renaissance Figures of Speech*, ed. Sylvia Adamson and Gavin Alexander (Cambridge: Cambridge University Press, 2007), 222.

71. I am deploying this sense of metalepsis carefully taking into consideration Valerie Traub's powerful argument against conflating the movements of and elisions of metalepsis with "queer analysis," itself wherein that which disappears—the metaleptic link—is sloppily equated to the unspeakability of queerness itself. Traub writes: "Metalepsis occurs when a present effect is attributed to a remote cause; it links A to D but only by eliding B and C. . . . Metalepsis can be rhetorically powerful, but it is vulnerable to critique as fuzzy logic . . . More interested in the status of metalepsis as a repressed or failed rhetorical device, Menon uses it to read absent sex scenes in Shakespearean drama, scenes of implied consummation that, despite their failure to be staged nonetheless link social cause to tragic effect . . . [yet] fails to translate into a cogent defense of metalepsis as a mode of queer argument." Traub, "The New Unhistoricism in Queer Studies," 31. Traub critiques the "fuzzy logic" of Menon's and Freccero's usage of the trope, specifically their overanalogized generalization, extending metaleptic usage as "embody[ing] the spirit of queer analysis" (Freccero, *Queer/Early/Modern*, 2), as if queer analysis (as an entity) could be embodied in a single trope. What I wish to emphasize here is that metalepsis' rejection of order and sequence does not in and of itself defy a heteronormative teleology. But what metalepsis does enact, especially and specifically in this instance in the play, is a type of rushing that cannot be merely dismissed as "fanaticism" or "fuzzy logic," but is actively employed by the two characters to express that which lies outside of representation and the representable.

72. Cummings, "Metalepsis," 230.

73. Cummings, "Metalepsis," 230.

74. René Descartes, *Abrégé de la musique* (Paris: Méridiens Klincksieck, 1990), 460.

75. Pedro Calderon de la Barca, *El médico de su honra* (Madrid: Catedra, 2012), lines 1211–20.

76. Thomas Street Christensen notes that Marin Mersenne touches on the same problem and hazards a guess, but is unable to fully explain it: "Eventually the correct theory occurred to Mersenne, to wit: 'it seems it is entirely necessary that [the string] beat the air five, four, three, and two times at the same time.' But Mersenne rejected this idea as 'impossible to imagine' and 'against experience.'" Christensen, *Rameau and Musical Thought in the Enlightenment* (Cambridge: Cambridge University Press, 1993), 136. Effectively, what Mersenne was puzzling over was this: hearing a higher pitched sound meant that the string had to vibrate more rapidly and frequently than the way the string would vibrate at a lower tone. But if only one string was being played, how could it vibrate both quickly and slowly at the same time?

Chapter 4

1. "à peine y a-t-il une action ici"; "depuis le commencement jusqu'à la fin, n'est qu'un tissu galant de Madrigaux et d'Élégies." Jean Racine, *Œuvres completes*, vol. 1, *Théâtre poésie*, ed. Georges Forestier (Paris: Gallimard, 1999), 517. This use of "galant" is akin to the aforementioned reference to *galanterie* in chapter 2; this was a heighted, formal politeness, a means of respectful or respectable seduction, and an idealized form of courtesy towards women.

2. Mitchell Greenberg summarizes the myth of the play's origin: "According to 'la petite histoire,' Henriette d'Angleterre supposedly suggested to both Racine and Corneille that they use the historical disguise . . . to represent an episode in Louis XIV's amorous career. As legend has it, Louis, when a young man, fell passionately in love with Marie Mancini, niece of his cardinal prime minister Mazarin. Despite their ardor, higher demands of the state worked inexorably against the match. A more politically motivated marriage awaited Louis, a marriage upon which the possibility of a generalized European peace depended." Greenberg, *Canonical States*, 139.

3. "Il y avait longtemps que je voulais essayer si je pourrais faire une Tragédie avec cette simplicité d'Action qui a été si fort du goût des Ancients." Racine, *Théâtre complet*, 469.

4. Racine, *Œuvres completes*, 517.

5. Racine, *Théâtre complet*, 479.

6. "Et qui doute, que ce qui a pu fournir assez de matière pour tout un Chant d'un Poème héroïque, où l'Action dure plusieurs jours et où la Narration occupe beaucoup de place, ne puisse suffire pour le sujet d'une Tragédie?" Racine, *Théâtre complet*, 479.

7. Racine, *Œuvres completes*, 517.

8. Racine, *Œuvres completes*, 511.

9. Racine, *Théâtre complet*, 481.

10. Forestier, *Jean Racine*, 1445.

11. Lynn Enterline, *Shakespeare's Schoolroom: Rhetoric, Discipline, Emotion* (Philadelphia: University of Pennsylvania Press, 2016).

12. Racine, *Bérénice*, in *Théâtre complet*, ed. Alain Viala and Sylvaine Guyot (Paris: Classiques Garnier, 2017); and *Racine, Berenice and Bajazet*, trans. Alan Hollinghurst (London: Faber and Faber, 2012. Translations of *Bérénice* adapted by Marie Satya McDonough.

13. Racine, *Œuvres completes*, 511.

14. According to Forestier, "In comparison to the couple, the role of Antiochus—a semi-historical figure linked to a historical duo—has persistently troubled critics over the last three centuries, to the point that some see in this figure the major weakness of the play. At worst, he is treated as a 'confidant who has been elevated in station'; at best, he is made into a purely functional character . . . In other words, under the pretext of allowing Titus to evade the spectacle of Bérénice's suffering, Antiochus's main function is to delay Titus's explanation. As a result, following the critical meeting of the lovers in Act IV, Antiochus's role seems to be at an end, and he appears only intermittently thereafter . . . As the Abbé de Villars remarks, the role of Antiochus is what allows the matter of a single scene to be turned into an entire play. And indeed, his appearance in fourteen scenes (in contrast to fifteen for Titus and eleven

for Bérénice) and the fact that Racine gives him 350 lines (barely fifty fewer than Bérénice) appear to be justified only by this concern for expansion in an extremely tenuous manner . . . However, if this character can be reduced to having a purely functional role, we must still understand why he reappears in Act IV after the decisive explanation between the two lovers, why Racine insists on the pathos of his own situation . . . and finally why the last sigh of the play falls to him." Forestier, *Jean Racine*, 1465.

15. Jacques Derrida, "Différance," in *Margins of Philosophy*, trans. Alan Bass (Chicago: University of Chicago Press, 1982), 7.

16. Derrida, "Différance," 7.

17. Patricia Parker, *Literary Fat Ladies: Rhetoric, Gender, Property* (London: Methuen, 1987).

18. Patricia Parker, "Deferral, Dilation, Difference: Shakespeare, Cervantes, Jonson," in *Literary Theory/Renaissance Texts*, ed. Patricia Parker and David Quint (Baltimore: Johns Hopkins University Press, 1986), 204.

19. Parker, *Fat Ladies*, 14.

20. Greenberg, *Canonical States*, 136.

21. Parker, *Fat Ladies*, 11.

22. In the play, dilation is most frequently associated with the East or the "Orient," a difference that often reappears in the play's invocation of Roman "virtue" (*vertu*) aligned with the Latin root "vir," for man or manliness against Eastern deferral or delay. This East-West difference was not only present in the characters' origins (Bérénice and Antiochus as representatives of the east, against Titus's Roman West); this imagined schism was also apparent in rhetorical prejudices. Patricia Parker writes: "Lipsius, the anti-Ciceronian humanist whose writings heavily influenced Jonson's *Discoveries*, wrote in 1586: 'I love Cicero; I even used to imitate him; but I have become a man, and my tastes have changed. Asiatic feasts have ceased to please me; I prefer the Attic.'" For Lipsius, a virile or "manly" style was the antithesis of a copious one: his *Institutio Epistolica* praises a style that is "clipped, strong, and truly manly" ("oratio stricta, fortis & vere virilis"). Patricia Parker, "Virile Style" in *Premodern Sexualities* ed. L. O. Aranye Fradenburg and Carla Freccero (New York: Routledge, 1996), 206, Kindle edition.

23. Roland Barthes, *On Racine*, trans. Richard Howard (New York: Octagon Books, 1977), 93.

24. Gilles Deleuze, *Masochism: Coldness and Cruelty and Venus in Furs*, trans. Jean McNeil (Princeton, NJ: Zone Books, 1991), 62.

25. Parker, *Fat Ladies*, 14.

26. Margaret Ferguson, "Hymeneal Instruction," in *Masculinities, Childhood, Violence: Attending to Early Modern Women and Men: Proceedings of the 2006 Symposium*, ed. Amy E. Leonard and Karen L. Nelson (Newark: University of Delaware Press, 2010), 98.

27. Ferguson, "Hymeneal Instruction," 98.

28. Jacques Derrida, "The Double Session," in *Dissemination*, trans. Barbara Johnson (Chicago: University of Chicago Press, 1988), 265.

29. Derrida, "Double Session," 222.

30. Parker shows in early modern rhetoric, overwrought, lengthy speech was considered particularly feminized, citing the "effeminate Ciceronian . . .

'bignesse'" (Parker, *Fat Ladies*, 14), but she reminds us of the other "bignesse" is that of pregnancy. As we saw in Paulin's speech warning of "fruits illegitimes," the proleptic specter of which is used as justification for Bérénice's departure.

31. Derrida, "Double Session," 223. "L'hymen, consommation des différents, continuité et confusion du coït, mariage se confond avec ce dont il parait dériver: l'hymen comme écran protecteur, écrin de la virginité, paroi vaginale, voile très fin et invisible, qui, devant l'hystère, se tient *entre* le dedans et le dehors de la femme, par conséquent entre le désir et l'accomplissement. Il n'est ni désir ni le plaisir mais entre les deux. Ni l'avenir ni le présent, mais entre les deux" (Derrida, *La dissémination*, 262).

32. Derrida, "Double Session," 223. "C'est l'hymen que le désir rêve de percer, de crever dans une violence qui est (à la fois ou entre) l'amour et le meurtre. Si l'un ou l'autre avait lieu, il n'y aurait pas d'hymen. Mais non plus simplement dans le non-lieu. Avec tout l'indécidabilité de son sens, l'hymen n'a lieu que quand il y a consumation sans violence, ou violence sans coup, ou coup sans marque, marque sans marque (marge), etc., quand le voile est déchiré *sans l'être*" (Derrida, *La dissémination*, 262).

33. Here, the ellipses are in the original play, indicating interruption. Arsace is unable to finish his speech because he is cut off by Antiochus.

34. Hollinghurst translates the line as "fame that shines as well on you," but it does not capture the erotic connotations of "éclat," which is a burst and here a near-orgasmic release or "rejaillir," which is commonly used to indicate a spurt or splash, in the context of a liquid.

35. A reference to Gayle Rubin, "The Traffic in Women: Notes on the 'Political Economy' of Sex" (1975), 175, in which women's oppression is reinforced through social rites that render women objects or gifts (to be given in marriage, traded, or bargained for); these rites solidify the male-male homosocial bonds of patriarchy since the trading and trafficking operations happen between men.

36. Jean-François Lyotard's remarks on silence specifically relate the breaking of silence with a "déchirement," underscoring the violent and sexual dynamics of the hymen: "Silence is the opposite of discourse, simultaneously violence and beauty; but silence is the very condition of discourse since it is also on the side of the things of which one must speak, that one must express. There can be no discourse without this opacity in trying to undo and restore this inexhaustible thickness. Silence is the result of the ripping-apart that allows discourse and its object to stand vis-à-vis each other, and the work of signification to begin; it is the result of the tear, integral to language, where the work of expression occurs. Lyotard, *Discourse, Figure*, trans, Antony Hudek and Mary Lydon (Minnesota: University of Minnesota Press, 2011), 8.

37. Derrida writes, ". . . nous ne tarderons pas, en effet, à buter sur ce motif du tiers dans la scène du témoignage possible-impossible, du témoignage possible *comme* impossible. Dans son étymologie latine, le témoin (*testis*), c'est celui qui assiste en tiers (*terstis*). Nous aurions à y regarder de très près pour comprendre ce que cela pourrait impliquer. *Testis* a un homonyme en latin. On l'utilise le plus souvent au pluriel pour dire 'testicule.' [. . .] *Testitrahus* veut dire à la fois entier et mâle, masculine." Marie-Louise Mallet and Ginette Michaud, eds., *Jacques Derrida* (Paris: L'Herne, 2004), 526.

38. Longino argues that "he [Antiochus] has allowed himself to be guided by his impossible love for Bérénice and his tortured fascination with Titus's power greater than his own, so that he has contributed to sow destruction in the very part of the world that would have been his to minister and protect. Expectations for a man are greater than for a woman, but a man from this part of the world, it is clear, is hardly a man by Western standards. Not only his hopeless love for Bérénice, but his compromised status as a man, make of him doubly a woman, and as such a strong signifier of the East for the West." Michèle Longino, *Orientalism in French Classical Drama* (Cambridge: Cambridge University Press, 2002), 168.

39. Greenberg's analysis redoubles a male-female binarism and reinscribes Bérénice in the slippery equivalences between "Oriental" and "feminine": "Behind Titus' military prowess and magnanimity stands the image of Bérénice. She leads him away from the easy road of sensual pleasure, away from the monstrous sexuality that reigned at Nero's court and down the thorny path of moral rectitude. She certainly appears to occupy a maternal rather than a passionate role in Titus' description of her. This maternal, in the sense of nonsexual, and wise pedagogue leads the child-man still captive of his senses out of the prison of his body's pleasure and into the light of mature, that is, sublimated, humanitarianism. At the same time she is presented as the embodiment of a conventional allegorical representation of the Orient: Bérénice is here garbed as Sophia, a traditional figure of Oriental wisdom whose historic abode was in the East (in Egypt) . . . It is precisely because of this doubling, of this combination of the love-object as maternal and Oriental, that Bérénice is doomed" (Greenberg, *Racine*, 127).

40. Leo Spitzer, *Leo Spitzer: Essays on Seventeenth-Century French Literature* (Cambridge: Cambridge University Press, 1983), 5.

41. For more on ellipses in Racine, see Michael Hawcroft, "Points de suspension chez Racine: enjeux dramatiques, enjeux éditoriaux," *Revue d'histoire littéraire de la France* 106, no. 2 (2006): 307–35.

42. Derrida, "The Double Session," 240. L'entr'acte ou l'entre-temps de l'hymen ne donne pas le temps, ni le temps comme existence du concept (Hegel), ni le temps perdu ni le temps retrouvé, encore moins l'instant ou l'éternité. Aucun présent en vérité ne s'y présente, fût-ce pour s'y dissimuler. Ce que l'hymen déjoue, sous l'espèce du présent (temporel ou éternel), c'est l'assurance de maîtrise (Derrida, *La dissémination*, 282).

43. Spitzer, *Essays*, 93.

44. Spitzer, *Essays*, 94.

45. Racevskis, "Time of Tragedy," 115.

46. Bryant C. Freeman and Alan Batson, *Concordance du théâtre et des poésies de Jean Racine* (Ithaca, NY: Cornell University Press, 1968).

47. Walter Benjamin, *The Origin of German Tragic Drama*, trans. John Osborne (London: NLB, 1977), 66. Agamben clarifies that this translation is slightly faulty, but the error is actually closer to what Benjamin intended to say: "An unfortunate emendation in the text of the Gesammelte Schriften has prevented all the implications of this shift from being assessed. Where Benjamin's text read, Es gibt eine barocke Eschatologie, 'there is a baroque eschatology,' the editors, with a singular disregard for all philological care,

have corrected it to read: Es gibt keine . . . 'there is no baroque eschatology.' And yet the passage that follows is logically and syntactically consistent with the original reading: 'and for that very reason [there is] a mechanism that gathers and exalts all earthly creatures before consigning them to the end [dem Ende].' The baroque knows an eskhaton, an end of time; but, as Benjamin immediately makes clear, this eskhaton is empty. It knows neither redemption nor a hereafter and remains immanent to this world." Agamben, *State of Exception*, 56.

48. Derrida, *Beast and the Sovereign*, 33.

49. Benjamin, *Origin*, 66.

50. Parker, "Deferral," 204.

51. Racine, *Œuvres completes*, 511.

Conclusion

1. Muñoz, *Cruising*, 25.

2. "To make such a claim I examine in this book the pervasive invocation of the Child as the emblem of futurity's unquestioned value and propose against it the impossible project of a queer oppositionality that would oppose itself to the structural determinants of politics as such, which is also to say, that would oppose itself to the logic of opposition." Lee Edelman, *No Future: Queer Theory and the Death Drive* (Durham, NC: Duke University Press, 2004), 3.

3. Munoz, *Cruising*, 22.

4. Munoz, *Cruising*, 31.

5. D'Aubignac, *La pratique*, 70. Translated by Marie Satya McDonough.

6. Muñoz, *Cruising*, 21.

7. Deleuze, *Foucault*, 92.

8. Stuart Sherman, "Dryden and the Theatrical Imagination," in *The Cambridge Companion to John Dryden*, ed. Steven N. Zwicker (Cambridge: Cambridge University Press, 2006), 18. John Dryden, *The Works of John Dryden*, vol. 2, ed. Walter Scott (London: Miller, 1808) 287.

9. Fabian, *Time*, 31.

10. Fabian, *Time*, 17.

11. Fabian, *Time*, 17–18.

12. Fabian, *Time*, 26.

13. Fabian, *Time*, 26.

14. Portions of these reflections were previously published with *Le Monde français du dix-huitième siècle* as "Alternative Intimacies, Sympathy and Sexuality in Voltaire's *Zaïre*."

15. François-René de Chateaubriand, "Chateaubriand, Lecteur de Zaïre," in *Zaïre*, by Voltaire, ed. Pierre Frantz (Paris: Gallimard, 2016), 198.

16. Freeman, *Beside You*, 14.

17. "On l'appelle [Zaïre] à Paris tragédie chrétienne, et on l'a jouée fort souvent à la place de Polyeucte" (Voltaire, *Zaïre*, 141.

18. Caroline Weber, "Voltaire's *Zaïre*: Fantasies of Infidelity, Ideologies of Faith," *South Central Review* 21, no. 2 (Summer 2004): 53.

19. Sedgwick, *Touching*, 130.

20. Sedgwick, *Touching*, 130.

21. Weber, "Fantasies,"44.

22. Aaron Hill's translation of Voltaire's *Zaïre* was published in 1736 as *The Tragedy of Zara.*

23. "Si tout est d'abord à découvert, on est rassasié; il ne reste plus rien à desirer, et on arrive tout d'un coup à la langueur en croyant courir à la volupté." Voltaire, "Seconde Lettre au même Monsieur Falkener," in *Zaïre*, ed. Pierre Frantz (Paris: Gallimard, 2016), 163.

24. "Ne dire que ce qu'il faut, et de la manière dont il le faut, est, ce me semble, un mérite dont les Français, si vous m'en exceptez, ont plus approché que les écrivains des autres pays." Voltaire, "Seconde Lettre au même Monsieur Falkener," 164.

25. Alain Badiou, *In Praise of Theatre*, with Nicolas Truong (Malden: Polity, 2015), 63.

BIBLIOGRAPHY

Agamben, Giorgio. *State of Exception*. Chicago: University of Chicago Press, 2005.

Apostolidès, Jean-Marie. *Le roi-machine*. Paris: Éditions de Minuit, 1981.

Aubignac, Abbé de [François Hédelin]. *La pratique du théâtre*. Edited by Hélène Baby. Paris: Honoré Champion, 2011.

Badiou, Alain. *In Praise of Theatre*. With Nicolas Truong. Malden, MA: Polity, 2015.

Barret, J. K. *Untold Futures: Time and Literary Culture in Renaissance England*. Ithaca, NY: Cornell University Press, 2016.

Barthes, Roland. *On Racine*. Translated by Richard Howard. Berkeley: University of California Press, 1992.

———. *Sur Racine*. Paris: Éditions du Seuil, 1963.

Beaune, Colette. *Naissan de la nation France*. Paris: Gallimard, 1985.

Bedini, Silvio. "European Timekeepers in China and Japan." In *Encyclopedia of Time*, edited by Samuel L. Macey, 188–92. London: Routledge, 2013.

Benjamin, Walter. *The Origin of German Tragic Drama*. Translated by John Osborne. London: NLB, 1977.

———. "Theses on the Philosophy of History." In *Illuminations: Essays and Reflections*. Edited by Hannah Arendt. Translated by Henry Zohn, 253–63. New York: Houghton Mifflin Harcourt, 1968.

Bennett, Jane. *Vibrant Matter: A Political Ecology of Things*. Durham, NC: Duke University Press, 2010.

Benserade, Isaac de. *Iphis et Iante: Comédie*. Edited by Christian Biet and Lise Leibacher-Ouvrard. Paris: Lampsaque, 2000.

Bersani, Leo. *A Future for Astyanax: Character and Desire in Literature*. Boston: Little, Brown, 1976.

Biet, Christian. "La veuve et l'idéal du mari absolu: Célimène et Alceste." *Cahiers du Dix-Septième* 7, no. 1 (Spring 1997): 215–26.

Biet, Christian, and Christophe Triau. *What Is the Theatre?* Translated by Joanne Brueton. New York: Routledge, 2019.

Bilis, Hélène E. *Passing Judgment: The Politics and Poetics of Sovereignty in French Tragedy from Hardy to Racine*. Toronto: University of Toronto Press, 2016

Blanton, Ward, and Hent de Vries, eds. *Paul and the Philosophers*. New York: Fordham University Press, 2013.

Blocker, Déborah. *Instituer un "art": Politiques du théâtre dans la France du premier XVIIe siècle*. Paris: Honoré Champion, 2009.

Boellstorff, Tom. "When Marriage Fails: Queer Coincidences in Straight Time." *GLQ: A Journal of Lesbian and Gay Studies* 13, nos. 2–3 (2007): 227–48. https://doi.org/10.1215/10642684-2006-032.

Boswell, John. *Christianity, Social Tolerance, and Homosexuality: Gay People in Western Europe from the Beginning of the Christian Era to the Fourteenth Century*. Chicago: University of Chicago Press, 1980.

Bourdieu, Pierre. *Distinction: A Social Critique of the Judgement of Taste*. Translated by Richard Nice. Harvard University Press, 1984.

Braider, Christopher. "*Cet hymen différé*: The Figuration of Authority in Corneille's *Le Cid*." *Representations* 54 (1996): 28–56. https://doi.org/10.2307/2928691.

Bray, René. *La formation de la doctrine classique en France: René Bray*. Paris: Librairie Nizet, 1974.

Butler, Judith. *Antigone's Claim Kinship between Life and Death*. New York: Columbia University Press, 2000.

———. *Bodies that Matter: On the Discursive Limits of "Sex."* 1st ed. New York: Routledge, 2014.

———. "What Is Critique? An Essay on Foucault's Virtue." In *The Judith Butler Reader*, edited by Judith Butler and Sara Salih, 302–22. Hoboken, NJ: Wiley-Blackwell, 2003.

Cacciari, Massimo. *Europe and Empire: On the Political Forms of Globalization*. Edited by Alessandro Carrera. Translated by Massimo Verdicchio. 1st ed. New York: Fordham University Press, 2016.

Calderón de la Barca, Pedro. *El médico de su honra*. Madrid: Catedra, 2012.

Calvin, John. *Institutio Christianae Religionis*. Paris, 1559.

Caruth, Cathy. *Unclaimed Experience: Trauma, Narrative, and History*. Baltimore: Johns Hopkins University Press, 1996.

Castioni, Barbara Selmeci. "Déjouer le saint: Le devenir de l'image du saint dans le théâtre religieux en France au XVIIe siècle, à l'interstice du théâtralisable et du théâtralisé." *LHT: Littérature Histoire Théorie* 19 (October 2017). https://www.fabula.org/lht/19/selmecicastioni.html.

Chapelain, Jean. "Lettre sur la règle des vingt-quatre heures." In *Opuscules critiques*, edited by Alfred C. Hunter and Anne Duprat, 222–34. Geneva: Librairie Droz, 2007.

Chateaubriand, François-René de. "Chateaubriand, Lecteur de *Zaïre*." In Voltaire, *Zaïre*, edited by Pierre Frantz, 196–202. Paris: Gallimard, 2016.

Chen, Mel Y. *Animacies: Biopolitics, Racial Mattering, and Queer Affect*. Durham, NC: Duke University Press Books, 2012.

Christensen, Thomas Street. *Rameau and Musical Thought in the Enlightenment*. Cambridge: Cambridge University Press, 1993.

Cipolla, Carlo M. *Clocks and Culture: 1300–1700*. New York: W. W. Norton, 2003.

Civardi, Jean-Marc. *La querelle du* Cid *(1637–1638): Édition critique intégrale*. Paris: Champion, 2004.

———. "Quelques critiques adressées au *Cid* de Corneille en 1637–1638 et les réponses apportées." *L'information littéraire* 54, no. 1 (2002): 12–26. https://doi.org/10.3917/inli.541.0012.

Corneille, Pierre. *Le Cid / Cinna / The Theatrical Illusion*. Translated by John Caincross. London: Penguin, 1975.

———. *Théâtre*. Vol. 2. Edited by Liliane Picciola. Paris: Classiques Garnier, 2017.

———. *Théâtre complet*. Vol. 2. Edited by Maurice Rat. Paris: Classiques Garnier, 2014.

———. *Trois discours sur le poème dramatique*. Edited by Bénédicte Louvat and Marc Escola. Paris: Flammarion, 2006.

Coviello, Peter. *Tomorrow's Parties: Sex and the Untimely in Nineteenth-Century America*. New York: New York University Press, 2013.

Crawford, Katherine B. "Love, Sodomy, and Scandal: Controlling the Sexual Reputation of Henry III." *Journal of the History of Sexuality* 12, no. 4 (2003): 513–42. https://doi.org/10.1353/sex.2004.0024.

Cummings, Brian. "Metalepsis: The Boundaries of Metaphor." In *Renaissance Figures of Speech*, edited by Sylvia Adamson and Gavin Alexander, 217–34. Cambridge: Cambridge University Press, 2007.

De Wilde, Marc. "Meeting Opposites: The Political Theologies of Walter Benjamin and Carl Schmitt." *Philosophy and Rhetoric* 44, no. 4 (2011): 363–81. https://philpapers.org/rec/DEWMOT.

———. "Politics between Times: Theologico-Political Interpretations of the Restraining Force (*katechon*) in Paul's Second Letter to the Thessalonians." In *Paul and the Philosophers*, edited by Ward Blanton and Hent de Vries, 105–25, 541–47. New York: Fordham University Press, 2013.

DeJean, Joan E. *The Reinvention of Obscenity: Sex, Lies, and Tabloids in Early Modern France*. Chicago: University of Chicago Press, 2002.

Deleuze, Gilles. *Foucault*. Minneapolis: University of Minnesota Press, 1988.

———. *Masochism: Coldness and Cruelty and Venus in Furs*. Translated by Jean McNeil. Princeton, NJ: Zone Books, 1991.

Derrida, Jacques. *The Beast and the Sovereign*. Translated by Geoffrey Bennington. Chicago: University of Chicago Press, 2009.

———. "Différance." In *Margins of Philosophy*. Translated by Alan Bass, 3–27. Chicago: University of Chicago Press, 1982.

———. *Dissemination*. Translated by Barbara Johnson, 187–316. Chicago: University of Chicago Press, 1981.

———. "'La 'Différance,' Séance du samedi 27 janvier 1968." *Bulletin de la Société française de philosophie* 63 (1968): 73–120.

———. *La dissémination*. Paris: Éditions du Seuil, 1972.

———. "The Double Session." In *Dissemination*. Translated by Barbara Johnson. London: Continuum, 2004.

———. *Margins of Philosophy*. Translated by Alan Bass. Chicago: University of Chicago Press, 1982.

———. *Poétique et politique du témoignage*. Paris: L'Herne, 2005.

———. *Séminaire: La bête et le souverain*. Paris: Galilée, 2008.

Descartes, René. *Abrégé de musique*. Paris: Méridiens Klincksieck, 1990.

Dictionnaire de l'Académie française. Vol. 2. Paris: Coignard, 1694. University of Chicago, ARTFL, Dictionnaires d'autrefois, https://artfl-project.uchicago.edu/content/dictionnaires-d'autrefois.

Dinshaw, Carolyn. *Getting Medieval: Sexualities and Communities, Pre- and Postmodern*. Durham, NC: Duke University Press, 1999.

———. *How Soon Is Now?: Medieval Texts, Amateur Readers, and the Queerness of Time*. Durham NC: Duke University Press, 2012.

———. "Temporalities." In *Oxford Twenty-First Century Approaches to Literature: Middle English*, Edited by Paul Strohm, 107–23. 1st ed. Oxford: Oxford University Press, 2009.

Dohrn-van Rossum, Gerhard. *History of the Hour: Clocks and Modern Temporal Orders*. Chicago: University of Chicago Press, 1996.

Dotoli, Giovanni. *Temps de préfaces: Le débat théâtral en France de Hardy à la Querelle du* Cid. Paris: Klincksieck, 1997.

Doubrovsky, Serge. *Corneille et la dialectique du héros*. Paris: Gallimard, 1982.

Duclos, Vincent, Tomás Sánchez Criado, and Vinh-Kim Nguyen. "Speed: An Introduction." *Cultural Anthropology* 32, no. 1 (February 2017): 1–11. https://doi.org/10.14506/ca32.1.01.

Dufallo, Basil, and Peggy McCracken. *Dead Lovers: Erotic Bonds and the Study of Premodern Europe*. Ann Arbor: University of Michigan Press, 2006.

Dryden, John. *The Works of John Dryden, Vol. 2*. Edited by Walter Scott. London: Miller, 1808

Edelman, Lee. "Ever After: History, Negativity, and the Social." *South Atlantic Quarterly* 106, no. 3 (2007): 469–76. https://doi.org/10.1215/00382876-2007-005.

———. *No Future: Queer Theory and the Death Drive*. Durham, NC: Duke University Press Books, 2004.

Enterline, Lynn. *Shakespeare's Schoolroom: Rhetoric, Discipline, Emotion*. Philadelphia: University of Pennsylvania Press, 2016.

Fabian, Johannes. *Time and the Other: How Anthropology Makes Its Objects*. New York: Columbia University Press, 2014.

Ferguson, Gary. *Queer (Re)Readings in the French Renaissance: Homosexuality, Gender, Culture*. Aldershot: Ashgate, 2008.

Ferguson, Margaret. "Hymeneal Instruction." In *Masculinities, Childhood, Violence: Attending to Early Modern Women and Men; Proceedings of the 2006 Symposium*, edited by Amy E. Leonard and Karen L. Nelson, 97–129. Newark: University of Delaware Press, 2010.

Forestier, Georges. *Jean Racine*. Paris: Gallimard, 2006.

Foucault, Michel. *Discipline and Punish: The Birth of the Prison*. Translated by Alan Sheridan. 2nd ed. New York: Vintage Books, 1995.

———. *Histoire de la sexualité*. Paris: Gallimard, 1976.

———. *The History of Sexuality, Vol. 1: An Introduction*. Translated by Robert Hurley. New York: Vintage Books, 1978.

———. *The History of Sexuality, Vol. 2: The Use of Pleasure*. Translated by Robert Hurley. Reissue edition. New York: Vintage, 1990.

———. *Surveiller et punir: Naissance de la prison*. Paris: Editions Gallimard, 2014.

———. "The Subject and Power." In *The Essential Foucault*, edited by Paul Rabinow and Nikolas Rose, translated by F. Durand-Bogaert, 126–44. New York: New Press, 2003.

Fradenburg, L. O. Aranye, and Carla Freccero, eds. *Premodern Sexualities*. New York: Routledge, 1996.

Freccero, Carla. *Queer/Early/Modern*. Durham, NC: Duke University Press Books, 2006.

———. "Queer Times." In *After Sex?: On Writing since Queer Theory*, edited by Janet Halley and Andrew Parker, 17–26. Durham, NC: Duke University Press, 2011.

Freeman, Bryant C., and Batson, Alan. *Concordance du théâtre et des poésies de Jean Racine*. Ithaca, NY: Cornell University Press, 1968.

Freeman, Elizabeth. *Beside You in Time: Sense Methods and Queer Sociabilities in the American Nineteenth Century*. Durham, NC: Duke University Press, 2019.

———. *Time Binds: Queer Temporalities, Queer Histories*. Durham, NC: Duke University Press, 2010.

Friedlander, Ari. "Desiring History and Historicizing Desire." *Journal of Early Modern Cultural Studies* 16, no. 2 (2016): 1–20. https://doi.org/10.1353/jem.2016.0016.

Frostin, Charles. "L'éveil scientifique de la France." In *La France de la monarchie absolue, 1610–1715*, edited by Joël Cornette, 325–40. Paris: Éditions du Seuil, 1997.

Frye, Northrop. *Anatomy of Criticism: Four Essays*. Princeton, NJ: Princeton University Press, 2001.

Furetière, Antoine. *Dictionaire universel, contenant generalement tous les mots françois tant vieux que modernes, & les Termes de toutes les sciences et des arts . . . / par feu Messire Antoine Furetière*. The Hague and Rotterdam: Arnout and Renier Leers, 1690. http://gallica.bnf.fr/ark:/12148/bpt6k50614b.

Georges, André. "L'appel de Polyeucte et de Néarque au martyre." *Revue d'Histoire littéraire de la France* 96, no. 2 (March 1996): 192–211. https://www.jstor.org/stable/40532616.

Goldberg, Jonathan. *The Seeds of Things: Theorizing Sexuality and Materiality in Renaissance Representations*. 1st ed. New York: Fordham University Press, 2009.

———. *Sodometries: Renaissance Texts, Modern Sexualities*. New York: Fordham University Press, 2010.

Goodkin, Richard. "A Choice of Andromache's." *Yale French Studies* 67 (January 1984): 225–47. https://doi.org/10.2307/2929917.

Greenberg, Mitchell. *Canonical States, Canonical Stages: Oedipus, Othering, and Seventeenth-Century Drama*. Minneapolis: University of Minnesota Press, 1994.

———. *Corneille, Classicism, and the Ruses of Symmetry*. Cambridge: Cambridge University Press, 1986.

———. *Racine: From Ancient Myth to Tragic Modernity*. Minneapolis: University of Minnesota Press, 2010.

———. *Subjectivity and Subjugation in Seventeenth-Century Drama and Prose: The Family Romance of French Classicism*. Cambridge: Cambridge University Press, 1992.

Greenblatt, Stephen. *The Swerve: How the Renaissance Began*. London: Bodley Head, 2011.

Guyot, Sylvaine. *Racine et le corps tragique*. Paris: Presses Universitaires de France, 2014.

Hall, A. R. "Robert Hooke and Horology." *Notes and Records of the Royal Society of London* 16, no. 2 (1951): 167–77. https://www.jstor.org/stable/3087198.

Habermas, Jürgen. *The Structural Transformation of the Public Sphere: An Inquiry into a Category of Bourgeois Society*. Studies in Contemporary German Social Thought. Cambridge, MA: MIT Press, 1989.

Halberstam, J. Jack. *In a Queer Time and Place: Transgender Bodies, Subcultural Lives*. New York: New York University Press, 2005.

Hammond, Paul. *Figuring Sex between Men from Shakespeare to Rochester*. Oxford: Clarendon Press, 2002.

Hampton, Timothy. *Fictions of Embassy: Literature and Diplomacy in Early Modern Europe*. Ithaca, NY: Cornell University Press, 2009.

Harris, Joseph. "Disruptive Desires: Lesbian Sexuality in Isaac de Benserade's *Iphis et Iante* (1634)." *Seventeenth-Century French Studies* 24, no. 1 (June 2002): 151–63. https://doi.org/10.1179/c17.2002.24.1.151.

———. *Inventing the Spectator: Subjectivity and the Theatrical Experience in Early Modern France*. 1st ed. Oxford: Oxford University Press, 2014.

Hartle, Robert W. "Racine's Hidden Metaphors." *Modern Language Notes* 76, no. 2 (1961): 132–39.

Hawcroft, Michael. "Points de suspension chez Racine: enjeux dramatiques, enjeux éditoriaux." *Revue d'histoire littéraire de la France* 106, no. 2 (2006): 307–35.

Hogg, Chloé. *Absolutist Attachments: Emotion, Media, and Absolutism in Seventeenth-Century France*. Evanston, IL: Northwestern University Press, 2019.

Horowitz, Louise K. "The Second Time Around." *L'Esprit Créateur* 38, no. 2 (1998): 23–33. https://doi.org/10.1353/esp.2010.0009.

Howe, Cymene. "Timely." Theorizing the Contemporary, *Fieldsights*, January 21, 2016. https://culanth.org/fieldsights/timely.

Ibbett, Katherine. "Classicism and the Creaturely: Pierre Corneille's 'Polyeucte.'" *Yale French Studies* no. 124 (2013): 108–20. http://www.jstor.org/stable/23646044.

———. *The Style of the State in French Theater, 1630–1660: Neoclassicism and Government*. Farnham, UK: Ashgate Publishing, 2009.

Kantorowicz, Ernst H. *The King's Two Bodies*. Reprint edition. Princeton, NJ: Princeton University Press, 1997.

Karsenti, Tiphaine. "From Historical Invention to Literary Myth: Ambivalences and Contradictions in the Early Modern Reception of the Franco-Trojan Genealogy." In *Early Modern Medievalisms*, edited by Alicia Montoya, Sophie van Romburgh, and Wim van Anrooij, 93–110, Leiden: Brill, 2010.

Klapisch-Zuber, Christiane. "La 'mère cruelle': Maternité, veuvage et dot dans la Florence des XIVe–XVe siècles." *Annales. Histoire, Sciences Sociales* 38, no. 5 (1983): 1097–109. http://www.jstor.org/stable/27581802.

Landes, David S. *Revolution in Time: Clocks and the Making of the Modern World*. Cambridge, MA: Belknap Press, 1983.

Lerner, Ross. *Unknowing Fanaticism: Reformation Literatures of Self-Annihilation*. 1st ed. New York: Fordham University Press, 2019.

Levine, Caroline. *Forms: Whole, Rhythm, Hierarchy, Network*. Princeton, NJ: Princeton University Press, 2015.

Leyerle, Blake. "Blood Is Seed." *Journal of Religion* 81, no. 1 (2001): 26–48. https://www.jstor.org/stable/1206937.

Longino, Michèle. *Orientalism in French Classical Drama*. Cambridge: Cambridge University Press, 2002.

Love, Heather. *Feeling Backward: Loss and the Politics of Queer History*. Cambridge, MA: Harvard University Press, 2007.

Luciano, Dana. *Arranging Grief: Sacred Time and the Body in Nineteenth-Century America*. New York: New York University Press, 2007.

Lupton, Julia Reinhard. "Ablative Absolutes: From Paul to Shakespeare." In *Paul and the Philosophers*, edited by Ward Blanton and Hent de Vries, 281–98. New York: Fordham University Press, 2013.

Lyons, John D. "Le démon de l'inquiétude: La passion dans la théorie de la tragédie." *XVIIe siècle* 185 (1994): 787–98.

———. *Kingdom of Disorder: The Theory of Tragedy in Classical France*. West Lafayette, IN: Purdue University Press, 1999.

Lyotard, Jean-François. *Discourse, Figure*. Translated by Antony Hudek and Mary Lydon. Minneapolis: University of Minnesota Press, 2011.

Mallet, Marie-Louise, and Ginette Michaud, eds. *Jacques Derrida: Les Cahiers de L'Herne* 83. Paris: Éditions de l'Herne, 2004.

McClure, Ellen. "Sovereign Love and Atomism in Racine's Berenice." *Philosophy and Literature* 27, no. 2 (December 2003): 304–17.

———. *Sunspots and the Sun King: Sovereignty and Mediation in Seventeenth-Century France*. 1st ed. Champaign: University of Illinois Press, 2006.

Menon, M. *Unhistorical Shakespeare: Queer Theory in Shakespearean Literature and Film*. Palgrave Macmillan US, 2008.

Merlin-Kajman, Hélène. *Public et littérature en France au XVIIe siècle*. Paris: Belles Lettres, 1994.

Mould, William A. "The 'Innocent Strategème' of Racine's Andromaque." *French Review* 48, no. 3 (1975): 557–65. https://www.jstor.org/stable/388244.

Muñoz, Jose Esteban. *Cruising Utopia: The Then and There of Queer Futurity*. New York: New York University Press, 2009.

———. "Ephemera as Evidence: Introductory Notes to Queer Acts." *Women and Performance: a journal of feminist theory* 8 (1996): 5–16. https://doi.org/10.1080/07407709608571228.

Muratore, M. J. "The Pleasures of Re-Enactment in 'Andromaque.'" *Dalhousie French Studies* 24 (1993): 57–70. https://www.jstor.org/stable/40836725.

———. "The Poetics of Indeterminacy: Corneille's *Le Cid*." *Romance Quarterly* 60, no. 4 (2013): 244–53.

Murray, Timothy. "'Animé d'un regard': The Crisis of Televisual Speed in Racine." *L'Esprit Créateur* 38, no. 2 (1998): 11–22. https://doi.org/10.1353/esp.2010.0005.

———. *Theatrical Legitimation: Allegories of Genius in Seventeenth-Century England and France*. Oxford: Oxford University Press, 1987.

Musser, Amber Jamilla. "Objects of Desire: Toward an Ethics of Sameness." *Theory and Event* 16, no. 2 (2013). muse.jhu.edu/article/509903.

Natan, Stéphane. "Les questions d'Andromaque: Entre révolte et révélation." *Seventeenth-Century French Studies* 36, no. 2 (November 2014): 125–40. https://doi.org/10.1179/0265106814Z.00000000045.

Orr, Bridget. *Empire on the English Stage, 1660–1714*. Reissue edition. Cambridge: Cambridge University Press, 2007.

Parker, Patricia. "Deferral, Dilation, Difference: Shakespeare, Cervantes, Jonson." In *Literary Theory/Renaissance Texts*, edited by Patricia Parker and David Quint, 182–209. Baltimore: Johns Hopkins University Press, 1986.

———. *Literary Fat Ladies: Rhetoric, Gender, Property*. London: Methuen, 1987.

———. "Metaphor and Catachresis." In *Ends of Rhetoric: History, Theory, Practice*, edited by John Bender and David E. Wellbery, 60–73. Stanford, CA: Stanford University Press, 1990.

———. *Shakespeare from the Margins: Language, Culture, Context*. Chicago: University of Chicago Press, 1996.

———. "Virile Style." In *Premodern Sexualities*, edited by Louise Fradenburg and Carla Freccero, 199–222. New York: Routledge, 1996.

Poselt, Gerard. "The Tropological Economy of Catachresis." In *Metaphors of Economy*, edited by Nicole Bracker and Stefan Herbrechter, 81–94. Amsterdam: Rodopi, 2005.

Quintilian. *Institutes of Oratory*. Translated by John Selby Watson (1856), revised and edited by Lee Honeycutt (2007) and Curtis Dozier (2015). 2015. Kindle.

Racevskis, Roland. *Time and Ways of Knowing Under Louis XIV: Molière, Sévigné, Lafayette*. Lewisburg, PA: Bucknell University Press, 2003.

———. "The Time of Tragedy: Andromaque, Britannicus, Bérénice." In *Racine et/ou le classicisme: Actes du colloque conjointement organisé par la North American Society for Seventeenth-Century French Literature et la Société Racine*, edited by Ronald W. Tobin, 113–25. Tübingen: Gunter Narr Verlag, 2001.

———. *Tragic Passages: Jean Racine's Art of the Threshold*. Lewisburg, PA: Bucknell University Press, 2008.

Racine, Jean. *Berenice and Bajazet*. Translated by Alan Hollinghurst. London: Faber and Faber, 2012.

———. *Œuvres complètes*. Vol. 1, *Théâtre poésie*. Edited by Georges Forestier. Paris: Gallimard, 1999.

———. *Œuvres complètes*. Vol. 1, *Théâtre poésie*. Edited by Raymond Picard. Paris: Gallimard, 1976.

———. *Théâtre complet*. Edited by Alain Viala and Sylvaine Guyot. Paris: Classiques Garnier, 2013.

Rancière, Jacques. *The Emancipated Spectator*. Translated by Gregory Elliott. Brooklyn: Verso, 2011.

Reeser, Todd. *Setting Plato Straight: Translating Ancient Sexuality in the Renaissance*. Chicago: University of Chicago Press, 2015.

Richelet, Pierre. *Dictionnaire françois*. Widerhold: Geneva, 1680

Rohy, Valerie. *Lost Causes: Narrative, Etiology, and Queer Theory*. 1st ed. Oxford: Oxford University Press, 2014.

Roussillon, Marine. "'Agréables différends': L'esthétique galante de la querelle dans deux dialogues de Jean Chapelain et Jean-François Sarasin." *Littératures classiques* 81, no. 2 (2013): 51–62. https://doi.org/10.3917/licla.081.0051.

Row, Jennifer. "Alternative Intimacies, Sympathy and Sexuality in Voltaire's *Zaïre*." *Le Monde français du dix-huitième siècle* 2, no. 1 (2017). https://ojs.lib.uwo.ca/index.php/mfds-ecfw/article/view/408.

———. "'Aux cendres d'un époux': Traumatisme et le temps du désir inexprimable dans *Andromaque* de Racine." In *Autour de l'extrême littéraire*, edited by Alastair Hemmens and Russell Williams, 73–87. Newcastle, UK: Cambridge Scholars, 2012.

———. "Queer Time on the Early Modern Stage: France and the Drama of Biopower." *Exemplaria: Medieval, Early Modern, Theory* 29, no. 1 (2017): 58–81. https://doi.org/10.1080/10412573.2017.1284366.

Saint-Girons, Claude. "Racine et l'amour maternel." *Dix-septième siècle* 7, no. 8 (1950): 229–37.

Sanchez y Sanchez, Samuel. "The Flesh and Bones of Politics in Early Modern Spain." In *Dead Lovers: Erotic Bonds and the Study of Premodern Europe*, edited by Basil Dufallo and Peggy McCracken, 106–27. Ann Arbor: University of Michigan Press, 2006.

Santner, Eric. *The Royal Remains: The People's Two Bodies and the Endgames of Sovereignty*. Chicago: University of Chicago Press, 2011.

Scherer, Jacques. *La dramaturgie classique en France*. Paris: Nizet, 1950.

Schmitt, Carl. *Political Theology: Four Chapters on the Concept of Sovereignty*. Translated by George Schwab. Chicago: University of Chicago Press, 2006.

Scott, Paul. "'Ma force est trop petite': Authority and Kingship in *Le Cid*." *Forum for Modern Language Studies* 45, no. 3 (July 2009): 292–304. https://doi.org/10.1093/fmls/cqp049.

Sedgwick, Eve Kosofsky. *Between Men: English Literature and Male Homosocial Desire*. 13th anniversary ed. New York: Columbia University Press, 2015.

———. *Touching Feeling: Affect, Pedagogy, Performativity*. Durham, NC: Duke University Press, 2003.

Seifert, Lewis. *Manning the Margins: Masculinity and Writing in Seventeenth-Century France* Ann Arbor: University of Michigan Press, 2009.

———. "Queer Time in Charles Perrault's 'Sleeping Beauty.'" *Marvels and Tales* 29, no. 1 (2015): 21–41. https://doi.org/10.13110/marvelstales.29.1.0021.

Semk, Christopher. *Playing the Martyr: Theater and Theology in Early Modern France*. Lewisburg, PA: Bucknell University Press, 2017.

Shannon, Laurie. *Sovereign Amity: Figures of Friendship in Shakespearean Contexts*. Chicago: University of Chicago Press, 2001.

Sherman, Stuart. "Dryden and the Theatrical Imagination." In *The Cambridge Companion to John Dryden*, edited by Steven N. Zwicker, 15–36. Cambridge: Cambridge University Press, 2006. https://doi.org/10.1017/CCOL0521824273.002.

———. *Telling Time: Clocks, Diaries, and English Diurnal Form, 1660–1785*. 1st ed. Chicago: University of Chicago Press, 1997.

Spenser, Edmund. *The Faerie Queene*. Edited by A. C. Hamilton, with Hiroshi Yamashita, Toshiyuki Suzuki, and Shohachi Fukuda. 2nd ed. London: Longman, 2007.

Spitzer, Leo. *Leo Spitzer: Essays on Seventeenth-Century French Literature*. Cambridge: Cambridge University Press, 1983.

Stedman, Allison. *Rococo Fiction in France, 1600–1715: Seditious Frivolity*. Lewisburg, PA: Bucknell University Press, 2012.

Stone, Harriet. *The Classical Model: Literature and Knowledge in Seventeenth Century France*. Ithaca, NY: Cornell University Press, 1996.

———. "The Tragic Implications of Andromaque's Sacrifice." *Romanic Review* 75, no. 4 (1984): 424–31.

Sorel, Charles. *De la connaissance des bons livres*. Paris: André Pralard, 1671

Taqa, Shathil Nawaf. "Polyeucte de Corneille face à la crise du sens," *PHILITT: Philosophie, littérature, et cinéma* (March 22, 2017). https://philitt.fr/2017/03/22/polyeucte-de-corneille-face-a-la-crise-du-sens.

Traub, Valerie. "The New Unhistoricism in Queer Studies." *PMLA* 128, no. 1 (2013): 21–39. doi:10.1632/pmla.2013.128.1.21.

———. *The Renaissance of Lesbianism in Early Modern England*. Cambridge: Cambridge University Press, 2002.

Ubersfeld, Anne. Introduction to *Andromaque*, by Jean Racine, 7–94. Edited by Anne Ubersfeld. Paris: Éditions sociales, 1961.

Valéry, Paul. "Calepin d'un poète." In *Œuvres*, vol. 1. Edited by J. Hytier. 1449–50. Paris: Gallimard, 1957.

———. "Propos sur la poésie." In *Œuvres*, vol. 1. Edited by J. Hytier. 1372. Paris: Gallimard, 1957

———. "Les droits du poète sur la langue." In *Œuvres*, vol. 2. Edited by J. Hytier. 1262. Paris: Gallimard, 1960.

Vialleton, Jean-Yves. "Les bienséances: Concept intraduisible ou notion apocryphe?" *Littératures classiques* 96, no. 2 (November 2018): 63–72. https://doi.org/10.3917/licla1.096.0063.

Voltaire. "Seconde Lettre au même Monsieur Falkener." In *Zaïre*, edited by Pierre Frantz. Paris: Gallimard, 2016.

———. *Zaïre*. Edited by Pierre Frantz. Paris: Folio, 2016.

Weber, Caroline. "Voltaire's *Zaïre*: Fantasies of Infidelity, Ideologies of Faith." *South Central Review* 21, no. 2 (2004): 42–62. https://www.jstor.org/stable/40039809.

Welch, Ellen R. *A Theater of Diplomacy: International Relations and the Performing Arts in Early Modern France*. Philadelphia: University of Pennsylvania Press, 2017.

Wiegman, Robyn. "The Times We're In: Queer Feminist Criticism and the Reparative 'Turn.'" *Feminist Theory* 15, no. 1 (April 2014): 4–25. https://doi.org/10.1177/1464700113513081a.

Wiegman, Robyn, and Elizabeth A. Wilson. "Introduction: Antinormativity's Queer Conventions." *Differences* 26, no. 1 (January 2015): 1–25. https://doi.org/10.1215/10407391-2880582.

Viala, Alain. "Un temps de querelles." *Littératures classiques* 81, no. 2 (2013): 5–22. https://doi.org/10.3917/licla.081.0005.

INDEX